The Political and Institutional Effects
of Term Limits

The Political and Institutional Effects of Term Limits

Marjorie Sarbaugh-Thompson,
Lyke Thompson, Charles D. Elder,
John Strate, and Richard C. Elling

THE POLITICAL AND INSTITUTIONAL EFFECTS OF TERM LIMITS
© Marjorie Sarbaugh-Thompson, Lyke Thompson, Charles D. Elder, John
Strate, and Richard C. Elling, 2004

First published 2004 by
PALGRAVE MACMILLAN™
175 Fifth Avenue, New York, N.Y. 10010 and
Houndmills, Basingstoke, Hampshire, England RG21 6XS
Companies and representatives throughout the world

PALGRAVE MACMILLAN is the global academic imprint of the Palgrave
Macmillan division of St. Martin's Press, LLC and of Palgrave Macmillan Ltd.
Macmillan® is a registered trademark in the United States, United Kingdom
and other countries. Palgrave is a registered trademark in the European
Union and other countries.

ISBN 1–4039–6514–5 hardback

Library of Congress Cataloging-in-Publication Data
    Political and institutional effects of term limits / Marjorie
Sarbaugh-Thompson ... [et al.].
      p.cm.
    Includes bibliographical references and index.
    ISBN 1–4039–6514–5
    1. Michigan. Legislature. House of Representatives. 2. Term limits
(Public office)—Michigan. 3. Legislators—Term of office—Michigan.
I. Sarbaugh-Thompson, Marjorie, 1949–

JK5878.P65 2004
328.774'073—dc22   2004046005

A catalogue record for this book is available from the British Library.

Design by Newgen Imaging Systems (P) Ltd., Chennai, India.

First edition: September 2004
10 9 8 7 6 5 4 3 2 1

Printed in the United States of America.

In the hope that elected officials will engage in the deliberative policy-making and bipartisan compromise needed to address the concerns and interests of all citizens

Contents

List of Tables and Figures

Tables

Figures

Acknowledgments

The "Term Limits Project," as our five years of persistent effort is known, has operated on a shoestring budget and succeeded only through the commitment of many, many people. Many of the individuals who made this project possible worked more than they were paid to or worked without pay to see that this research was completed. As principal investigator, let me first thank my faculty coauthors. All of us worked on this project for several summers without being paid to do so and contorted our schedules during the fall and winter semesters to fit trips to Lansing around our teaching and other duties.

Next we all thank our graduate research assistants without whose work the project would have been unmanageable. We are especially indebted to J.P. Faletta and Lisa Marckini, our first two graduate research assistants on the project, who endured endless debates during the planning stages of the project and contributed immensely to the collection and organization of pre–term limits baseline data. They became outstanding field interviewers in their own right. Next we thank Eric Rader and Shannon Orr, two more outstanding graduate students, who helped code campaign finance data from boxes of microfiche to provide a baseline and helped develop codebooks for open-ended questions. We are also grateful to Jovan Trpovski and Chris Wilson, who helped us with the second round of interviews and more data coding and codebook development. We also thank Kelly LeRoux and Pam Walsh, who coded lots and lots of campaign finance data, even tracking down illusive, obscure PACs so that we could classify them correctly. Finally, we thank Meg Comins and P.J. Pettipren. Meg went on more interviews than any other graduate assistant and coded almost all the open-ended questions for the third round of interviews. P.J. used her extensive knowledge of Lansing to determine what legislators did after they were termed out of office. Doug Drake of the State Policy Center helped us arrange some of the interviews with representatives, and we appreciate his willingness to help us. We also thank our student assistants, Simone Dietrich, Nirupma Banka, Tricia Ketterer,

Jennifer Wilson, and Jason Hardacre. Heidi Alcock, Charo Hulleza, Chris Lobb, Marie Olson, and Susan Tobbe all volunteered their time when we needed help with interview notes, and Alec Thompson helped code campaign finance data. This book would not have been possible without all these outstanding students.

We also received financial and material support from several generous sources. First, the Wayne State University Policy Center and its Director, Peter Eisinger, supported us for multiple years, providing money to pay some of our graduate students and to cover some of our travel expenses. We are also grateful for funding provided by the Vice President for Research, Wayne State University; the Hewlett Packard Corporation; and the College of Liberal Arts, Wayne State University. The Department of Political Science at Wayne State University generously provided us with office space and support. Amie Meixner in the Political Science office helped us with typing when she could and tracked us down when we were on the way to Lansing to save us hours on the highway when interviews were canceled.

We are also deeply indebted to Mark Grebner of Practical Political Consultants for generously giving us the 1990 campaign finance reports on microfiche and a microfiche reader. We are equally deeply indebted to Edwin Bender of the Institute for Money in State Politics for giving us the 2000 and 2002 campaign finance data for the Michigan House. We are also grateful to Bill Ballenger of Inside Michigan Politics for his prompt assistance in providing information about legislators' ages. Additionally we thank Drs. Mary Herring and Stanley Caress for their earlier involvement in the project.

Last, but certainly not least, we thank the Michigan Representatives and State Senators who gave us their time and endured our questions. Several of them were interviewed more than once, a few even agreed to be interviewed for all three rounds of the research project. We are especially grateful to some of the veteran legislators who spent multiple hours with us explaining in great detail and with great candor how the legislature "really" worked. Clearly we could not have done this research without them.

We embarked on this project partly out of academic interest in what happens when legislatures confront mass turnover. But, we also were motivated by public service and a sense of commitment to the citizens of Michigan. We are convinced that citizens have a right to know how the initiatives they pass affect their government and their state. Our fascination with the changes we observed in the legislature spurred us on. We hope the book provides information that Michigan citizens as well as citizens and observers of state politics nationally find as intriguing as we did.

Introduction

In 1998 nearly two-thirds of Michigan's State House Representatives were banished forever from their positions. They had served too long according to nearly 59 percent of the state's voters, who in 1992 constitutionally limited the maximum years of service for several state elected offices.[1] The 1998 exodus from the Michigan House of Representatives included most of the chairs of standing committees and most of the caucus and chamber leaders.

Michigan's actions were not unique. Term limits spread to 19 states during the 1990s. Despite their popularity, there was little systematic information about their effects on government and governing. Proponents' optimistic promises and opponents' dire prognostications were both speculative.

Ongoing Political Debates About Term Limits

Although in 2001 the CATO Institute pronounced term limits a rousing success, citizens and politicians, even some who admit that they were elected because of term limits and supported them in the past, are not so certain. In 2002 Idaho's legislature repealed term limits, while in California citizens tried but failed to modify them. In a survey conducted in March 2001, Michigan voters were evenly divided over whether to repeal term limits, but a majority of those surveyed (58 percent) favored lengthening the term for state house members from six to eight years (EPIC-MRA, 2001).[2] In Summer 2003, 62 percent of Michigan adults said that they would not support a ballot initiative to repeal term limits and only 35 percent said that they would support lengthening the limits to 12 years in each chamber (Wayne State University, Center for Urban Studies, 2003).[3] On the other hand, Michigan State Representative John Pappageorge reported that in 2003, 62 percent of Michigan voters supported his proposal to lengthen the service of state legislators to 14 years of combined service in either or both chambers. This would supplant the current limits of six years in the House and eight in the Senate.[4] Thus, the debate over term limits seems likely to persist in the coming decade creating the need for comprehensive, systematic information about their effects.

In states in which term limits have been implemented, it is now possible to assess their effects. Potential impacts are far-reaching, including (1) changes in the political environment of state politics, (2) changes in personal characteristics of elected officials, and (3) institutional changes in the way state government works. Using highly detailed longitudinal data about the Michigan House of Representatives and comparative data from other states where appropriate and feasible, we provide a comprehensive assessment of the impacts of limits on legislative terms of service.

Effects on the Political Environment

There were two primary effects on the political environment that term limits proponents hoped to achieve: more competitive elections and less interest group influence on elected officials. Open seat elections tend to be more competitive (Gaddie & Bullock, 2000). Therefore term limits proponents reasoned that the increased number of open seat races produced by "terming" officials out of office would increase electoral competition. In chapter 1, we examine changes in competition in both primary and general elections in Michigan and in California after term limits took effect. We find some modest increases in primary competition, but surprising declines in competitiveness overall.

Open seat elections tend to be more expensive, so experts in campaign finance warned that term limits would increase the importance of money in politics (Gierzynski, 1998). In chapter 2, we analyze campaign contributions to see who receives how much money and from whom after term limits. Despite total increases in campaign spending for all House races, the average amount raised by individual candidates decreased after term limits. Interestingly, we found a dramatic increase in money channeled through political parties and legislative caucus political action committees (PACs) and also more reliance on personal resources to fund campaigns.

Incumbents generally receive more money than challengers do, with much of it coming from special interests. By reducing the number of incumbents, proponents hoped that term limits would sever the ties between organized interest groups and elected officials. Thus, term limits offer an alternative way to reform campaign funding. In chapter 3, we explore postelection contributions from special interests and the effect of committee service and leadership positions on these contributions. We found that after term limits PACs seemed more, not less, likely to target their giving toward members serving on committees handling issues of interest to them.

Effects on Individual Legislators

Term limits change the opportunities elected officials have to hold office and so were expected to change the types of people seeking these positions. Proponents promised that purging legislatures of entrenched incumbents would attract a "new breed" of citizen legislators who would return to their communities after brief stints of public service to live under the laws they had passed. Proponents also speculated that because many incumbents termed out of office were white males, more women and more candidates from other ethnic groups would be elected. In chapter 4, we compare the physical characteristics of the pre– and post–term limits members of the state house. We found that the "new breed" bears a striking resemblance to the "old guard," but that ethnic diversity of legislators may increase.

Highly professional legislatures, such as Michigan's, provide reasonable salaries and benefits, as well as opportunities to achieve specific policy goals. Absent term limits, representatives could view service in the state legislature as a career. Limiting the length of service in an elected office changes its payoff and consequently could appeal to candidates with different motives and aspirations (Schlesinger, 1966; Ehrenhalt, 1991). Instead of luring citizens with discrete or limited political aspirations into legislative service, term limits may attract candidates with what Schlesinger (1966) calls progressive ambition, who view the State House as a stepping stone to higher office. Term limits mean that there will be numerous vacancies in the State Senate and in statewide offices for State Representatives who want to seek higher office. In chapter 5, we explore the reasons representatives ran for office and their goals and career paths after they are termed out of office. We found that post–term limits legislators are more likely than their pre–term limits counterparts to have held a prior political office and that termed-out legislators often run for other statewide, county, or municipal offices, exhibiting what we call sustained ambition.

Under term limits everyone will know that representatives elected to their last term in office are lame ducks. Will this make them less accountable to their constituents? Or will limiting the time that a representative can serve keep them more closely tied to their constituents and their district? In chapter 6 we explore the responsiveness of term-limited representatives to their constituents. We do this by asking how they reconcile conflicts between their personal views and the views of their constituents and between what is best for their district versus statewide interests. We also compare the extent to which pre– and post–term limited representatives say they rely on constituents, key local officials, and advisors in their districts when making up their minds about how to vote on difficult issues. We find that under term limits, lame ducks serving their last term in office appear relatively more concerned with their future employment opportunities than about their districts and constituents.

Institutional Effects

Although Carey et al. (1998) found relatively few effects of term limits, they predicted that institutional effects would be among the more profound changes wrought by term limits. In our section on institutional effects, we explore changes in the informal structure of the legislature, such as vote cuing and friendships, as well as changes in the formal roles, such as committee chair, and in constitutionally prescribed relationships, such as oversight of the bureaucracy.

Among the institutional effects of term limits, Carson (1998) predicted that term limits would make it harder for legislators to build coalitions to pass legislation because long-term relationships, especially those that cross party lines, will be less common with higher turnover in the chamber. Francis (1962) finds that friendship and influence are correlated in non–term limited legislatures. Using network analysis techniques, we examine the structure of friendships before and after term limits and compare patterns of friendship and influence attributed to legislators by their colleagues. After term limits, we found that fewer representatives were seen as influential by their colleagues. We also found that friendships were even more numerous, and also more homogeneous. These findings are presented in chapter 7.

Committee chairs often control the work of their committees, typically through a combination of their formal position and their expertise in both the substance of the issues before the committees and their knowledge of the legislative process. Under term limits freshman sometimes replace veterans in the role of committee chair. During our interviews with legislators, we asked them about the work of specific committees and the role the chair played. Our findings are presented in chapter 8. We find that the influence of committee chairs has declined while the influence of caucus leaders has increased leading to a greater concentration of power in the caucus in the term-limited Michigan House.

Confronted by myriad complex, technical issues, legislators learn quickly that they cannot be experts on every issue. Thus they rely on fellow legislators and other actors to help them decide how to vote (Kingdon, 1989). Becoming an expert on even a few issues requires time, perhaps more time than term-limited representatives have. Therefore, the sources of information upon which representatives rely are likely to change under term limits. In chapter 9 we investigate these sources of information. Contrary to the hopes of term limits proponents, we find a slight increase in the extent to which term-limited legislators report relying on lobbyists for information and guidance on issues that reach the floor of the chamber.

Although term limits proponents promised that citizen legislators would be more independent and have fewer ties to special interests, their lack of experience in state government may have ceded substantial power to the bureaucracy, to their staff, to the governor, and to lobbyists, just as term limits opponents warned. In addition to a large, predictable influx of freshmen, term limits regularly produces a flock of lame ducks whose status is known for the duration of their final term. Lobbyists have less need to maintain ongoing trust with these "short-timers," and bureaucrats can out wait their requests. In chapter 10, we explore the shifts in the balance of power among the branches of state government and between the legislature and outside actors.

Variation Across the States

In a comparative 50-state study of anticipatory effects of term limits, Carey, Niemi, and Powell (1998) found evidence that majority party leaders lose power and governors gain power under term limits. Yet, these authors found that term limits had no effect on the composition of the legislature. Further they found no differences in ideology for newly elected legislators in term-limited and non–term limited states. Finally, they found only small differences in behavior between old-timers and newcomers in term-limited and non–term limited states.

There are two problems with the Carey, et al study that may have limited its ability to discern the full effects of term limits. First, the authors did not distinguish between passing term limits laws and implementing the law by forcing legislators from office. In 1995, when their survey was conducted, several states had passed term limits laws but none had termed anyone out of office. Therefore, their study explores changes that occur when a state is waiting for or anticipating the implementation of a term limits law.

Although anticipatory effects are possible with sweeping reforms such as term limits, they may differ from the effects after implementation. Additionally, because of court challenges to the constitutionality of term limits laws, anticipatory effects may have been muted in some states. In Michigan the constitutional question was not settled by the state's Supreme Court until March of 1998, barely six months before they were to take effect. Legislators were first termed out of office at the end of the 1998 session, less than a year later. Given the uncertain status of the law, very few legislators opted for early voluntary retirement, leading to a mass exodus of 64 veterans from the Michigan State House when term limits were finally implemented in 1998. So even if there were anticipatory effects in some states, in others these effects may have been muted or absent.

Second, term limits' effects are likely to differ dramatically across the states due to the differences in the severity of the term limits laws and differences between state legislatures. We summarize these in table I.1. Across the states the length of service permitted varies dramatically from a low of 8 years total combined service in both chambers in Nebraska to a maximum of 24 years (12 in each chamber) for Louisiana, Wyoming, and Nevada. Many states with term limits restrict consecutive years of service, and often the years "off" can include service in the other chamber of the legislature. Fewer states impose lifetime limits. Michigan is one of these. As one representative quipped, "only convicted felons and former members are prohibited from running for the House, and even felons can run after 25 years" (interview notes 1997–1998).

In states that restrict only consecutive years of service and permit more than two decades of service, term limits are less likely, perhaps even unlikely, to have noticeable effects. Term limits are more likely to have noticeable impacts in states with more stringent limits on service. Michigan is among the states with the most severe limits on the length of service. Members of the Michigan House of Representatives can serve for six years and State Senators can serve for eight years.

The type of legislature a state has is also likely to interact with the impacts of term limits. Some states have part-time legislatures that meet less than once a year, and then for only a few months. Other states have

Table I.1 State term limits provisions and level of professionalization

Limit in years	Consecutive	Lifetime ban
8 total	*Nebraska (2006/2006)*	
12 total		*Oklahoma (2004/2004)*
6 House/8 Senate		Arkansas (1998/2000) **California (1996/1998)** **Michigan (1998/2002)**
8 House/8 Senate	*Arizona (2000/2000)* *Colorado (1998/1998)* *Florida (2000/2000)* Maine (1996/1996) Missouri (2002/2002) Montana (2000/2000) *Ohio (2000/2000)* *South Dakota (2000/2000)*	
12 House/12 Senate	Louisiana (2007/2007) Wyoming (2006/2006)	Nevada (2008/2008)

Note: Numbers in parentheses indicate year of impact in the House first and Senate second. States listed in bold type are those with highly professionalized legislatures, those in italics have moderately professionalized legislatures, and those the regular type are part-time legislatures. Levels of professionalization are based on Squire (1992).

Source: Barnhart, 1999 and National Conference of State Legislatures, 2003.

highly professionalized, full-time legislatures that meet year round. A third group of states have what are called "moderately professionalized" legislatures (Squire, 1992), which share some characteristics with full-time legislatures and some with part-time legislatures. If the states with more lenient term limits laws are also those with part-time legislatures, we would expect term limits to have few, if any, noticeable impacts. In other states, especially those with lifetime bans on service and stringent limits on the years of service permitted, term limits are likely to have much more dramatic impact. This is especially true when restrictive term limits are put in place in states with highly professionalized legislatures. This is the case in Michigan.

The Value of Michigan in Testing Term Limits

With so much variation among the states with term limits laws, a cross-sectional study may obscure instead of illuminate the impacts of this reform. Further, anticipatory effects may differ from effects when legislators are termed out of office, especially in states in which constitutional questions were not settled for several years. To resolve these challenges, term limits' effects need to be explored initially using longitudinal case studies, focusing first on the states in which any effects, either positive or negative, are most likely to be found. Because Michigan is a state with a highly professionalized state legislature where severe term limits have been imposed, it is one of the states where any effects should be most readily apparent. Thus, this longitudinal study of Michigan term limits is key to understanding the effects of the term limits "experiment."

As we noted earlier, Michigan is one of only two states with term limits that also have highly professionalized legislatures (Squire, 1992).[5] This means that Michigan's elected officials work full time conducting the state's business. They are paid more than $70,000 annually, and each chamber employs numerous partisan and nonpartisan staff. Each legislator also has money to hire personal staff to perform constituent service and maintain offices both in the district and in the state capital. Further, professionalized legislatures are more likely than part-time legislatures to attract members who serve for decades.

Michigan is one of three states that impose the shortest tenure in the lower chamber of the legislature—six years.[6] For the decade prior to the imposition of term limits for the Michigan House of Representatives, the mean tenure of members of the House was in the range of 7.5–8.5 years. Between 1986 and 1994 the percentage of incumbent members of the Michigan House seeking reelection was greater than 80 percent (Faletta et al., 2001). Prior to term limits, Michigan had the ninth most stable legislature in the nation (Brace & Ward, 1999) with an average tenure in office of 9.5 years and a median tenure of nine years during 1996. This clearly exceeded the tenure prescribed under Michigan's term limits law. Therefore, not surprisingly, term limits increased legislative turnover in the Michigan House and produced more open seat elections. In the first session of the Michigan House following the imposition of term limits, the mean tenure of members dropped to 2.2 years.

One of the overarching questions we attempt to answer throughout this book is whether higher legislative turnover and more open seat elections produce the effects term limits opponents fear or those that their advocates desire. For example, some term limits proponents believed that by limiting the length of service a "new breed" of candidate would be attracted to state legislative service. Therefore, in several chapters we return to the theme of legislators' motivations for seeking office, the characteristics of those serving in the term-limited Michigan House, and the political career paths that are unfolding in Michigan's term-limited political environment.

Methodology

Voters adopted term limits in Michigan in 1992. Legislators were first "termed out" of office in 1998. Therefore we knew when term limits would take effect and had a unique opportunity to use quasi-experimental designs to study rapid, dramatic change in a state legislature. To seize this opportunity, a group of Wayne State University researchers began in 1998 to gather baseline data on Michigan's pre–term limits House of Representatives. They followed changes in the House through 2000, gathering comparable data about the first cohort of post–term limited representatives. In the following chapters, we focus primarily on comparing the last pre– and first post–term-limited Michigan House of Representatives. Whenever possible we compare Michigan's and California's experiences with term limits because they are the two most highly professionalized legislatures with term limits and both have six-year limits for service in the lower chamber. Both had expelled legislators from the lower chamber, so they were beyond the anticipatory phase between passing the law and implementing it. Additionally, we use the Michigan State Senate as a control group in some of our analyses because implementation of term limits in Michigan was staggered, taking effect in the House in 1998 and in the Senate in 2002. Therefore, the experiences of our first cohort of term-limited Michigan State Representatives can be compared to non–term limited Michigan State Senators. For example, we used the Senate as a control group in our analyses of campaign contributions.

Throughout our investigation, we integrate three sources of data. First we interviewed 95 members of the last pre–term limits cohort of representatives and 93 of first post–term limits cohort of representatives. We also interviewed 93 members of the second post–term limits cohort (serving in 2001–2002). Second, we analyzed election results and characteristics of office holders for both Michigan and California from 1988 through 2002. Third, we analyzed campaign contributions made by different types of contributors to all candidates for the Michigan House and Senate in 1990 and 1998 and for the 110 members of the Michigan House in the post election years of 1997 and 1999. Finally, we examine aggregate campaign contributions made to Michigan House candidates in 2000 and 2002.

Our interviews with legislators were semi-structured and combined open- and closed-ended questions. These were face-to-face interviews that lasted approximately one hour. Although face-to-face interviews, especially those incorporating multiple open-ended questions, are time consuming to conduct and code, we view them as vital given the probability that term limits may have subtle or unanticipated consequences. Open-ended questions allow legislators to respond in their own words, to volunteer their own insights, and to convey the strength of their opinions and feelings. Further, in a face-to-face interview, legislators can clarify their answers to closed-ended questions, thus preserving the complexity capturing ability of qualitative data (McCracken, 1988) while providing the precision and coding efficiency of quantitative data. Finally, face-to-face interviews provide an opportunity for the researchers to probe for more information and clarify ambiguous responses. Given the newness of term limits and the necessarily exploratory nature of initial research on their effects, we believe the advantages of face-to-face interviews justified the extra work.

The research team opted for written notes instead of tape recording because former legislators on whom we pilot-tested the interview questions advised us that tape recording would be likely to reduce candor and that some legislators might refuse to be tape recorded. Generally, one interviewer and at least one notetaker were present at the interviews. This procedure allowed the interviewer to maintain eye contact with the legislator and conduct the interview in a conversational style that encouraged candor. We transcribed the notes after the interview combining information for the notes taken by the interviewer and the notetaker(s). Given that we relied on handwritten notes, the comments we use from the interviews preserve the meaning conveyed by our respondents, but only the approximate wording. Thus, even when we designate them with quotation marks, they are not literal quotes. Following these comments, we note the legislative term in which the respondent served after these comments. The interviews were confidential, hence we cannot identify the person making the comment in any more precise way. Additionally, when the comments include details that we believe might identify the specific respondent, we have paraphrased or omitted that part of the comment.

We provide our interview questions in appendix A. We encourage other scholars to use them to replicate our work and would welcome collaborators who would like to extend the investigation of term limits effects to other states. Even readers who have no plans to embark on their own term limits research are encouraged to at least scan the list of questions. We will refer to specific questions frequently throughout our discussion of our findings, and it is likely to help all readers if they are somewhat familiar with these questions. Many of the questions at the beginning of the interview are open-ended questions. To analyze these we developed a codebook consisting of a list of categories of responses with numerical values associated. Two members of the research team coded these responses independently. Differences between their coding were then resolved by rereading the responses. Ultimately these were entered into an SPSS dataset and analyzed using the multiple response routine. Therefore, we were able to include the different responses made by each respondent and, also, to report the percentage of our respondents making similar comments—comments that fell into the same general category of responses in our "codebook" for each question.

There are also several "closed-ended" questions, in which the respondent was given specific categories and asked to respond using those categories. These questions can be treated as two series of questions. One series asked about the amount of time respondents spent doing 11 activities that legislators typically perform. The other series asked about the extent to which the respondent relied on a source of information and guidance, for example, the committee chair or partisan staff, in trying to decide how to vote on a difficult issue considered by a committee on which the respondent served. The response categories for both series of questions were "an enormous amount of time," "a lot," "some," "little," or "none." These responses were arranged along a continuum, and respondents were allowed to designate responses that fell between the categories. We treated these responses as ordinal data, coding "an enormous amount" as a value of four and "none" as a value of zero and using decimal increments to denote responses that fell between the categories.[7]

In addition to the categories of time spent on the 11 activities, we also calculated the relative amount of time spent on each of them. We did this by computing the average amount of time each respondent spent on the 11 activities and then calculated the difference from the mean for each specific activity. For example, one of the activities we asked about was time spent communicating with constituents. The difference measure allows us to assess whether the respondent spent more than his or her personal average time on this activity. Conceptually this allows us to adjust for the possibility that new representatives might report spending large amounts of time on everything. Thus a specific activity might receive relatively less attention than other activities even though newly elected legislators reported spending more time on it than their predecessors. Similarly, we thought that lame ducks might spend less time on all their activities, but still spend more than the average amount of time on some activities, for example constituent service. If this were the case, the actual amount of time spent on constituent-related activities could decrease, while the relative priority placed on the activity increased or remained the same.

During our interviews, we also asked representatives to identify a difficult issue that had been seriously considered by a committee on which they served. The second series of closed-ended questions addressed this. We asked about the extent to which the representative relied on 17 different sources of information and guidance to help him or her decide what position to take on the difficult issue. Here again we were concerned that shifts in overall levels of consulting for a group of respondents (e.g., lame ducks or newcomers) could obscure the priority given to different sources of information. With the series of questions about consulting, we had an additional reason to rely on deviations from the average amount of consulting done by the individual representative. First, when asking this series of questions, we used a committee on which the respondent served. Second, the questions were asked about a specific issue chosen by the representative. Therefore, both the committees and the issues differed across respondents. Some issues lend themselves to more or less consulting than do others. Therefore, we wanted to assess the *relative* weight, or priority, the respondent gave to different sources of information and guidance.[8]

Finally, given that interviews were conducted with 80–90 percent of the total membership of each House session, the statistical measures used to assess their responses are more like population parameters than sample-based statistics. As a consequence, the conventional standards of statistical significance used in hypothesis testing based on small samples from large populations hardly seem apposite. Still, we are interested in knowing to what extent the observed patterns are attributable to chance. To insure that we were not ignoring differences that were real, we lowered the usual standard for statistical significance, typically at least 90 percent confidence that the difference is real, to 85 percent, an adjustment that might still be too conservative given the high response rate we achieved.

To explore both the institutional and the individual impacts of term limits, we generally include in our analyses both a measure of the status of term limits and a measure of some characteristics of the individual legislators, such as number of terms of served.[9] This often produces an interaction effect between the institutional and individual-level factors.

An example may help readers unfamiliar with "interaction effects" understand this concept. With term limits not only will newcomers flock into the Michigan House, there will be many representatives serving their last term of office. These so-called lame duck representatives will not only be more numerous than they were before term limits, but their imminent "retirement" will be known for the duration of their last term in office. It is not uncommon for representatives who plan to leave office to announce this only a few months before they voluntarily step down or, if they leave after losing an election, they are only known to be lame ducks for the waning days of the legislative session. Thus being a lame duck is likely to mean something different under term limits than it did before. Prior knowledge of which legislators are lame ducks could lead other actors to treat them differently. Additionally, lame ducks may behave differently knowing that they won't be returning. Often legislators don't decide that they are leaving until it is time to file for reelection. Therefore, we would expect there to be lame duck effects in our pre– term limits cohort and also lame duck effects in our post–term limits cohort, and further we would expect these effects to differ from each other indicating an interaction between length of service (lame duck or not) and status of term limits (before and after).

In our analyses that include institutional effects of term limits, we treat the 1997–1998 term as the pre–term limits benchmark, referring to it with the shorthand, "before term limits." We consider the 1997–1998 chamber to have been in the "pre–term limits" era because it was populated by many veteran legislators, and as noted earlier, given the lengthy court battle over the constitutionality of Michigan's term limits law, those elected prior to 1992 weren't sure until March of 1998 whether they would be term-limited out of office or not. Occasionally, we distinguish between the years prior to the passage of the term limits law (1992 and earlier) as the pre–term limits state and the period between 1992 and 1998 as the "anticipatory period" during which the law had been passed, but no representatives had yet been expelled from office. When we make this distinction, we indicate this clearly in the text. The period from 1998 onward, after the first representatives were forced from office, is designated with the abbreviated phrases "after term limits" or "post–term limits" throughout the book even though it is more technically correct to describe this time period as "after term limits expulsions began." The latter, longer phrase proved to be distractingly cumbersome when it appeared repeatedly in the same paragraph.

Datasets we use in our analyses include interview responses, characteristics of the legislator (e.g., age, ethnicity, gender), campaign contributions, district-level election data, and district demographic data. These datasets are linked by codes that identify the legislator, the district, the chamber, and the legislative term. Linking these datasets facilitates analysis by individual legislator, by district, by groups of legislators sharing specific characteristics (e.g., political party, gender, ethnicity, years in office, margin of electoral victory) or by groups of legislative districts sharing specific characteristics (e.g., competitive versus safe districts). This permits us to address the far-reaching claims of term limits advocates and detractors.

Summary

Limiting the length of time that a legislator can hold office is a dramatic change in state governance. There is a clear need to investigate the impacts of this change, but it is difficult to study impacts of term limits because they interact with the state's system of government. There is great diversity across the United States in the ways states choose to organize their political and policy-making systems. We found that effects of term limits depend on the specific institutional rules of the legislative chamber and the ways that the state's electoral system operates. For example in some states, like California, lower and upper chamber legislative districts are nested; in other states, Michigan for example, there may be only a tiny overlap between House and Senate Districts. In some states everything that is considered by a standing committee is sent to the floor of the chamber. Maine does this. In others, such as Michigan, only bills approved by the majority on the committee are sent to the chamber. These differences in the state's political institutions interact with the specific type and length of term limits to produce differential effects on state government and governing. In large cross-sectional studies, it is difficult, perhaps impossible, to control for these numerous differences. Thus, much that is interesting and important about term limits is likely to be canceled out by state-level differences that obscure profound impacts. Therefore, we believe that longitudinal single-state studies and comparisons among small groups of similar states with similar limits on service are essential to understand the effect of term limits. Further, given the limited findings to date on the impacts of term limits, it is important to begin by studying states in which term limits are most likely to have impacts—those with stringent limits and highly professionalized legislatures. Michigan and California are the two states with this combination of characteristics.

Elected officials and other government actors need information to help them govern under term limits. Voters need information to help them decide whether to modify or to repeal current term limits laws. Academics are interested in effects on political institutions and in information that can be generalized to other instances of political reform and legislative turnover. In the chapters that follow, we try to provide information that will be valuable to all these audiences. In our efforts to please all three groups of readers, we risk pleasing none of them. Therefore, we request your patience as we explain concepts that some of our academic readers know quite thoroughly or when we belabor methodological or other technical details likely to bore other readers. We have used endnotes extensively to report technical details, such as statistical tests used. We also provide appendices to provide more quantitative and technical details. Finally, we have tried to signal within the text sections that one or another segment of our audience may want to skim or skip.

As academics, we have tried to provide a balanced view of both the pros and cons of term limits throughout the chapters of this book—and there are both. Our frequent refrain of "on one hand . . ." and "on the other hand . . ." may lead some readers to yearn for a one-handed political scientist, much as Harry Truman famously begged that someone find him a "one-handed economist." Therefore, in the concluding chapter we doff our academic caps, at least partially, and make some specific recommendations and draw some specific conclusions.

PART ONE

Political Impacts of Term Limits

CHAPTER 1

Electoral Competition and Incumbency Advantages[1]

Imagine at least two candidates either of whom might win a majority of the votes cast by actively involved citizens—a competitive election. In reality, candidates for state legislatures often run unopposed in primary elections that attract less than 20 percent of the voters. General elections attract more voters, but few are competitive with most candidates winning by a landslide. In this chapter we explore some of the reasons that state legislative electoral reality falls short of the competitive ideal, and we investigate whether term limits increase electoral competition.

Open seat elections generally attract more candidates, spark more interest, and bring more voters to the polls (Gaddie & Bullock, 2000). So by increasing the number of open seat elections, term limits proponents reasoned that they would increase electoral competition. This seems like a plausible assumption, yet we found little evidence that this happened. Even more surprising, when an incumbent runs for reelection term limits seem to suppress competition. So term limits appear to make elections even less competitive overall despite substantially increasing the number of open seat contests.

To explore the effects of term limits on electoral competition, we examined the lower chambers of the California and Michigan legislatures. Readers are reminded that voters in both states adopted extremely stringent lifetime limits on legislative service, with a maximum of six years in the lower chamber and eight years in the upper chamber. Given their short terms of service and their highly professionalized legislatures, the effects of term limits should be more powerful in California and in Michigan than in any other states with term limits. Hence, if term limits do *not* affect electoral competition in these two states, it is less likely that they will anywhere.

As we noted in the introduction, the Michigan House of Representatives and the California General Assembly share many characteristics, but also differ on some key variables that might affect electoral competition. One of these differences is partisan competition. Political parties are important brokers of political competition. The strength of the political parties can be measured by their ability to exert control over the candidates appearing on primary ballots. Using this metric California's political parties are weak (Debow & Syer, 2000), and Michigan's are strong (Palm & Smith, 1995). Third-party candidates are less common and less important in Michigan than they are in California, where third-party candidates occasionally win elections and sometimes make a difference in the outcome of the election.

Although the two major political parties are active in both states, in the last decade and a half, statewide partisan competition was more common in Michigan than in California. Both Michigan and California have had Republicans and Democrats in control of legislative chambers during the 1990s, and each has had governors from both political parties. From 1942 to 1992, nearly two-thirds of Michigan's governors won with less than 55 percent of the vote. During the same time period, only 41.7 percent of California governor's races were decided in similarly close contests (G. Scott Thomas, 1994, p. 314). Michigan was a battle ground state in the 2000 presidential election, while California was safely Democratic. Partisan control of Michigan's State House of Representatives was closely contested and changed regularly in the pre-term limits years. The Democrats (and Willie Brown) maintained control of the California General Assembly in the years preceding term limits.

Although Michigan appears to have both stronger political parties and more partisan competition than California, Michigan's parties have distinct geographic bases of power. So statewide partisan competition does not usually translate into partisan competition within individual State House districts. Base party voting strength is lopsided in almost all of Michigan's races for the State House.[2] Thus we would expect Michigan's two parties to manage competition strategically to protect their most vulnerable candidates, and given the strength of the state's parties, we would expect them to succeed.

Design

To explore impacts of term limits–induced open seat elections on electoral competition, we relied on data for elections from 1988 through 2002 in Michigan and in California. Readers are reminded that California's voters passed a term limits law in 1990 that forced General Assembly members out of office beginning in 1996. Michigan voters adopted term limits in 1992 and ejected legislators from the State House for the first time in 1998. Hence, the implementation of term limits in the lower chamber of the legislature of these two states is offset by two years and provides some help, albeit limited, in distinguishing between some effects of history (e.g., reapportionment) and the effects of term limits. Additionally, the implementation of term limits was offset by four years in Michigan, affecting the House in 1998 and the State Senate and other statewide offices in 2002. In California, State Senators were termed out of office in 1998, two years after General Assembly members were first ejected.

Term Limits and Electoral Competition

To see whether term limits changed elections in California and Michigan, we examined three features of the electoral environment: (1) the *number of open seat elections* (2) levels of citizen participation measured by *voter turnout* in elections for the state's lower legislative chamber, and (3) whether the election was *competitive* or at least whether voters had a *choice among viable candidates* measured by the margin of victory in primary and general election contests. To see whether open seat races have the same effect on electoral competition when they occur at regular, frequent intervals, we analyzed these three facets of competition separately for open seat races and races in which an incumbent ran for reelection. We call the latter "closed seat" races.

In our analyses, we compare Michigan House elections before term limits were adopted (the baseline, from 1988 to 1992) to the period after voters adopted term limits but when no one was being forced out of office (the anticipatory effects, which would have occurred in 1994 and 1996 in Michigan) to the first three elections when legislators were forced from office (the direct effects, which occurred beginning in 1998). In California, voters adopted term limits in 1990, so the pre-term limits baseline includes 1988 and 1990. During the 1992 and 1994 elections, candidates could have been anticipating the onset of term limits. General Assembly members were first termed out of office in 1996, so the four California General Assembly elections from 1996 through 2002 were all post–term-limits elections.

Increases in the Number of Open Seat Races

With the constitutionality of Michigan's term limits law in question until a few months before term limits took effect in 1998, most of Michigan's State House members served until they were expelled from office. Thus, looking at table 1.1, we see only limited anticipatory impacts of term limits in Michigan. Sixty-four of the 110 members of the House were expelled in 1998. In 2000, only 21 House members were termed out of office. In both 1998 and 2000 all the incumbents eligible to run sought and won reelection. Although 85 incumbents could have run for reelection in 2002 for the Michigan House, only 58 chose to do so. Some incumbents who were not termed out did not run for reelection, and newly drawn districts pitted some incumbents against each other. This produced 52 open seat primary races and 53 open seat general election races in Michigan in 2002 after one incumbent lost in the primary. Although this might lead one to assume that term limits will produce periodic massive turnovers in the State House, it is more likely that this is an ephemeral effect of redistricting and a bumper crop of open seats in the State Senate. (In 2002, 30 Michigan State Senators were termed out of office, and new district boundaries were drawn to reflect the 2000 census.)

Looking at table 1.1, in California in 1992 and 1994 an usually high number of incumbents chose not to run for reelection. This might be the effect of anticipating term limits or the impact of redistricting or a combination of the two. New district boundaries may make campaigning more difficult, and sometimes redistricting pits incumbents against each other. Therefore, it typically produces some voluntary retirements from incumbents who know that they will have a tough fight to win reelection. A tough reelection battle might be even more likely to dissuade an incumbent from running when he or she will be termed out of office soon anyway.

In California in 1996, 28 of the 80 members of the California General Assembly were expelled from office. Although only 12 General Assembly members were termed out of office in 1998, 13 more incumbents chose not to run. Only 24 incumbents were "termed" out of office in 2000, yet there were 30 open seat general election contests. Clearly other factors continue to influence incumbents' decisions about running for reelection to the California General Assembly even when they are

Table 1.1 Impact of term limits on electoral competition

Election year	Number of incumbents who did not run for reelection		Number of incumbents losing either a primary or general election		Number of competitive general elections		Number of competitive primary elections	
	California 80 seats	Michigan 110 seats	California 80 seats	Michigan 110 seats	California 80 seats	Michigan 110 seats	California 160 primaries	Michigan 220 primaries
1988	3	5	4	3	15	16	10	16
1990	7	16	5	4	34	19	19	24
1992	24	19	4	6	44	35	50	49
1994	23	16	6	3	29	29	36	39
1996	31*	16	2*	7	37	22	36	31
1998	25	64*	2	0*	25	27	33	62
2000	30	21	1	0	21	24	29	22
2002	34	52	0	2	11	29	33	50

Notes: * First-year term limits implemented. Boldface type indicates term limits implemented.
Shading indicates first elections following redistricting, which are typically much more competitive than other elections.

legally permitted to run again. One of these factors is the opportunity to run for an open seat for another political office. Nine of the 13 who voluntarily departed from General Assembly in 1998, ran for open State Senate seats.

During the 1990s in both Michigan and California, there were more open seat primary election races for the lower chamber of the legislature. Given the severity of their limits on service, it is not surprising that we found this. Can we attribute all of this increase in open seats to term limits, however? The answer is not as simple as one might expect. As demonstrated later, it is not clear that term limits are wholly responsible for this change, but they probably contributed to it.

In California, before voters adopted term limits, open seat races for the General Assembly were uncommon with only three incumbents choosing not to run in the 1988 primary elections and only seven making this choice in 1990. After term limits were adopted, the number of open seats increased, ranging approximately between 25 and 35 open primaries from 1992 to 2002. Although it is tempting to attribute this increase in open seat races to the passage of term limits, evidence from Michigan's elections suggests that we need to be cautious about this. In Michigan, open seat elections increased at similar levels, but these increases occurred beginning in 1990, the election *before* voters adopted term limits. In 1988 only 5 of Michigan's 110 incumbent State Representatives did not seek reelection. In 1990–1996, between 15 and 20 incumbents chose not to run.[3] Michigan voters did not adopt term limits until 1992, so the number of open seat races in 1990 and in 1992 cannot be an impact of term limits. We infer from Michigan's increase in open seat elections that in California there may also have been factors other than anticipation of term limits that dissuaded incumbents from running for reelection. Changes in the political climate or the increased cost of running for office might have produced more open seat races.

Redistricting also is likely to increase open seat elections. Redistricting in 1992 coincided with the first year in which California's General Assembly members might decide not to run for reelection in anticipation of term limits, which passed in 1990. Redistricting may convince incumbents not to run in what would be a hotly contested race that they might lose. The voluntary vacancies in the General Assembly in 1992 and 1994 were nearly as high as those in 1996 when General Assembly members were expelled from office. It is hard to tell how many General Assembly members voluntarily retired from office because of term limits or because reelection in their newly drawn district would have been tough.

The number of incumbents defeated in California General Assembly primaries—one in 1990, three in 1992—suggests that shifting demographics and the newly drawn district boundaries changed the electoral landscape substantially in California in the early 1990s, even without term limits. In Michigan redistricting had similar effects, with three incumbents losing to non-incumbents, three pairs of incumbents running against each other in the primary elections, and one pair of incumbents running against each other in the 1992 general election. Given that Michigan voters did not adopt term limits until the 1992 election, redistricting is the most likely explanation for the increase in open seats and losses by incumbents there. This leads us to infer that redistricting is responsible for at least some of the open seats in California in 1992 and 1994.

We find a similar effect of redistricting in 2002 in both Michigan and California. In California 21 General Assembly Members were termed out of office in 2002, while 11 incumbents chose not to run for reelection. In 2002, term limits expelled members of the Michigan's State Senate for the first time. Additionally, the newly drawn district boundaries pitted incumbent representatives against each other or in districts with a majority of voters who had not been part of their old district. Faced with a tough election battle for only two more years in the State House, many of these representatives told us that they decided to run for a State Senate seat that would give them an opportunity to serve for eight more years. Although they acknowledged that a State Senate race would be challenging, many said it would be no more difficult than running against an incumbent in a newly redrawn district for their State House seat (interview notes, 2001–2002). This probably explains the high number of voluntary departures, which combined with the 24 forced departures, produced 52 open seat primary races in 2002 for the Michigan House of Representatives.

Despite the relatively high levels of stability in Michigan's and California's legislatures before term limits, incumbents did not seek reelection indefinitely and did not always win reelection. In the ten-year period from 1979 to 1989, 70 percent of California's legislative districts had at least one new incumbent, as did 65 percent of Michigan's (Thomas, 1994, p. 316). Incumbents for various reasons choose not to run for reelection, and incumbents can and do lose primary races as well as general election races. Referring again to table 1.1, prior to term limits, even though most incumbents were reelected, in both California and Michigan an average of between four and five incumbents per year lost either their primary or their general election race in addition to the incumbents who chose not to run again. After term limits, it became even more rare for an incumbent to lose a reelection bid, less than one per year. So it appears that term limits increase the power of incumbency, even as they increase the number of open seat races. We explore this in more depth when we discuss the competitiveness of elections before and after term limits.

Voter Turnout

Figure 1.1 presents evidence of the effects of term limits on voter turnout in Michigan and California.[4] Both states exhibit a saw-toothed pattern with peaks in presidential election years and troughs in the years of the midterm congressional and gubernatorial races in both states. To adjust for the effects of presidential elections, we compare turnout in the general elections in four-year cycles (1990 compared with 1994, 1998, and 2002; and 1992 compared with 1996 and 2000). In both Michigan and California, voter turnout in general elections appears virtually unaffected by term limits.

Given the partisan basis on which many legislative districts are drawn, often the only competitive races for seats in the state legislature occur in the primary. Turnout in General Assembly primaries in California did increase with the advent of term limits in 1996. This

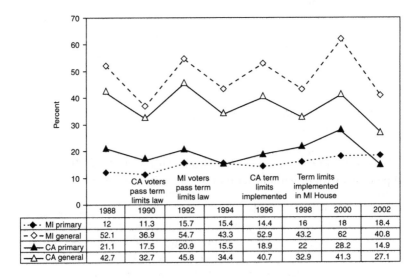

	1988	1990	1992	1994	1996	1998	2000	2002
··◆·· MI primary	12	11.3	15.7	15.4	14.4	16	18	18.4
– ◇ – MI general	52.1	36.9	54.7	43.3	52.9	43.2	62	40.8
—▲— CA primary	21.1	17.5	20.9	15.5	18.9	22	28.2	14.9
—△— CA general	42.7	32.7	45.8	34.4	40.7	32.9	41.3	27.1

Figure 1.1   Voter turnout in Michigan and California

might reflect the increased voter interest in the open seats produced by term limits. Interestingly, although the number of open seats *decreased* by six in California from 1996 to 1998, turnout for General Assembly primaries *increased* further. The "blanket primary" adopted in 1996 and taking effect in 1998 may account for this anomaly.[5]

In 1996 California voters passed a ballot initiative that authorized blanket primaries in which voters who are not self-identified members of a political party could vote in the primaries to help choose the parties' candidates. Without the blanket primary, voters not registered as members of a political party were/are barred from participating in primary elections, contributing to California's relatively low primary turnout (Hyink & Provost, 2001). In Michigan, although voters designate a party preference when they register, they can choose to vote in one or the other party's primary election. Additionally, voters who register as independents in Michigan can still vote in a primary election, while in California, independents without the blanket primary, received a primary ballot with only the nonpartisan candidates. Obviously the blanket primary gave California independents a chance to vote in the primary and could easily account for the increased turnout in 1998 and 2000.

During the 1998 and 2000 California primaries, voters received a ballot that listed all the candidates in all the parties' primaries and could choose to vote in different parties' primaries for different offices. Therefore, a voter could vote in the Democratic primary for General Assembly and in the Republican primary for Governor. In June 2000, the U.S. Supreme Court declared the blanket primary unconstitutional. With two simultaneous political experiments, term limits and the blanket primary, in effect in California in 1998 and 2000, it is difficult to determine the sources of California's increased turnout. Given that the demise of the blanket primary coincides with a dramatic decline in primary turnout in California, we suspect that the blanket primary may have had more impact on turnout than term limits did.

Voter turnout in primaries in Michigan continues to be low (less than 20 percent), with or without term limits. Despite a dramatic increase in open seat races, turnout in 1998 Michigan House primary races increased only slightly after term limits took effect. This effect in Michigan cannot be attributed to a change in the rules governing primaries as it could be in California. Yet, it is not clear that more open seat elections increased voter turnout. A greater percentage of Michigan's voters cast ballots in primaries for State House candidates in 2000 than did in 1998 despite a dramatic decline in the number of open seat races. The competitiveness of the primary races may be one factor that influences turnout more than an open seat, especially in primary races in which only one candidate, or at least only one viable candidate, may be running.

In short, an increase in the number of open seats may stimulate voter turnout slightly in the primaries for those seats, but overall post–term limits primary turnout remains low in both states and is subject to a wide variety of influences. Even though reapportionment produced fewer open seat contests than term limits did for the lower chamber of the legislature in both Michigan and California, it seems to have spurred primary turnout just as much. In general elections, we cannot find any lasting effect of term limits on voter turnout. Therefore, we conclude that simply increasing the number of open seat elections is not a prescription for increasing voter turnout.

Landslide Margins of Victory

One way to assess electoral competition involves the margin of victory, with landslide elections indicating very little electoral competition. To explore whether the level of competition between the two major parties is affected by term limits, we used a very generous measure of landslide elections, a 20 percent margin of victory. Often elections are not considered competitive unless the margin of victory is 10 percent or less, but it is very rare in Michigan for State House elections to be this competitive. Therefore, we are exploring elections that would be considered highly competitive to somewhat competitive. Given the tendency of politicians to design districts that are safe for a particular party, we were not surprised to find that most candidates for the Michigan House of Representatives won by a landslide. In California's more raucous political environment (Daniel & Lott, 1997; Hyink & Provost, 2001), landslide margins of victory for seats in the lower legislative chamber were less common than they were in Michigan, at least before term limits.

We give readers an overview of competitive general elections in table 1.1. Given the difference in the number of legislative districts in California (80) and Michigan (110), it is difficult to compare the patterns across these two states using the actual number of elections. Therefore, we rely on percentages in our discussion. As figure 1.2 demonstrates, the 1992 redistricting was associated with the highest percentage of competitive general election races for the lower legislative chamber in both states, but especially in California. In California, implementation of term limits is associated with another, albeit smaller, peak in the percentage of competitive elections. In Michigan the percentage of competitive elections in 1998 increased, but only slightly. The effect of term limits on electoral competition appears ephemeral, however. Following an increase in the percentage of competitive general election races during the year in which members were expelled by term limits (1996 in California and 1998 in Michigan), the percentage of competitive elections drifted back down toward the pre–term limits level. Even more surprising, in 2002 the usual redistricting peak in competitiveness was conspicuously absent for general elections for the lower legislative chamber in California and muted in Michigan. This was especially surprising in Michigan given that the mass exodus from the State Senate triggered a game of musical chairs in which more than two dozen Michigan representatives left office early in addition to the two dozen expelled by term limits.

Once again, we wondered whether general election landslide victories in closed seat races masked increased competition in open seat elections. Our findings are summarized in figure 1.3. Scanning across the bar charts for both states affirms the conventional wisdom that open seat races are more competitive than closed seat races, but there clearly are exceptions to this. Amazingly, term limits seem to have had little effect on the percentage of competitive open seat races for the California

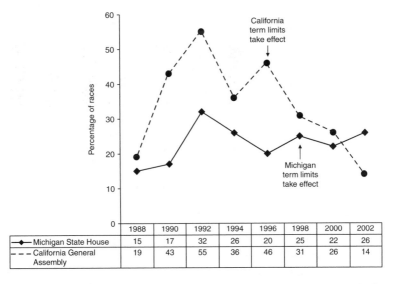

	1988	1990	1992	1994	1996	1998	2000	2002
Michigan State House	15	17	32	26	20	25	22	26
California General Assembly	19	43	55	36	46	31	26	14

Figure 1.2 Percentage of general election contests that were competitive (won by less than 60 percent of the votes)

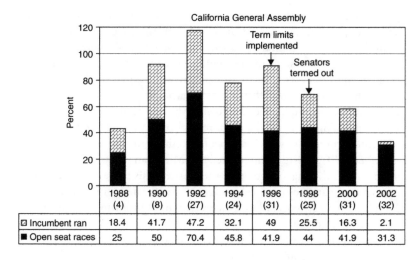

	1988 (4)	1990 (8)	1992 (27)	1994 (24)	1996 (31)	1998 (25)	2000 (31)	2002 (32)
☑ Incumbent ran	18.4	41.7	47.2	32.1	49	25.5	16.3	2.1
■ Open seat races	25	50	70.4	45.8	41.9	44	41.9	31.3

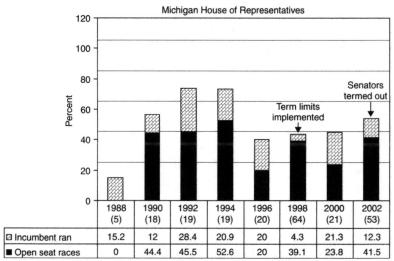

	1988 (5)	1990 (18)	1992 (19)	1994 (19)	1996 (20)	1998 (64)	2000 (21)	2002 (53)
☑ Incumbent ran	15.2	12	28.4	20.9	20	4.3	21.3	12.3
■ Open seat races	0	44.4	45.5	52.6	20	39.1	23.8	41.5

Figure 1.3 Competitive general election races as a percentage of open seats and a percentage of closed seats

Note: The number of open seat races appears in parentheses beneath the election year.

General Assembly. The percentage of open seat general election races that were competitive peaked in 1992, when redistricting and anticipation of term limits coincided. Subsequently, the percentage of open seat elections that were competitive hovered between 40 and 45 percent until the 2002 redistricting. Then instead of rebounding, the percentage of open seat competitive general elections for General Assembly seats dropped by approximately 10 percentage points! Returning for a moment to table 1.1, readers will see that the percentage of competitive elections in California declined after term limits, and, as figure 1.3 demonstrates, the decline is not an artifact of less competition in closed seat races. California's experience clearly challenges the assumption that term limits would increase electoral competition.

In California, we found that the percentage of *closed* seat races that were competitive spiked in 1996, the year in which General Assembly members were expelled. After term limits took effect in California, competitive closed seat elections became less and less common, however. Instead of rebounding in 2002 with newly drawn district boundaries, competition all but disappeared for general elections in which an incumbent ran. Therefore, both open and closed seat general election races in California are less likely to be competitive in the post–term limits era.

In Michigan the evidence appearing in figure 1.3 is more ambiguous. There seems to be a roller coaster pattern of increases and decreases in general election competition for open and closed seats in the Michigan House of Representatives. Further, these rolling cycles seem to be mirror images of each other. In the Michigan House in 1998 with 64 open seats, competition all but disappeared in the 46 closed seat races. In a similar, but less pronounced slump, the percentage of competitive closed seat races dropped in 2002 as the number of open seat general election races soared to 53. In 1998 and 2002, the percentage of competitive elections for open State House seats rebounded almost to their pre–term limits levels. Just prior to and in the immediate aftermath of term limits expulsions, in 1996 and 2000 respectively, the percentage of these open seat general election races that were competitive dropped to approximately 20 percent.

The number of open seats in Michigan still exhibits peaks and valleys that reflect the way term limits were implemented. As we noted earlier, in Michigan expulsion effects were very large. Also because term limits did not affect the State Senate until 2002, there were attractive opportunities to run for higher office that affected some House members' decisions about whether to run for reelection. Looking at this pattern it appears that when open seats are numerous, competition for closed seats drops and when open seats are less numerous, competition for closed seats rises. This pattern suggests a partisan strategy in which finite resources can be spread over only a limited number of competitive races, and these resources are concentrated in those races in which the party believes it has the highest probability of winning, regardless of whether they are open or closed seat races. Comparing the two redistricting elections, 1992 and 2002, we see the number of competitive races trending downward, but less dramatically than in California. We suspect that, except when there is a "shock" to the electoral system (e.g., redistricting, mass term limits expulsions), partisan decisions will overwhelm any long-term impact of term limits on electoral competition. We will continue to watch this pattern in Michigan as the secondary impact of term limits' implementation in the State Senate filters through the electoral politics in Michigan House districts.

Contested Primary Elections

Although fewer citizens vote in primary elections, these are often important races. The primary election, especially in districts with a lopsided partisan split, may be crucial in selecting the candidate who will be anointed in uncontested or at least uncompetitive general elections. For example, Michigan House of Representatives Districts within the City of Detroit often have a base Democratic voting strength of 80–90 percent or more. Competition in primary elections is the only electoral competition voters in these districts are likely to see—with or without term limits.

In figure 1.4, we see that, overall, primary elections seem to have become more competitive in California after term limits, although it is difficult to isolate the effects of term limits and the effects in 1996 and 1998 of the blanket primary. In Michigan we find the same swings that we observed in the open and closed seat races for the general election. When there are many open seats, there are more competitive primaries, and when there are fewer open seats there are fewer competitive primary elections. Even so the percentage of competitive primary races for the Michigan State House remains low, less than one-quarter overall, except in 1998 when it peaked at 28 percent with the massive term limits expulsions.

Given the differing impacts we found on open and closed seat general election races, we examined these two types of primary elections separately for each state. Looking at figure 1.5 we find that competition in closed seat primary races for the California General Assembly seems to vanish after term limits. This pattern persisted even in 2002 when redistricting would lead us to expect the some incumbents might have to run against each other. The percentage of California open seat primary races that were competitive drifted downward from a "redistricting" high in 1992—seemingly unaffected by term limits expulsions in 1996.

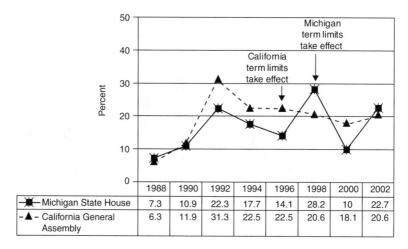

Figure 1.4 Competitive primary elections (percent won with less than 60 percent of the votes cast)

	1988	1990	1992	1994	1996	1998	2000	2002
Michigan State House	7.3	10.9	22.3	17.7	14.1	28.2	10	22.7
California General Assembly	6.3	11.9	31.3	22.5	22.5	20.6	18.1	20.6

Looking at figure 1.5, we see that in Michigan competition in races for closed seats declined steadily from the 1992 redistricting peak through 2000. The percentage of competitive primary races for closed seats in 2002 with redistricting does increase slightly, but less than expected compared to 1992. Referring to table 1.1 again, we see that, even with the more than 2.5 times as many open seat elections, the total number of competitive primary races increased by only one (from 49 competitive primaries in 1992 to 50 competitive primaries in 2002). What is more surprising is that the percentage of open seat primary races that are competitive declines after term limits expelled members of the Michigan House of Representatives. The decline reverses but only mildly in 2002 with redistricting. To our surprise, there was a 20 percentage point drop in the percentage of open seat primary races that were competitive in 2002 compared to 1992, both redistricting elections.

Here again we suspect that political party control over the resources candidates need to run a competitive election influences the number of competitive primaries as well as the number of competitive general elections. These findings remind us that electoral competition is a complex process that is influenced by many different factors other than simply increasing the number of open seat contests.

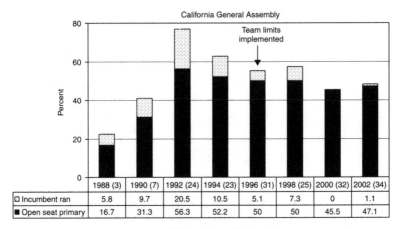

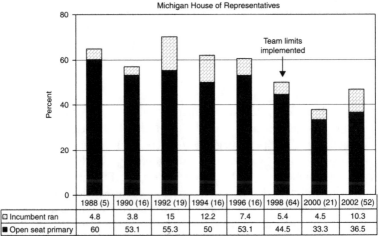

Figure 1.5 Competitive primary elections for open seats and closed seats

Note: The number of openseat races appears in parentheses accompanying the election year.

Conclusions

Term limits' effects on Michigan and California state legislative elections surprised us. Although there were more open seat elections, this did not increase voter turnout or provide a lasting increase in electoral competition. We found more competitive elections for the lower legislative chamber in both states when term limits initially expelled veteran legislators but, this appears to have been transient. Indeed, if we look only

at California General Assembly elections in the years following implementation of term limits, we would conclude that term limits are a
powerful way to depress electoral competition, even in years when
districts have been redrawn. In Michigan, we found a very slight
rebound in competitive elections in 2002 with redistricting, but overall
the picture is similar. Increasing the number of open seat races is no
guarantee that voters will be interested enough to vote and may actually
decrease the number of races that are competitive after the novelty of
term limits wears off. Usually open seat elections are more competitive
and attract more interest. Therefore we found these findings surprising.

The role of political parties in elections provides one plausible explanation for these puzzling results. Political parties can suppress competition even for open seats (Jewell, 1998). This may account for the stable
or declining levels of competition we found for open seat primary
elections for the lower chamber in Michigan and California after term
limits. With higher turnover jeopardizing their control of the chamber,
political parties might target scarce resources toward districts that are
critical to partisan control.[6] This may decrease electoral competition for
other seats.

This explanation fits the evidence in Michigan particularly well.
When open seats for the Michigan House of Representatives were
scarce, closed seat races were more competitive. When open seat races
were numerous, competition for closed seats dwindled. Political parties
raise and spend a lot of money, but not infinite amounts. Therefore, the
parties are likely to target their resources toward races in which the
candidate has the best chance of unseating an incumbent or winning an
open seat. The number of seats chosen for these infusions of scarce
resources may remain fairly constant regardless of the number of open
seats. Prior to term limits, there may have been enough money to spend
extra resources on any of the open seat primary races with money left
over to fund some challenges to incumbents. With the influx of open
seats precipitated by term limits, the political parties may have to pick
and choose among open seat races with little or nothing left to fund
challenges to incumbents. The strength of Michigan's political parties
may make these strategic calculations a more prominent feature of its
political landscape.

There have always been electoral advantages of incumbency (Breaux &
Jewell, 1992), yet prior to term limits a handful of incumbents lost every
year. After term limits were adopted, incumbents rarely lost, suggesting
that the incumbency advantage is more intense, although it is legally
truncated. This is consistent with our speculation that scarce resources

leave little money to help newcomers challenge incumbents when there are so many open seat races. Our findings suggest that the six-year cap on tenure in the Michigan House and the California General Assembly may well become the normal length of service with potential challengers willing to wait for an open seat instead of challenging an incumbent or political parties unwilling to fund viable challengers until the seat is open. This will lead to episodes of electoral competition over open seats. But even these periodic bursts of electoral competition will be confined to primaries instead of the general elections that most candidates increasingly win by landslide margins of victory.

Thus, elections for closed seats may be less competitive than they were prior to term limits, if the trends seen in these elections in Michigan from 1998 to 2002 and in California from 1996 to 2002 persist. In the term-limited electoral environment, we conclude that political parties may suppress competition for closed seats so that they can concentrate limited time and money on a subset of open seats that offer the best opportunity of winning majority control of the chamber. We also suspect that "rational" candidates for seats in the states' lower chambers will wait until their prospects of victory are better, especially when the wait is short—only six years at most.

CHAPTER 2

Funding Campaigns in a Term-Limited House[1]

Legislative term limits are likely to affect the costs of state legislative campaigns in opposing ways. On the one hand, they might increase the cost of elections because there will be more open seat contests, which tend to be more expensive (Gierzynski, 1998). On the other hand, they might reduce the cost of elections in two ways.

First, with shorter terms of service, a legislative seat might be a less valuable commodity, so candidates and their patrons might not be willing to spend as much money to win the office (Mitchell, 1991). From the point of view of an organized group, there may be little point in using campaign contributions to establish an ongoing relationship with a state legislator who will be expelled from a given chamber of the legislature in a few years.

Second, some proponents believed that term limits would increase the proportion of legislators attracted to public service for ideological or policy reasons instead of aspirations for a political career. They also believed that this "new breed" of term-limited legislator would be less inclined to provide the kinds of legislative services that organized interests expect. Therefore they predicted a decline in campaign contributions if people with such orientations entered state legislatures in greater numbers and if special interests saw a declining return on their investment in candidates' elections (Brown, Powell, & Wilcox, 1995).

In practice, both effects could coexist. With more open seats available in every election cycle, aggregate spending might increase. Yet the average level of contributions per individual candidate (incumbent or nonincumbent) might decrease compared to pre–term limit days if seats are less valuable and organized groups are more reluctant to spend money because the return on their investment is more uncertain.

Beyond the impact of term limits on the amount of money spent, they may influence how different types of contributors target their contributions and the relative importance of different sources of campaign funds for state legislative seats. Various studies have found that political action committees (PACs) tend to concentrate their contributions on incumbents of either party and also tend to target legislative leaders.[2] The committee assignments of incumbents seeking election are also seen as an important factor in the decisions of interest groups considering contributions to legislative candidates.[3] There is only one study that explores these patterns with respect to the impact of term limits, however. Gordon and Unmack (1999), focusing on California, identify what they call "juice committees." These are committees that, among other things, have the authority to regulate or otherwise impact the activities of powerful interests in a state. In their study they focus on the California Assembly's (lower house) committees relating to transportation, finance and insurance, and agriculture. Traditionally PACs of organized groups contributed heavily to members of these committees because of the "help" these legislators might provide in blocking or facilitating the progress of bills through the committee. Gordon and Unmack hypothesized that after term limits took effect the committee assignments of legislators would be a weaker predictor of corporate PAC contributions. Like others,[4] Gordon and Unmack also identified the ideological inclinations of candidates as factors that influence the strategies of contributors. They hypothesized that ideology also would become a less significant predictor of corporate PAC contribution after the implementation of term limits.

Last, but certainly not least, term limits may affect the role that party organizations—whether national or statewide or within each chamber of the legislature—play in the financing of state legislative campaigns. With a larger number of open seat election contests, term limits increase the odds that majority control may shift from one party to another—except in one-party dominated states. This should increase the importance of campaigns for the state legislature in the eyes of state party leaders. Moreover, with legislative service presumably less attractive because an extended legislative career is thwarted by the existence of term limits, recruiting good candidates to run for the legislature becomes simultaneously more essential and more daunting. This, too, may cause party organizations to play a bigger role. Using data from the mid-1980s and early 1990s for 11 states, Gierzynski and Breaux (1998) find that, while the extent of party organizations' support for state legislative candidates varies across states, parties commonly target aid to their candidates running for open seats and especially to those running in districts that are closely competitive. Thus, we would expect that the increase in open seats that inevitably accompanies term limits will prompt state party organizations to become even more involved in campaigns for these seats.

Term limits may affect the role played by party organizations in state legislative campaigns and campaign finance in yet another way. Earlier we discussed the contribution patterns typical of political action committees. While the partisan affiliation of a legislator has always been of some importance in interest groups' decisions to contribute to campaigns (Gopoian, 1984; Grier & Munger, 1991 and 1993), it is not the only or even necessarily dominant factor in some elections. PACs frequently concentrate on incumbents regardless of party. Grier and Munger (1986) found that party was not an important variable when attempting to understand corporate donations. This may change under term limits, however, because not only will there be fewer incumbents running for reelection in any given election cycle, but even those who do run for reelection can do so only a few times. Therefore, it will be difficult for interest groups to accumulate the wealth of information about candidates that they can when the "track record" is longer. Gordon and Unmack argue that with newcomers' political ideology less well known and committee service less valuable to organized interests, organized groups' decisions to fund campaigns will depend more heavily on the party affiliation of a candidate. Therefore, political party will become a more significant predictor of corporate PAC contributions after the full implementation of term limits. Funneling contributions to party organizations may be one way for donors to cope with heightened uncertainty and information asymmetry about the candidates.

Methodology

While nearly two-thirds of the races in 1998 for the Michigan House of Representatives were for open seats, in the Senate numerous incumbents who had served for many years ran for reelection. The fact that term limits did not take effect in the Michigan Senate until 2002 means that we can use the Senate to control for state and national political dynamics other than term limits that might have affected various dimensions of campaign finance in the Michigan House races in 1998. Hence, if term limits impact patterns and dynamics of campaign finance, these effects should be clearly evident in the case of the House but not the

State Senate. One reason that having the Michigan Senate as a control group is important relates to the sharp increase in so-called soft money contributions since the mid-1990s. As Gierzynski and Breaux (1998) have observed:

> The 1996 election was a watershed for "soft money" (that is, unregulated money with no limits as to who can contribute or how much can be contributed). Soft money is raised by the national party committees for purposes of party building. More specifically, soft money is used for paying a portion of state party overhead; for campaign activity that bene-fits federal, state, and local elections (e.g., voter registration and get-out-the-vote drives); issue advocacy; and generic party advertising. (p. 204)

Because we have campaign finance data for both House and Senate candidates[5] we are in a better position to rule out the "soft-money explosion" or other outside influences on Michigan's electoral politics as alternative source of changes in spending for House races.[6]

In this chapter we have two central purposes. First, we explore whether or not the imposition of term limits for the lower house of the Michigan legislature has had the effect of increasing campaign contri-butions for House candidates—measured both as the aggregate amount raised by all candidates and on a per candidate basis. This is important because, while an increase in open seats may increase the stakes for parties and interest groups and prompt them to contribute more, the existence of more open seats may well prompt so many more candidates to seek their party's nomination that there will not be enough money available to support each of these candidates at the levels received by their predecessors.

Second, this chapter investigates whether the significance of different sources of campaign funds for Michigan House candidates changed as a consequence of the advent of term limits. One question here is whether the contribution allocation patterns of interest groups changed so that factors such as the past committee assignments of incumbent candidates or the partisan affiliation of all candidates matter relatively more or less than they once did. A second question is whether or not party organizations became more important sources of funds for candidates running for a term-limited legislative body. This might have occurred as interest groups increasingly funneled contributions through the party organizations rather than contributed directly to candidates. It might also have occurred because the stakes for the parties grew as term limits increased the number of open seats, making partisan control less certain. Fierce competition for partisan control of the chamber increased the need for parties to recruit good candidates, perhaps by promising them a substantial level of financial support.

Data

We gathered data for two time points for the Michigan State House and Senate: a pre–term limits election year, 1990, before term limits were enacted in 1992, and a term limits election year, 1998, the first election in which term limits took effect for incumbent House members. There were a sizable number of contribution records to code. For example, for 1998, we coded approximately 39,000 House contribution records including contributions for both the primary and general election periods. Until recently, the State of Michigan was legally prohibited from maintaining campaign finance records for more than six years.[7] Therefore, when we began this research project in 1998, the 1990 campaign finance records were not available from the Michigan Secretary of State (SOS). We were given a microfiche reader and many boxes of microfiche, including the 1990 campaign finance records, by Mark Grebner of Practical Political Consultants.

We used data on contributions to all candidates actually participating in the 1990 and 1998 primary or general elections. Some contribution records were submitted to the Michigan SOS for politicians who created campaign committees, but did not run. These we excluded. In addition, some candidates who ran did not report contributions. In the vast majority of cases these candidates had filed for waivers from the SOS, permitting them not to file so long as they collected no more than $1,000 in the primary and $1,000 in the general election. The amount of contributions that these candidates actually received is unknown, possibly ranging from $0 to $2,000, so in most of our analyses we excluded them. Excluding these contributions could, however, bias our results, so, as we explain later, in some of our analysis we estimate the amounts raised by these candidates.

We classified contributions by 15 broad types of donors: individual, corporate, trade association, educational labor unions, public sector labor unions, regular labor unions, non-unionized public sector, citizens' groups, legal groups and lobbyists, member PACs, legislative leadership and coalition PACs, agricultural groups, medical professionals, party organizations, and unidentified. Additionally, we subdivided individual contributions to reflect personal or family members' contributions whenever we could identify them separately. These categories represent the major sources of campaign contributions in Michigan.

The Michigan Secretary of State no longer enters campaign contributions electronically. They only provide scanned copies in PDF format for candidates who do not choose to provide the information electronically. This means that these data are so incomplete that researchers such as ourselves cannot systematically assess patterns in campaign contributions without assistance. We overcame this problem through the generous assistance of Edwin Bender of the National Institute for Money in State Politics (NIMSP). He and his staff provided us with the 2000 and 2002 election contribution data for Michigan. We provide some preliminary evidence from the 2000 and 2002 elections years here. Additionally, we refer readers who are interested in more technical treatment of these to data to our previous work (Sarbaugh-Thompson et al., 2002) and suggest they contact us if they are interested in future analyses.

Changes in Campaign Contributions from 1990 to 1998

It is useful before examining specific hypotheses to explore the overall patterns of campaign contributions between 1990 and 1998. In 1990 and 1998 respectively there were 30,603 and 39,375 contributions made to candidates running for the Michigan House of Representatives. In 1990 there were 321 candidates running for election to the 110 House seats, but only 167 filed campaign finance reports. Therefore, some data were clearly missing, although some of these "missing" candidate records are likely to reflect waivers filed by those who raised less than $1,000.[8] In 1998, there were 541 candidates running and 445 who filed reports, also indicating missing campaign finance reports. Using an estimation formula,[9] we adjusted the total contributions for both elections. We estimate that the campaign contributions for 1990 totaled approximately 7.5 million dollars. In 1998, this total rose to slightly more than $11 million, an increase of 46 percent or nearly 3.5 million dollars. In order to compare these amounts without the effect of inflation, we deflated the 1998 dollars to their 1990 value by dividing the 1998 dollars by the Consumer Price Index estimate for inflation between 1990 and 1998.[10]

For the Senate there were 27,713 contributions in 1990 and 22,147 in 1998, a *decrease* of 21 percent. In 1990, 128 candidates ran for the 38 seats in the Michigan State Senate. We had campaign finance reports for only 71 of these. In 1998, 122 candidates ran, but only 86 filed campaign finance reports. Using the same technique, we estimated that in 1990 the total amount contributed to candidates for the Michigan

State Senate totaled nearly $9 million. In 1998, we estimated that contributions to State Senate candidates declined to slightly more than $7 million, a decrease of approximately $1.9 million or 21 percent.

Clearly the trends differ for overall amount contributed to campaigns for the House and the Senate for the period from 1990 to 1998. For the Senate the amount of contributions decreased, while in the House they rose dramatically. Part of the increase in total House contributions can be explained by the dramatic increase in the number of candidates running for office. Despite a decrease of 36 percent in the average amount raised by each candidate, the sheer number of candidates running in 1998 increased the total amount raised to fund House races. This lower average amount raised for House races was not entirely surprising. First, we suspect that many of the candidates may have been the type of political novice that term limits advocates hoped would throw their hats into the ring. Their inexperience and lack of political connections are likely to have left them at a disadvantage in fundraising, and so their political coffers may have been empty or nearly so.

We did not expect the pattern that emerged in State Senate contributions, however. With a fairly stable number of candidates running, the average amount raised by individual candidates for the Senate was lower than it had been in 1990. Assuming that the deep pockets of special interests and other donors to political campaigns are not bottomless, there may be limits to the amounts available or at least the amounts donors are willing to spend on campaign contributions. Thus, the increase in total contributions to the House may have limited the amount available to support campaigns for Senate seats. Evidence nationally suggests that campaigns in general have become more not less costly. The drop in Senate contributions suggests that campaign contributions may be, at least to some extent, zero–sum commodities.[11]

Contributions to Open Seat Races

To compare the impact of term limits on the amounts of money given in open seat election contests, we used an average for House districts across the state. We did this because occasionally there are candidates who receive exceptionally large amounts of money and also candidates who raise extremely small amounts of money (e.g., those who run a very limited campaign in the primary). We wanted to look at the overall trend in giving to open seat races without being distracted by exceptional cases that might skew the pattern in one direction or the other. These very big or very small values are called "outliers."

Looking at table 2.1, we see that in 1990 the average amount given to candidates in open seat races was more than the average amount contributed to candidates in closed seat races. In all three elections after term limits took effect, we find the opposite pattern. In all three elections after term limits (1998, 2000, and 2002), the average amount received by candidates running in closed seat races was larger than the average amount received by candidates running for open seats. As we discussed earlier, contributors may not know the ideology, the likely committee assignment, or the willingness or ability of new candidates running in open seats to provide some return on the donors' campaign "investment." This uncertainty may make them reluctant to give money.

During the 2000 election, there were relatively few open seats races, only 21—a modest number of open seat races for the term-limited Michigan House—and none of these were in competitive districts. Yet in this election, we find the widest disparity between the average amount given to those running in open or closed seat races. For races in which an incumbent ran—closed seat races—the average amount contributed was about $15,000 more per district (approximately $39,000 compared to $24,000 in open seat races using constant 1990 dollars [see table 2.1]). With "only" 21 new candidates, we thought special interests and other donors might have an opportunity to gather information about these newcomers. In our previous work (Sarbaugh–Thompson et al., 2002), we speculated that the smaller number of open seats before term limits might explain the higher giving we found in 1990 (before term limits) in open seat races. If uncertainty about candidates limits giving, then it appears that even the smallest cohort of newcomers after term limits, in 2000, was still too large for donors to resolve the uncertainty about the candidate's value.

In 2002, as House members sought seats in the State Senate, there was another major upsurge in open seat Michigan House races, with 54 open seats in the general election—almost as many as in 1998. The gap between the average amounts raised in open and closed seat races in 1998 and 2002 was small (between $2,500 and $4,000). Yet, more money still flowed to the cohort of candidates running in closed seat races. We suspect that part of the reason the gap between open and closed seat giving is so large in 2000 is that there were no open seat races in competitive districts.

In Michigan both before and after term limits, competitive elections attract more money. As we noted in chapter 1, partisan control of the Michigan House of Representatives changes fairly regularly. Therefore,

Table 2.1 Campaign contributions to the Michigan House and Senate before and after term limits

	House 1990	House 1998	House 2000	House 2002	Senate 1990	Senate 1998
Contributions in 1990 dollars						
Factor used to divide current dollars to convert to 1990 dollars	1.00	1.23	1.33	1.36	1.00	1.23
Mean for all candidates reporting	$36,446.00	$18,829.69	$27,292.70	$22,518.38	$87,104.00	$76,038.04
Mean in open seat races	$41,201.00	$22,695.09	$24,061.37	$28,752.21	$93,305.95	$100,328.06
Mean in closed seat races	$34,584.00	$25,134.06	$39,043.04	$32,618.38	$85,442.94	$75,296.24
Mean in competitive races	$44,020.00	$31,057.72	$73,579.43	$36,630.62	$114,734.49	$107,902.21
Mean in noncompetitive races	$33,116.00	$19,166.65	$32,443.05	$28,702.48	$69,112.28	$73,284.37
Total amount spent on all seats	$6,086,562.00	$8,379,483.86	$6,479,537.83	$11,995,755.88	$6,184,394.00	$5,296,957.57
Raised by Democratic candidates	$3,484,827.00	$4,004,506.13	$2,538,385.38	$4,218,801.47	$2,269,352.00	$1,743,090.00
Raised by Republican candidates	$2,601,735.00	$6,261,313.53	$3,957,573.20	$7,772,890.44	$3,915,042.00	$4,796,050.00
Ratio in 1990 dollars	$1.34	$0.64	$0.64	$0.54	$0.58	$0.36
Contributions not adjusted to constant 1990 dollars						
Mean for all candidates reporting	$36,446.00	$23,246.00	$36,167.00	$30,625.00	$87,104.00	$93,872.00
Mean in open seat races	$41,201.00	$28,018.00	$31,885.00	$39,103.00	$93,305.95	$123,859.00
Mean in closed seat races	$34,584.00	$31,029.00	$51,738.00	$44,361.00	$85,442.94	$92,956.22
Mean in competitive races	$44,020.00	$38,342.00	$97,504.00	$49,817.64	$114,734.49	$133,209.60
Mean in noncompetitive races	$33,116.00	$23,662.00	$42,992.00	$39,035.86	$69,112.28	$90,472.48
Total amount spent on all seats	$6,086,562.00	$10,344,808.00	$8,586,379.00	$16,314,228.00	$6,184,394.00	$6,539,306.00
Raised by Democratic candidates	$3,484,827.00	$4,943,723.00	$3,363,749.00	$5,737,570.00	$2,269,352.00	$2,151,914.33
Raised by Republican candidates	$2,601,735.00	$7,729,842.00	$5,244,390.00	$10,571,131.00	$3,915,042.00	$5,920,915.57

the outcome of a few competitive elections can determine partisan control of the chamber, which has profound impacts on policymaking in the state. There are very few competitive districts in Michigan—only 10 out of the 110 based on the districts drawn after the 1990 census, and 28 in the districts drawn after the 2000 census.[12] so it is feasible to concentrate both time and money on these few crucial seats. In 1990, we find an increment of approximately $11,000–$12,000 between the average amounts raised by candidates running in competitive districts over the average amounts raised by other candidates for the State House. In 2000 we found an astounding difference of $41,000 between the average amounts raised by candidates running in competitive elections— all of which were closed seat races—and the average amounts raised by other candidates.

One might assume that open seat races in competitive districts would attract the most money because there would be a good chance to win a seat that should be valuable in the partisan competition to control the chamber. Prior to term limits these assumptions would have been correct. Not so after term limits, however. In our previous work (Sarbaugh-Thompson et al., 2002), we reported that prior to term limits, contributions to candidates in open seat races in competitive districts were much higher than the average amount given to candidates running in closed seat races, regardless of whether the closed seat race was in a competitive district or not. Additionally in open seat races in districts that were not competitive, candidates received the lowest average amount of money—less than they did in any of the other situations. In the same work, we demonstrated that this was not true in the post–term limits election of 1998. We cannot test this effect using the 2000 election data because there were no open seat races in competitive districts. We can, however, explore this in the 2002 election. We find again that the interaction effect between open seats and competitiveness of the district has vanished and that the main factor predicting the average amounts of campaign funds candidates raised is the competitiveness of the district. Increasingly it appears that the competitiveness of the district not whether there is an incumbent running determines whether the race attracts large sums of money.

With more open seats after term limits, open seats seem less important. Just as we saw electoral competition decrease for open seat races, we now see less "economic" competition over open seats after term limits. We infer from this that the significance of open seat elections may have changed after term limits in ways that their advocates are not likely to have anticipated. Further, this finding suggests to us that even the deep pockets of special interests are not bottomless. Therefore, when there are competing reasons to donate money, even wealthy donors are forced to make choices. Competitive districts, with their potential to determine partisan control of the chamber, yield a higher return on the contributor's investment than a relatively unknown candidate running in a "safe" district.

Money Available to Candidates from the Two Major Political Parties

Term limits seem to change the amounts that candidates from the two major political parties receive for their campaigns. In 1990, prior to term limits and after a period of more than a decade of Democratic control of the chamber, the total amount raised by Democratic candidates for Michigan House races exceeded the amount raised by Republican candidates. Thinking of this as a ratio, the Democrats running for the House raised approximately $1.35 for every dollar raised by the Republican House candidates. With the advent of term limits in 1998, we find Republicans with a substantial fund raising advantage. In 1998 the Democratic House candidates as a group raised about 65 cents for every dollar raised by all the Republican House candidates. This ratio remained at the same level before tilting even further toward the Republicans. In 2002, all the Democratic State House candidates raised about 55 cents for every dollar raised by all the Republican candidates for State House.

Clearly this could be part of the national trend in which Republicans have a substantial fundraising advantage over Democrats. To see whether this simply reflects that broader pattern or is associated with the shift to term limits, we examined the change in this pattern of fundraising from 1990 to 1998 in races for the Michigan Senate. In 1990, with majority control of the State Senate in Republican hands for almost a decade, the total amount raised by all Democratic candidates running for the State Senate was 58 cents for every dollar raised by the group of Republican candidates running for the State Senate. By 1998 the Republican fundraising advantage had increased dramatically. As a group, all Democratic candidates running for the State Senate raised 36 cents for every dollar raised by all the Republican candidates running for the State Senate.

The comparison with the State Senate suggests two factors that are likely to account for the partisan fundraising disparity. First, majority control of the chamber is associated with receiving more contributions for campaigns. This reflects the potentially greater return on a contributor's investment that members of the majority party can provide. This advantage results in large part from the way bills in the Michigan legislature are sent to the floor of the chamber. Committee chairs, who are always members of the majority party in the chamber, and the majority party leaders have an enormous amount of influence on this, as we explain in greater detail in chapter 8. Partisan control of the State Senate remained constant between 1990 and 1998 and state Senators were not yet termed out of office. Therefore, we suspect that the increased fundraising advantages of Republican State Senate candidates reflect the national funding disparities between the two major political parties. Thus we conclude that partisan control of the House by the Republicans after term limits and the national fundraising trends, not term limits, are the principal explanations for the severe decline in money faced by Democratic candidates for the Michigan State House. On the other hand, the ratio of Democratic to Republican fundraising declined more dramatically in the House than in the Senate from 1990 to 1998, so we suspect that term limits also had an impact, just not the principal impact.

Changes in the Types of Contributors and Their Share of Campaign Contributions

To look at overarching patterns of contributions by types of contributors, we grouped the contributions into three very general categories of givers—organized groups, partisan political sources, and individual sources (including personal and family contributions). This comparison is presented in a bar chart in figure 2.1. The bars in the chart are clustered by the three broad types of contributors. Within each cluster the 1990 and 1998 House appear side-by-side followed by the 1990 and 1998 Senate. To assess the pattern of change in contributions within each chamber, we looked at the steps between 1990 and 1998 for each of the two legislative chambers. We compare the two chambers to determine whether term limits had an impact on these groups of contributors by looking at the relative size of the steps between the two pairs of bars.

The patterns of change for the House and the Senate between 1990 and 1998 for these three broad categories of contributors appear to move in tandem and to be approximately the same proportion. Contributions from organized groups shrank by 13 percent for the House races and by 12 percent for the Senate. Contributions from partisan political sources increased by 5 percent for the House and 4 percent for the Senate, no doubt reflecting the national increase in soft money

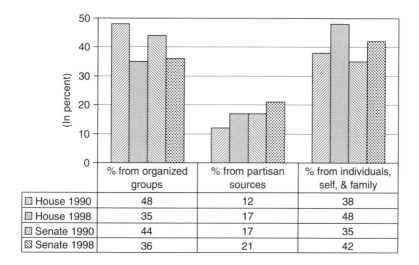

	% from organized groups	% from partisan sources	% from individuals, self, & family
▨ House 1990	48	12	38
▤ House 1998	35	17	48
▨ Senate 1990	44	17	35
▨ Senate 1998	36	21	42

Figure 2.1 Proportion of contributions from types of donors

funneled through political parties of which Gierzynski and Breaux (1998) speak. Finally, we found that individual contributions to both the House and Senate campaigns increased by 10 percent in the House and 7 percent in the Senate. This would suggest that term limits had little or no effect on the proportion of contributions coming from different types of donors to state legislative candidates, at least not in Michigan.

Looking at the major subgroups within these three broad categories, however, reveals some crucial differences that seem to be associated with the onset of term limits in the Michigan House of Representatives in 1998. The dollar amounts given by each type of subgroup are provided in table 2.2. We discuss these amounts as a proportion of the total contributions because we want to explore the relative significance of these different subgroups in the overall fundraising efforts by the House and Senate. Figure 2.2 presents the proportions graphically.

First, before term limits the campaign funds given by corporate donors and peak trade groups accounted for approximately the same proportion of the total funds given for House and the Senate races. In 1998, with the onset of term limits in the House, the proportion of total funds given by these sources declined by 8 percent from the 1990 proportion. For the Senate the change from 1990 to 1998 in the proportion of campaign funds coming from this source was only a 4 percent

Table 2.2 Money contributed by different types of donors

	House 1990 ($)	House 1998* ($)	Change 1990–98	Senate 1990 ($)	Senate 1998* ($)	Change 1990–98
Individual	1,973,278.00	3,010,685.00	1,037,407.00	1,990,502.00	2,468,028.00	477,526.00
Personal or family	329,605.00	1,935,383.00	1,605,778.00	174,954.00	254,259.00	79,305.00
Corporate	519,921.00	608,840.00	88,919.00	612,212.00	568,425.00	−43,787.00
Peak trade groups	1,067,363.00	1,272,201.00	204,838.00	965,867.00	866,386.00	−99,481.00
Sum business	1,587,284.00	1,881,041.00	293,757.00	1,578,079.00	1,434,811.00	−143,268.00
Education associations	148,357.00	254,812.00	106,455.00	134,170.00	111,742.00	−22,428.00
Public sector unions	98,169.00	87,843.00	−10,326.00	57,125.00	44,315.00	−12,810.00
Private unions	460,050.00	418,500.00	−41,550.00	439,451.00	192,142.00	−247,309.00
Sum labor	706,576.00	761,155.00	54,579.00	630,746.00	348,199.00	−282,547.00
Political candidates	18,059.00	99,108.00	81,049.00	59,073.00	39,555.00	−19,518.00
Leaders & caucus	537,187.00	1,450,135.00	912,948.00	541,109.00	306,829.00	−234,280.00
Political parties	162,735.00	229,288.00	66,553.00	437,196.00	1,049,718.00	612,522.00
Sum political	717,981.00	1,778,531.00	1,060,550.00	1,037,378.00	1,396,102.00	358,724.00
Medical professionals	240,470.00	205,899.00	−34,571.00	169,771.00	203,918.00	34,147.00
Ideological groups	131,155.00	110,208.00	−20,947.00	112,628.00	74,102.00	−38,526.00
Lawyers & lobbyists	128,605.00	301,848.00	173,243.00	120,550.00	154,181.00	33,631.00
Agriculture	24,716.00	63,137.00	38,421.00	35,923.00	20,212.00	−15,711.00
Government sector	100,049.00	164,391.00	64,342.00	55,949.00	107,539.00	51,590.00
Total reported	6,086,562.00	10,344,808.00	4,258,246.00	6,184,394.00	6,539,306.00	354,912.00

Note: * Deflated to 1990 dollars.

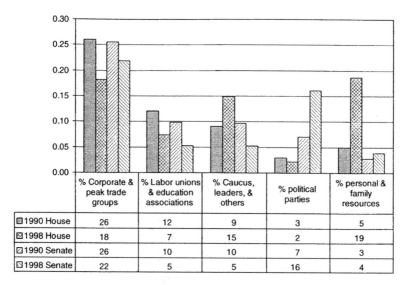

	% Corporate & peak trade groups	% Labor unions & education associations	% Caucus, leaders, & others	% political parties	% personal & family resources
1990 House	26	12	9	3	5
1998 House	18	7	15	2	19
1990 Senate	26	10	10	7	3
1998 Senate	22	5	5	16	4

Figure 2.2   Proportion of contributions by specific subgroups

decline. Readers are reminded that the dollar amount that corporate and peak trade associations gave to House candidates increased, but that their share of overall giving declined. The proportion of funds given by labor unions and education associations declined from 1990 to 1998 by approximately the same proportion for both chambers—4.2 percent for the House and by 4.5 percent for the Senate. This suggests that labor's strategy of deciding to whom to contribute may differ from that of corporate donors and peak trade organizations. As we discuss shortly, labor seems to give its funds to those it knows it can count on—possibly because it has so much less money to spread around. Corporations on the other hand seem to use their funds more strategically, giving to members of committees likely to consider bills of interest to them (see Sarbaugh-Thompson et al., 2002).

Interestingly, there were five groups of donors who increased their total contributions to House races and still managed to increase the total amount they gave to candidates for the State Senate. Looking at table 2.2, we see that these "deep-pocketed" donors were individual donors, political parties, the candidates themselves or their family members, lawyers and lobbyists, and the government sector. Medical professionals decreased their total contributions to House candidates by approximately $34,500 and increased their contributions to State Senate candidates by approximately the same amount. Public sector unions and private sector unions and ideological groups decreased their contributions to both the House and Senate. The six remaining groups of donors, corporate donors, peak trade groups, education associations, chamber leadership and caucus PACs, other political candidates' PACs, and agriculture PACs, offset at least some of their increased giving to House candidates by reducing their giving to Senate candidates. This finding nuances our earlier speculation that for many but not all groups, there is only a fixed amount of money for campaign giving. This appears to be true for most groups of donors, but not all.

Returning to figure 2.1 we see that the vastly increased amounts of money partisan political sources gave meant that their share of the money received by candidates increased for both the House and the Senate. But in the House these funds were channeled through intermediaries in the chamber. In the Senate these funds were given directly by the political parties. Given the increased role played by the leadership in the House after term limits, which we discuss at length in several of the coming chapters, we find it particularly interesting that House chamber and caucus leaders also are the mechanism through which the political parties distribute money to candidates. This has the potential to increase the sense of dependence of representatives on their chamber's party caucus and to increase the power of its leaders, potentially making representatives more inclined to comply with the wishes of these leaders on floor votes or in committees.

During our interviews with representatives we asked what factors they considered when electing caucus leaders. One of the many factors representatives mentioned was fundraising for the caucus. After term limits nearly 15 percent of the interview respondents said that this influenced their vote for party leaders, such as speaker or floor leader. Before term limits, only 9 percent of our respondents mentioned this as important when they chose a leader. Control of such a large pot of money for campaigns could easily enhance the power of the speaker or minority party leader because members of the caucus might worry that a vote against the caucus position might be remembered when the time came to dole out these caucus funds for the campaign season. Indeed we found in our other work that the amount money given to candidates from leadership PACs was a powerful predictor of who would win leadership positions (Faletta et al., 2000).

Finally, looking at the proportion of the funds given by all individual donors for both chambers we see that there was a little larger proportional increase for the House between 1990 and 1998 than for the Senate—an increase of 10 percent for the House compared to an increase of 7 percent for the Senate. This masks one of the largest increases in contributions in these data, however. That is the 15 percent increase in the share of funds for House campaigns that are from the candidate him or herself or from his or her relatives. Compared to the 1 percent increase in the proportion of Senate funds between 1990 and 1998 that were given by these personal sources, this is a very dramatic change. This reflects a whooping $1.9 million dollars given by candidates and their relatives compared to approximately $330,000 given by candidates and their relatives in 1990, before term limits. This dramatic increase leads one to question whether personal wealth is becoming an increasingly important factor for candidates running for the state legislature after term limits.[13]

Conclusions

Term limits advocates believed more open seat elections would produce many positive consequences for Michigan's political environment and its government. More electoral competition was among these positive outcomes. Yet, as we discussed in chapter 1, there are many open seat elections in which there is very little choice for voters either because very few candidates are running or because most House districts are drawn so that they are "safe" seats for one or the other political party. There are relatively few competitive districts for the Michigan State House. Between 10 and 25 percent of the 110 House districts might be considered at least somewhat competitive. This did not change with term limits. Regardless of the number of open seat elections, there is minimal competition even in primary elections across the state as a whole. That said, there is intense partisan competition in the few competitive districts. The impact of district competitiveness on campaign contributions has intensified after term limits. This is because partisan control of the chamber is increasingly important—a theme we return to repeatedly throughout the book.

As Gierzynski (1998) suggests, we found that term limits increase the total amount of money contributed to the full set of House races. This is accompanied by a decline in the contributions per candidate. This is probably because there are so many new candidates competing for funds, and many are very inexperienced fundraisers. With finite, albeit in some cases extremely large, amounts of money to contribute, donors seem to have had to make a choice about whom to support. The demand for cash in House races seems to have reduced the amount of money contributed to candidates for the State Senate as well.

Some might argue that the smaller average amount raised by candidates for the Michigan State House represents a decline in the value of the seat. We disagree. Our data suggest instead that the value of some seats has increased, especially if the seat might determine partisan control of the chamber. These seats have become not only exceedingly valuable, but extremely expensive to win. This, in turn, draws contributions away from other districts in which the partisan advantage virtually guarantees a victory for one party's candidate. The high cost and high stakes surrounding a handful of competitive House seats means that the fundraising capacities of the two major political parties, which are always important to electoral success, have become even more crucial.

Republican candidates increasingly raise more money and outspend the Democratic candidates overall, especially after term limits. Given the tendency of special interests to contribute to the party in majority control of the chamber and the national advantages the Republican Party has in raising money, it is not clear how much of this change is the result of term limits. Campaign contributions have become increasingly lopsided with Republican House candidates holding an almost 2 : 1 financial advantage over the Democratic candidates in 2002. We found a similar, but less pronounced fundraising advantage for the Republican candidates between 1990 and 1998 for the State Senate. Given that partisan control of the Senate did not change during this time period and that term limits did not take effect in the State Senate until 2002, this further supports our suspicion that majority control and national trends account for at least some of the Republican fundraising prowess in the House. Indirectly term limits might have cost the Democrats control of the House, and as the minority party, Democrats would typically receive less money from special interests. Therefore, we suspect that term limits have contributed to, but are not solely responsible for, the increasing partisan imbalance in fundraising for State House races.

At a very general level we see similar patterns of giving by three broad groups (i.e., individuals, organized groups and political sources) to House candidates and to Senate candidates between 1990 and 1998. This broad treatment, however, obscures some important differences within these categories. Particularly important was the increase in personal or family resources, which raises questions about the wealth of the "new breed" of term limits candidates. We are especially interested in one major difference between the patterns we found in the House and the Senate between 1990 and 1998—the far greater role played by the House party caucus and House leaders in funding candidates campaigns. We turn our attention to this in chapter 3.

CHAPTER 3

The Interest Group Connection:
Money, Access, and Support

B oth proponents and opponents of term limits foresaw this reform altering the relationship between legislators and organized interests, but in very different ways. For proponents, term limits promised to reduce the influence of interest groups by undermining both the opportunities and incentives for the development of mutually supportive and self-serving relationships between legislators and lobbyists. For opponents, term limits were a recipe for enhancing group influence. By forcing out experienced legislators and foreclosing the opportunities for their successors to develop comparable expertise over time, term limits would make legislators more dependent upon lobbyists while simultaneously leaving them less able to assess the credibility of information or its sources.

Interaction between legislators and interest groups is a two-way relationship whether viewed as vertices of an iron triangle, embedded in issue networks or linchpins of lobbying enterprises (Ainsworth, 1997). Often this relationship is examined from the perspective of interest groups or their lobbyists, from the outside looking in (e.g., Moncrief and Thompson, 2001b). These studies have yielded valuable insights about the range and diversity of lobbying strategies and tactics (e.g., Schlozman & Tierney, 1986). Less attention has been paid to how legislators relate to the activities and services provided by interest groups—the view from the inside looking out (Ainsworth, 1997; Bearry, Harelson-Stephens & Uhlir, 2001). Yet this perspective is important to understanding the relationships between interest groups and legislators and how this relationship is affected by changes in the rules of the game such as the imposition of term limits. Here we investigate this "inside looking out" perspective of legislators in the context of Michigan's implementation of term limits.

In this chapter we focus on three aspects of the relationship between organized interests and legislators. The first relates to money given to candidates by interest groups. The second involves interest group access to legislators, a factor often linked closely to campaign contributions. We discuss this both in terms of legislators socializing with interest groups and raising money from them. Then we explore legislators' reliance on interest groups as a source of information. We discuss this briefly here and more extensively in chapter 9 along with other sources of information and guidance that legislators use to make policy decisions. We are interested in how and to what extent term limits have affected each of these aspects of legislator-interest group relations.

One of the distinctions that needs to be made when discussing the relationships between legislators and lobbyists is the difference between "buying" influence versus "buying" access. Influence, of course, is notoriously difficult to measure. It is impossible to determine whether the money given to a legislator "buys" his or her vote unless the legislator claims this is so—an unlikely prospect. Therefore, we do not claim to be able to isolate the influence of money on representatives, but we can shed light on lobbyists' access to legislator. Although access does not necessarily translate into influence, it would be harder to influence a legislator without talking to him or her. Therefore, access is valuable to lobbyists, even though it does not guarantee that the legislator will be swayed. To explore this we asked how much time legislators spent fundraising and how much time they spent attending interest group sponsored events in the state captial. Additionally we examine selective giving by interest groups to legislators whose votes might be valuable.

The Role of Money in Legislator–Lobbyist Relationships[1]

As we demonstrated in chapter 2 interest groups give large amounts of money to political candidates, and candidates who raise the most money generally win elections (Gaddie & Bullock, 2000). During our interviews we asked House members if some person or group had asked them to run when they initially sought their office. Most past members of the Michigan House were self-starters, needing little or no prodding from anyone to run. However, by foreclosing long-term service, term limits have altered the opportunities a would-be office holder can pursue and have changed the incentives to run. We know that interest groups are active participants in candidate recruitment (Rozell & Wilcox, 1999). Certainly, one of the surest ways of securing access to a legislator is to recruit your own. Nearly 15 percent of those newly elected in 1998 or 2000 said that interest groups had asked them to run. Approximately half this number, 7.4 percent of our respondents who were elected during or before 1992, said that interest groups had asked them to run. It appears that term limits have enhanced both the opportunities and incentives for groups to participate in the candidate recruitment process. Interest groups that recruit these candidates are likely to contribute to their campaigns in order to help them win election.

As we noted earlier, it is difficult to tell whether interest groups give to candidates because they want to see like-minded candidates elected and reelected or whether they want to influence elected officials to vote in ways that they might not otherwise vote. It is the latter possibility that is particularly troubling to campaign finance reformers and to some term limits advocates.

In an effort to try to isolate the use of money to influence incumbent legislators from its use to help candidates win elections, we limited our analyses to contributions given to candidates in the calendar year *after* the candidate won an election.[2] These contributions are less likely to have been given to help elect the representative and more likely to have been given to gain access to or to curry favor with a representative in a position to help an interest group achieve its policy goals.

In our previous work (Sarbaugh-Thompson et al., 2002), we found that after term limits were implemented, there was a significant increase in the total amount of money contributed during the year after the election. Pre–term limits House veterans collectively received $919,301 in the postelection year of 1997. After term limits, in the postelection years of 1999 and 2001, House members collectively received $1,920,507 and $2,742,495. This clearly is a major increase in the amount of money given to candidates during the year after they are elected. This outpouring of postelection contributions after the first post–term-limits election might reflect the uncertainty about who to support that confronted campaign contributors with 64 open seat races and a sea of new faces. By waiting until candidates were elected and waiting until committee assignments were made, interest groups would know which representatives would be a worthwhile investment.

During the second post–term-limits election, in 2000, there were only 21 open seat elections and incumbents' ideology and committee preferences would have been at least somewhat known to interest groups. Therefore, uncertainty and its effects on giving cannot account for the continued rise in postelection year giving. We are forced to conclude that something fundamental has changed in the relationship between legislators and major financial contributors.

Much of the work in the Michigan House is performed in committees; and it is likely that interest groups would want to increase their access to or influence over members of committees with jurisdiction over issues that concern them. Thus, in our previous work, we expected and found that interest groups target their postelection giving toward legislators serving on specific committees. This was true both before and after term limits took full effect in Michigan, but we found that giving was targeted even more toward members of key committees after term limits than before (Sarbaugh-Thompson et al., 2002).

After term limits, postelection year contributions also favor members of the majority party in the House. This was only somewhat true before term limits. A few minority party members who received exceedingly large amounts of money after the election inflate the mean for the minority party so that it is slightly higher than the mean for the majority party.[3] Prior to term limits the majority party received a mean of $8,853 and the minority party members received a mean of $8,985. After term limits the gap widens dramatically. In 1999 majority party members received an average of $29,592 and the minority party received $13,294, less than half as much. This is a sizeable increase over the 1997 amounts even deflating to 1990 dollars. The amount of postelection year giving rises even more in the second post–term-limits session and the gap persists. In 2001 majority party members received an average $34,781 and the minority party received an average of $15,613 (again deflated to 1990 dollars for purposes of comparison). These are sizeable and statistically significant differences, especially for the majority party.

The reason to give to the majority party after the election is its power to vote bills out of committee and into law on the floor of the chamber. The minority party cannot do that unless the majority party has some reasons or incentives to compromise. The dramatic increase in the amount of money given after the election and the wide gap between the majority and minority party suggest that this money is intended to influence legislators. Why did the amount increase in the second post–term-limits session? This was after all an election with only 21 open seat races, and many of the candidates were known quantities. We will continue to pursue the sources and changes in campaign contributions with the hope that we can provide more definitive answers to this question sometime in the future.

In our previous work we found that only labor PACs did not contribute differentially to members and nonmembers of key committees. They contributed to Democrats regardless of their committee assignments and regardless of the partisan control of the chamber. We were puzzled about why labor's giving strategy did not change when other interest groups' giving patterns did. Again we hope to answer this question in the future.

Lobbyists and Interest Group Access to Legislators

To explore further the relationships between legislators and interests groups we asked how much time they spent attending the numerous receptions and gatherings to which these groups regularly invite them. Specifically, we asked legislators about how much time they spent attending events sponsored by groups in Lansing, the state capital. Responses to the question were recorded on a 5-point scale, coded from 0 (none) to 4 (an enormous amount). Respondents were allowed to give responses between two values on the scale. Additionally, we calculated a difference between the amount of time spent at these Lansing events and the average amount of time legislators spent on all 11 activities we asked them about. Negative values indicate that the legislator spent less time attending these events than his or her average amount of time spent on all activities, while positive values indicate more than the average amount of time was spent attending these events.

Attending events sponsored by groups in Lansing was not a high priority for legislators either before or after term limits—a fact that some citizens may find reassuring. All cohorts of representatives we interviewed reported spending less time than their average doing this.[4] After term limits, second-term legislators expended relatively less of their time hobnobbing with interest groups in Lansing than did their newly elected colleagues or than the post–term-limits lame ducks. They probably already knew who was who and where the groups were coming from. Additionally, given their rapid rise to power in the term-limited environment, this may reflect the increased demands on their time by other activities, such as developing new legislation or building coalitions within the chamber to pass legislation.

On the other hand, the time spent by lame ducks before and after term limits indicates a different pattern. Before term limits, lame ducks gave this activity a lower priority in their allocation of their time than did their second-term colleagues. Perhaps with their forced retirement looming many felt less need to maintain these relationships. After term limits, the priority lame ducks gave to attending events in Lansing increased. Given their increased political ambitions, which we describe in chapter 5, we suspect they needed to cultivate new friends and prospective campaign contributors. Therefore, they took more time to hobnob with potential donors and patrons.

Indeed we found that those legislators who reported spending more time attending events sponsored by groups in Lansing also reported spending more time fundraising. This was true both before and after term limits. Hence we infer that attending these events is part of the effort legislators make to raise money from lobbyists. There was a statistically significant correlation between the time spent attending these events and the time spent fundraising for both pre– and post–term limits legislators.[5]

Legislators' Efforts to Raise Money

Campaign contributions are often treated as a one-sided effort by lobbyists to curry favor with elected officials. Yet there is evidence that some legislators pressure lobbyists and others into giving.[6] To explore this we asked legislators how much time they spent fundraising. Once again they responded on the same five-point scale used in the question described earlier. And again, we compared responses about the time they spent on this activity to their average responses for all 11 activities we asked them about.

Fundraising is an unpopular activity among our respondents, and term limits did not change this. In fact, it appears to have an even lower priority than does attending events in Lansing. We examined time spent by six groups, based on the status of term limits (before and after) and their level of experience (first, second, or last term in office). Again all six groups reported spending less than their average amount of time on this activity. Other than a slight increase in the relative amount of time that second-term representatives, both before and after term limits, spent fundraising, there was virtually no difference among the six groups.[7] The absence of any difference is interesting, however. While the lame ducks were all ineligible to run for reelection, they continued to give this activity about the same priority that their other colleagues did. This perhaps reflected the reluctance of the pre-term limits lame ducks to abandon hope of a last-minute judicial reprieve overturning term limits. We suspect it also reflected the aspirations of many lame ducks to continue in politics and public life wherever and whenever a promising opportunity presented itself.

Interestingly, despite their professed aversion to fundraising, it appears that legislators' efforts are effective. We found a statistically significant correlation between the time spent fundraising and the amount of postelection year money the legislator received. We found this relationship both before and after term limits.[8]

Legislators' Consulting with Lobbyists and Organized Groups

Do postelection contributions from interest groups prompt legislators to rely more on such groups for information and guidance? Given that we found that interest groups target their postelection giving based on committee assignments of legislators, we focus our analysis on legislators' self-reported behavior in committees. Our dependent variable here is based on scaled responses to a question about the extent to which a legislator relied on groups or lobbyists for information and guidance on a particularly difficult issue considered by a major committee on which he or she served. The response categories were defined by the five-point scale previously discussed and ranged from "an enormous amount" (coded as 4) to "none" (coded as 0), and again we calculated the difference between the average amount of consulting and the amount of consulting with groups and lobbyists.

Given that postterm limits representatives seem to provide more access to groups and their lobbyists and receive more money from them, especially in the year after they are elected, we wanted to see whether there was a difference in the extent to which representatives reported relying on information or guidance from these sources. To explore this, we again divided House members into six groups, based on those serving before or after term limits and whether they were newcomers, in their second-term, or lame ducks. All six groups of House members relied on groups and lobbyists for information and guidance more than they typically relied on other sources of information. Somewhat surprisingly, we found that newcomers to the Michigan House after term limits said that they relied on groups and lobbyists more extensively than their lame duck colleagues while newcomers before term limits relied on this source less than their lame duck colleagues.[9]

We had expected that newly elected representatives after term limits would share the negative view of lobbyists held by term limits proponents and rely less heavily on this source of information. We thought, also, that they would hesitate to rely on this source of information extensively until they learned which lobbyists were trustworthy. No doubt this may be true for some House members, but in the aggregate those newly elected to the Michigan House after term limits were more willing than their predecessors to rely on lobbyists—at least when considering a difficult issue at the committee level. This may also reflect the greater likelihood after term limits that candidates were recruited to run for office by groups, an increasingly common phenomenon that we noted earlier.

After term limits, we also found a statistically significant correlation between the amount of time representatives spent attending events sponsored by groups in Lansing and the extent to which they relied on groups and lobbyists as a source of information about a difficult issue considered in a committee. From this we infer that the access organized interests gained through these receptions and other events encourage representatives to consult with them. Prior to term limits, we found no correlation between attending these events and the extent of consulting. This may be because the relationships between legislators and organized groups were established firmly enough before term limits and lobbyists representing these groups could call or stop by the representative's office without the need for a formal event to bring them together. On the other hand, as we demonstrate in chapter 9, organized groups do seem to have become a more important source of information and guidance for post-term limits representatives.

In addition to asking about a difficult issue considered in a committee, we asked legislators to tell us who they would rely on for information and guidance about two specific issues, school choice and licensing or regulating health care professionals, if these issues reached the floor of the chamber. These two questions were open-ended. Respondents could name any source of information and could name as many or as few sources as they wished. We discuss these data in greater detail in chapter 9, noting here only findings related to our analyses of the legislator–lobbyist relationships. Before term limits 74 percent of our respondents said that they would consult groups or lobbyists on a bill about school choice. After term limits this rose to 82 percent of our respondents. Eighty percent of our respondents both before and after term limits said that they would rely on groups or lobbyists for information and guidance about a bill licensing or regulating health care professionals.

With the full implementation of term limits, groups do seem to get a significant benefit from the events they sponsor in Lansing. Representatives who report spending more time going to such events also report greater reliance on groups for information and guidance. In our ongoing investigation of term limits, we are asking legislators to tell us more specifically about their relationships with lobbyists.

Conclusions

The first two cohorts of term-limited legislators rely more heavily on groups and their lobbyists for information and guidance in making substantive policy decisions in committees. Before and after term limits, legislators who spent more time fundraising also spent more time attending receptions and other events in Lansing sponsored by groups. Before term limits time spent on these two activities did not seem to lead legislators to consult groups more heavily about issues considered in House committees. After term limits, however, the time spent fundraising and attending these events was associated with greater reliance on groups for information and guidance on issues considered in committee.

Using data from campaign finance records, we find that term limits coincide with a stunning increase in the amount of money given to representatives *after* they are elected. This postelection giving is targeted toward representatives serving on committees with jurisdiction over issues the interest groups care about. This was true before term limits as well. But after term limits, the targeting of postelection money toward legislators serving on committees in which they might be able to "help" the organized group increased a lot. From all of this, we conclude that term limits have not diminished the role that interest groups play in the legislative process. If anything, interest group input has become more important, not less.

Term limits have certainly not attenuated the ties between legislators and lobbyists. Indeed, our findings suggest that term limits are an effective means of strengthening these ties, making legislators somewhat more accessible to lobbyists and the groups they represent. And term limits increase the prominence of lobbyists and organized groups as sources for information about issues.

This is probably more disquieting to term limits advocates than it is to political scientists such as ourselves. We expect interest groups and lobbyists to provide information about issues. Indeed, they are often experts in their subject area. While the mutual benefits of communication between lobbyists and legislators are, almost by definition, self-serving, they need not be narrowly so, although skeptics including most term limit advocates seem inclined to think so. Many members of organized groups represented by lobbyists are also a legislator's constituents. Therefore, lobbying includes, although it is clearly not limited to, representing the views of voters.

In any case, for the mutual benefits of lobbying exchanges to occur, mutual credibility is a critical ingredient (Milbrath, 1960; Wright,

1996). Legislators need to trust lobbyists to reveal fully and accurately the implications of a policy position. Lobbyists need to know that if a legislator says he or she will support a bill in a specific form—with a specific provision added or eliminated—that the legislator's "word is his or her bond" (interview notes, 1997–1998). Establishing and maintaining such credibility seemingly would be more difficult, and intendedly so, under term limits. It is this latter issue that we find troubling.

In the social sciences a field called game theory explores various situations in which people could behave in a trustworthy or a devious way. In situations where there is a known endpoint to the relationship between the parties, it is "rational" for the actors to behave deviously toward each other. In situations where the relationship continues indefinitely or at least the end point is unknown, then it is often more beneficial for both parties to behave in a trustworthy or credible manner (Axelrod, 1984). Under term limits, the relationship between lobbyists and some legislators is not likely to continue long term, unless the legislator is running for another state-level political office. Additionally the endpoint of the relationship is known well in advance by both parties, providing increasing incentives to behave deviously as the endpoint draws closer and closer.

After term limits politically ambitious legislators have the potential to extend the endpoint of their relationship with lobbyists, making it a long-term relationship. In long-term relationships, game theory predicts that it is less likely that either the legislator or the lobbyist will behave deviously. Political ambition could do this. Thus, politically ambitious legislators might be more likely to behave honestly toward lobbyists and lobbyists might be more likely to be forecoming and truthful with legislators if they expect to continue working with them in the future. Given that the relationship between lobbyists and legislators has benefits as well as costs, conditions that encourage both sets of actors to behave honorably toward each other would seem to be valuable to all parties, but especially to the citizens of Michigan.

PART TWO

---

*Term-Limited Representatives: Who They
are and Where They're Going*

CHAPTER 4

The New Breed of Term-Limited State Legislators[1]

Many people, both those supportive of and opposed to term limits, assumed that once entrenched white, male incumbents—the good ol' boys—were termed out of office, women and ethnic minority group members would win more elections (Bell, 1992). Additionally, some scholars (Petracca, 1996) believed that reducing the length of service would discourage middle-aged males from abandoning established careers to run for the state legislature. Thus, some opponents of term limits consoled themselves that at least term-limited state legislatures would become more diverse.

The number of women and ethnic minority group members elected to state legislatures increased steadily during the past decades. Yet, white men continue to dominate state legislatures, and women and ethnic minority group members are still underrepresented compared to their numbers in the population. Nationally, women held 23.5 percent of the State Assembly or State House seats in 2003, despite constituting more than 50 percent of the electorate. Although the 2000 census identifies 12 percent of the U.S. population as African American, only 8.2 percent of those serving in state legislatures in 2003 had African American ancestry.[2]

When term limits removed the "drag of incumbency," it seemed reasonable to assume that women would win more seats in state legislatures. Men and women have similar probabilities of winning open seat elections (Karnig & Walter, 1976; Burrell, 1988 and 1990; Bledsoe & Herring, 1990; Welch & Studlar, 1996) and in special elections, women tend to be more successful than men (Gaddie & Bullock, 2000). Yet, because incumbency provides an edge at the ballot box and most incumbents are men, the advantages of incumbency impede women's electoral gains.

Additionally, truncated legislative service imposed by term limits might undermine the career incentives thought to attract male candidates. In professionalized legislatures, such as Michigan's House of Representatives and California's General Assembly, with high salaries, staff, and year-round sessions, prior to term limits elected office often became a lifetime career.[3] Ehrenhalt (1991) found that the prominence of women in the Colorado legislature (a part-time chamber with relatively low compensation) could be partially explained by the unattractiveness to men of a job requiring long hours with low compensation. Therefore, women might be more interested than men in running for office in term-limited state legislatures. As one woman serving in the Michigan House of Representatives quipped, men are looking for a career; women are looking for a job (interview notes, 1997–1998).

Most voters tend to be loyal to incumbents regardless of the incumbent's ethnicity. In open seat elections, however, voters tend to support people of their own ethnicity (Herring & Forbes, 1994; Herrnson & Stokes, 2001). State electoral districts often concentrate ethnic group members into majority-minority districts (i.e., districts drawn so that more than 50 percent of its potential voters are members of an ethnic minority group). Yet prior to term limits, veteran "white" incumbents represented some of these majority-minority districts, in some cases for decades. Once these incumbents were termed out of office, many observers predicted that someone from the district's dominant ethnic group would win election. The assumption was that term limits would increase electoral opportunities for ethnic minorities, but primarily in districts where the "pent up voting strength" of ethnic minority voters was thwarted by long-serving white incumbents (Caress et al., 2003).

Given that term limits preclude a long-term career in a legislative chamber, middle-aged candidates might be reluctant to leave careers for a short hiatus in public service. Polsby (1993) argues that term-limited legislative service would be attractive to older people at or near the end of their career. Alternatively, ambitious people in their twenties might view the contacts and name recognition garnered during a stint in public office to be a good launch pad for a future career, political or otherwise.

In short term limits were expected to change the age distribution in state legislatures, as well as changing the gender and ethnic composition of those bodies. In this chapter we explore the impact of term limits on the composition of the Michigan State House of Representatives and the

California General Assembly. Does the membership of these term-limited chambers more closely reflect the gender and ethnic composition of the state's population? Did the age distribution of those serving in the lower chamber of the legislature shift after term limits?

Substantive Versus Descriptive Representation

This discussion about the composition of the legislature might seem arcane and detached from the potential for term limits to affect policy making. Yet, a key assumption underlying this debate involves questions about descriptive versus substantive representation. The basic question is whether someone who shares physical characteristics of voters (descriptive representation) also works more passionately on issues that tend to resonate with these voters and reflects their views on these issues more closely (substantive representation). There is evidence that elected officials' personal attributes affect their ability to represent constituents who share those attributes, but there is evidence to the contrary also. Those who seek greater diversity in the composition of a legislature assume that women do a better job of representing the issues of concern to women in the electorate. This reasoning also suggests that ethnic group members more consistently address concerns of constituents who share their ethnic identity or that senior representatives tend to represent the views of other senior citizens. Examples such a Clarence Thomas or Phyllis Schlafly suggest that there is at least some slippage between substantive and descriptive representation.

Gender differences on some issues of public concern are well established. Public opinion polling suggests that women are more likely than men to think that issues such as poverty and homelessness are highly important and men are nearly twice as likely as women to think these two issues are not at all important (Harrison, 2003, p. 49). Further, women are more likely than men to like bigger government and to think that government should provide jobs to anyone who wants to work (Harrison, 2003). Although one would assume that Republican women and Democratic women might propose and support different solutions to these problems, their inclination to view these as serious issues would be likely to move them onto the decisionmaking agenda. And, agenda setting (Cobb and Elder, 1983; Kingdon, 1995) is clearly a, some might even say *the,* crucial step in public policy-making.

Similar differences in public opinion abound between members of different ethnic groups. Thus, we agree with scholars (Hero & Tolbert, 1995; Johnson & Secret, 1996) who conclude that there is some value in descriptive representation, while at the same time acknowledging that choosing a candidate based on ideology and issue positions, regardless of gender, ethnicity, or age is also important.

Women in Term-Limited State Legislatures

Following the 1992 elections, women held 20.5 percent of the seats in state legislatures nationwide, up from 4 percent in 1969, but still far below their presence in the population of the nation as a whole. As table 4.1 indicates, in Michigan and California after the 1992 elections women held 24.5 percent and 27.5 percent, respectively, of the seats in the lower house, slightly above the average for all state legislatures.[4]

By 1996, women held 28.2 percent of the seats in the Michigan House of Representatives, and with the implementation of term limits in 1998, there was no change. In fact, the percentage of women

Table 4.1 Women elected to the Michigan House and California Assembly, 1990–2002

Year elected	Democratic Party, percent in caucus (number)	Republican Party, percent in caucus (number)	Total, percent in chamber (number)	Total, representativeness ratio for chamber***
1990 Michigan	18.3 (11)	14.0 (8)	16.4 (19)	0.32
1992 Michigan	27.3 (15)	21.8 (12)	24.5 (27)	0.48
1994 Michigan	31.5 (17)	23.2 (13)	27.3 (30)	0.53
1996 Michigan	29.3 (17)	26.9 (14)	28.2 (31)	0.55
1998 Michigan	34.6 (18)	22.4 (13)	28.2 (31)	0.55
2000 Michigan	28.8 (15)	20.7 (13)*	25.5 (28)*	0.50
2002 Michigan	31.9 (15)	14.3 (9)	21.8 (24)	0.43
1990 California	18.8 (9)	21.9 (7)	18.8 (15)	0.38
1992 California	36.7 (18)	12.9 (4)	27.5 (22)	0.55
1994 California	41.0 (16)	9.76 (4)	25.0 (20)	0.50
1996 California	39.5 (17)	8.10 (3)	25.0 (20)	0.50
1998 California	33.3 (16)	12.5 (4)	26.3 (21)**	0.53
2000 California	40.0 (20)	13.3 (4)	30.0 (24)	0.60
2002 California	41.7 (20)	15.6 (5)	31.3 (25)	0.62

Notes
* Although 13 Republican women won election in 2000, one died two weeks after the election and was replaced by a man.
** One additional woman won election as an independent.
*** This is the ratio of the percentage of female members serving in a chamber divided by the female percentage of a state's total population. Values less than 1.000 indicate women are underrepresented in a given chamber in a given year while values greater than 1.000 indicate overrepresentation relative to the presence of women in a state's population. Ratios for 2000 and 2002 use 2000 census data. All others use 1990 census date.

Sources: Center for American Women and Politics, Eagleton Institute of Politics, The State University of New Jersey, http://www.rci.rutgers.edu.

subsequently declined in 2000 and 2002, under term limits. The representativeness ratio in the rightmost column of table 4.1 makes this change even clearer. Following the 1998 election, women were "only" underrepresented in the Michigan House by about half. But following the 2002 election, they were more underrepresented than they were in 1992. In California, we find a slightly different pattern. In 1994, the election before term limits, 25 percent of legislators elected were women—a representativeness ratio of 0.50. But in 1998 through 2002 this ratio rose to 0.62 with the number of females in the California General Assembly exceeding 30 percent.

So, in the years following the first term limits expulsions, California and Michigan followed different paths. The number of women in the Michigan State House remained unchanged in the election in which representatives were first termed out of office and then began a steady decline. In 2002 women won only 24 seats, comprising a mere 21.8 percent of the Michigan State House of Representatives. This was a smaller proportion than the female cohort serving in 1992 in the Michigan House. This might lead one to assume that term limits had not only failed to help women make further gains, but had unraveled the progress made during the "year of the woman" (1992) and in the decade afterward.

In California, however, we find the opposite pattern. Even though term limits expulsions created many open seats and anticipation of term limits increased the number of special elections, the number of women fell slightly between 1992 and 1996 from 22 to 20. After the initial term limits expulsion, the number of women in the General Assembly climbed steadily, albeit incrementally, so that the representativeness ratio reached 0.62 by 2002 when 31.3 percent of the members of the California Assembly were women. Thus, in California, term limits seem to have halted an erosion of women's victories in the General Assembly and, over time, provided opportunities for gradual gains.

What accounts for this difference between the two states? One factor that could explain the trajectory of women's electoral victories in both states is the fate of the Democratic Party. In Michigan Democrats lost control of the House of Representatives when term limits expelled veteran legislators; while in California Democrats retained control of the General Assembly. In both states, female legislators are more likely to be Democrats than Republicans. So, one factor predicting the number of women in the chamber is the number of Republicans and Democrats elected overall.

After a peak in 1990 of seven electoral victories for Republican women, the number of women in the Republican caucus in the

California General Assembly hovered between three and five from 1992 to 2002. The number of Democratic women serving in the California General Assembly during these years rose dramatically from a low of nine in 1990 to fluctuate between 16 and 20 from 1992 to 2002. During this decade, there were four or five times more Democratic women than Republican women serving in the California General Assembly, a sizeable partisan gender gap.

During the 1990s the partisan gender gap in Michigan was present, but nowhere nearly as pronounced as it was in California. The largest number of victories for Republican women running for the Michigan House, fourteen, occurred during the year before term limits expulsions, in 1996. The lowest number of victories for Republican women, nine, occurred in 2002. Given the increase in the size of the Republican caucus, this meant that the number of Republican women dropped to a mere 14.3 percent of their caucus, much lower than the 26.9 percent they had achieved before term limits. Therefore, term limits seem to have thwarted progress made by Republican women in Michigan, even though in 1998 four wives of veteran Republican representatives won seats previously held by their husbands.

Although the number of women in the Michigan Democratic House caucus rose slightly during the year of term limits expulsions, in 2002 it slid back to its 1992 level of 15. However, given the losses the Democratic Party suffered in the State House races, this is 31.9 percent of the Democratic caucus. So as a percentage of their caucus, Democratic women have held onto the gains they made during the 1990s, but term limits have not unleashed a tidal wave of victories for Michigan Democrats, either male or female.

One of the major predictors of women's electoral success is the political parties' recruitment and support of women in elections. Looking at table 4.2, we find that, until 2002, Michigan Republicans did almost as well as their Democratic counterparts in recruiting female candidates to run for State House seats. However, this misses a crucial factor that we discussed in chapter 1, the viability of the candidate. In Michigan women candidates represented the GOP in several state house districts that are extremely safe Democratic districts. For example, the GOP ran women in City of Detroit districts, some of which have a base Democratic voting strength above 90 percent. Therefore, in looking at the number of women candidates recruited by each political party, we identified "sacrificial lambs," those candidates who stood no chance of winning, but were simply carrying the party standard. We considered candidates who won less than 20 percent of the vote to be sacrificial

Table 4.2 Political parties' efforts to recruit women to run for seats in the lower state legislative chamber

	Total Republican woman candidates	Sacrificial lambs among Republican women candidates	Viable Republican women candidates, percent of chamber districts (number)	Total Democratic women candidates	Sacrificial lambs among Democratic women candidates	Viable Democratic women candidates, percent of chamber districts (number)
Michigan 1990	20	6	12.7 (14)	20	0	18.2 (20)
Michigan 1992	19	6	11.8 (13)	23	0	20.9 (23)
Michigan 1994	25	5	18.2 (20)	36	1	31.8 (35)
Michigan 1996	27	6	19.1 (21)	30	0	27.3 (30)
Michigan 1998	34	9	22.7 (25)	33	0	30.0 (33)
Michigan 2000	25	6	17.3 (19)	29	0	26.4 (29)
Michigan 2002	15	3	10.9 (12)	34	0	30.9 (34)
California 1996	12	2	12.5 (10)	30	0	37.5 (30)
California 1998	17	4	16.3 (13)	24	0	30.0 (24)
California 2000	15	1	17.5 (14)	28	0	35.0 (28)
California 2002	13	1	15.0 (12)	30	0	37.5 (30)

Table 4.3 Ethnic minority group members elected to the California Assembly and Michigan House, 1990–2002

Year elected	African American		Hispanic		Asian American or Other		Total Minority	
	Percent (number) in chamber	Representativeness ratio**	Percent (number) in chamber	Representativeness ratio**	Percent (number) in chamber	Representativeness ratio**	Percent (number) in chamber	Representativeness ratio**
1990 Michigan	10.0 (11)	0.72	0.0 (0)	0.00	0.0 (0)	0.00	10.0 (11)	0.56
1992 Michigan	10.0 (11)	0.72	0.0 (0)	0.00	0.0 (0)	0.00	10.0 (11)	0.56
1994 Michigan	10.0 (11)	0.72	0.0 (0)	0.00	0.0 (0)	0.00	10.0 (11)	0.56
1996 Michigan	10.9 (12)	0.79	0.0 (0)	0.00	0.0 (0)	0.00	10.9 (12)	0.62
1998 Michigan	12.7 (14)	0.92	1.8 (2)	0.83	0.9 (1)	0.52	14.6 (17)	0.82
2000 Michigan	15.5 (17)	1.10	1.8 (2)*	0.55	0.9 (1)	0.22	18.2 (20)	0.85
2002 Michigan	13.6 (15)	0.96	0.0 (0)	0.00	0.9 (1)	0.22	14.5 (16)	0.68
1990 California	8.8 (7)	1.25	5.0 (4)	0.19	0.0 (0)	0.00	13.8 (11)	0.32
1992 California	7.5 (6)	1.07	16.3 (13)	0.63	1.25 (1)	0.13	25.0 (20)	0.58
1994 California	7.5 (6)	1.07	15.0 (12)	0.58	1.25 (1)	0.13	23.8 (19)	0.56
1996 California	5.0 (4)	0.71	20.0 (16)	0.77	2.5 (2)	0.25	27.5 (22)	0.64
1998 California	5.0 (4)	0.71	21.3 (17)	0.82	2.5 (2)	0.25	28.8 (23)	0.67
2000 California	5.0 (4)	0.78	25.0 (20)	0.77	3.75 (3)	0.26	33.8 (27)	0.63
2002 California	5.0 (4)	0.78	21.3 (17)	0.66	7.5 (6)	0.52	33.8 (27)	0.63

Notes

* One Hispanic member was elected but only served a few weeks before being elected to the State Senate in a special election. He was not replaced by an ethnic minority member.

** This is the ratio of the percentage of legislative members of a given racial or ethnic background serving in a given chamber in a given session divided by the percentage of that state's population that is comprised of people of a similar ethnic background. Ratios below 1.00 indicate that members of a particular ethnic background are underrepresented in the legislature while ratios greater than 1.00 indicate over representation relative to a group's presence in the population overall. Ratios for 2000 and 2002 were calculated using 2000 population census figures while ratios for elections in the 1990s use 1990 census date. This means that there is a shift in these ratios in 2000 that results from the shift to 2000 census data in addition to any trends within the state.

lambs. During the seven election cycles we examined, we found only one Democratic woman candidate who was a sacrificial lamb. During those same seven elections, a total of 41 Republican women candidates ran as sacrificial lambs. Both parties occasionally ran men who were sacrificial lambs, but they were never sacrificed at the same level as the Republican women.

In California, we were able to determine the gender of candidates in the four most recent election cycles. In these elections, we found that the Republican Party recruited fewer women candidates than did the Democratic Party. In these elections the California Republican Party recruited eight women to run as sacrificial lambs, while the Democratic Party ran no sacrificial lambs at all. Interestingly, the Republican Party in California ran no men as sacrificial lambs in these elections.

Republicans in both California and Michigan are not recruiting as many women candidates as Democrats are, and those women who are recruited are less likely to be running in a district in which a Republican has any reasonable chance of victory. This is consistent with the national trend for the two political parties. Term limits in and of themselves are not a boon to women's electoral prospects, and they may undermine women's electoral success if they inhibit the number of Democrats winning election. The key factor in producing victories for women involves recruiting and supporting women candidates in elections where their political party stands at least some reasonable chance of victory. Thus we conclude that partisan differences in recruiting and supporting women candidates appear to explain the changes in gender composition of the Michigan House of Representatives and the California General Assembly.

Ethnic Minority Group Members in Term-Limited State Legislatures

In 1992 African Americans held 5.6 percent of the seats in the state legislatures nationally, slightly less than half of their 11.75 percent share of the nation's population. In Michigan and California, the picture was much different, however. According to the 1990 census, 7 percent of California's citizens were African American and 13.8 percent of Michigan's citizens were African American. In 1992 there were six African Americans elected to the California General Assembly and 11 African Americans elected to the Michigan House of Representatives. This constituted 7.5 percent and 11 percent of these chambers, respectively. As the "representativeness ratios" included in table 4.3 make clear, as a proportion of the chamber, African Americans were slightly over represented in California and only slightly underrepresented in Michigan in the early 1990s.

One of the major differences between California and Michigan is California's greater ethnic diversity. According to the 1990 census, California's Hispanic population was almost 26 percent of the state's total population, while in Michigan Hispanics comprised only about 2 percent of the state's population. Also, California has a sizeable Asian American population, which in 1990 constituted slightly more than 9 percent of the state's population. In Michigan Asian Americans constituted only slightly more than 1 percent of the state's population in 1990. Not surprisingly then, there were no Hispanic or Asian American ethnic group members elected to the Michigan House of Representatives in 1992. In 1992 in California, however, 13 Hispanic candidates won election and 1 Asian American won a General Assembly seat. But as the representativeness ratios indicate both ethnic groups were substantially underrepresented, especially early in the 1990s.

By forcing entrenched white incumbents to retire, many observers assumed that term limits would provide opportunities for more ethnic minority group members to win election, particularly in the so-called majority-minority legislative districts. In Michigan, there were two white males who had represented state house districts within the City of Detroit, which has an overwhelming African American population. In 1998 African American candidates replaced both of these termed-out veterans. Additionally, in Michigan's 1998 election, the first in which veteran legislators could not run for reelection, two Hispanic candidates won seats in the state house. These results seemed to support the contention that the presence of white incumbents had thwarted the "pent up voting strength" of ethnic minority group members, and supported arguments that in open elections voters tend to vote for candidates of their own ethnicity (Gaddie & Bullock, 2000; Caress et al., 2003).

In Michigan in 2000, an incumbent Hispanic legislator was defeated in the primary by a white male in a district in which Hispanic and African American voters form a majority. During the 1998 election cycle, three African American candidates won election in districts where members of their ethnic group comprised a small portion of the population— only 18 percent of the population in one district, 16 percent in another, and 41 percent in the third. When asked whether they had endorsed one of these candidates, two of the former district incumbents replied that they had not and that the voters in the district simply picked the best candidate based on ability and experience (interview notes,

1997–1998). Results of these four election contests suggest that ethnic identification with the candidate is only one factor Michigan voters consider.

After three election cycles in which many incumbents were barred from running for reelection, the Michigan House of Representatives membership reflects the ethnic diversity in the state fairly well, with the exception of Hispanics. Of those elected in 2002, 13.6 percent of state house members were African American compared to 14.1 percent in the population, resulting in a representativeness ratio of nearly 1.0. No Hispanics won election to the state house in 2002, despite an increase in the state's Hispanic population to 3.3 percent by 2000.

This might suggest that term limits have helped ethnic minority group members win elections. Although prior to term limits the Michigan State House of Representatives members reflected the diversity of the state fairly closely, in the case of African Americans representativeness ratios improved from 0.72 in the early 1990s to greater than 1.00 by 2000. Despite a slight decline to 0.96 in 2002, overall the Michigan State House is more representative of the state's African American population in 2002 than it was before term limits. Without a "control" group to isolate the effects of term limits, it is difficult to say whether term limits or the increasing diversity of the state's population or the redrawn legislative districts or some combination of these factors (the explanation we think is most likely) contributed to the increased diversity among state house members in Michigan. We can at least say with some confidence that, unlike their effect on women's electoral fortunes, in Michigan term limits did not undermine gains by ethnic minority group members—as long as the overall decline that occurred between 2000 and 2002 does not continue.

In the early 1990s, the level of diversity among members of the California General Assembly substantially underrepresented the level of diversity in the state's population. In 1990 only 13.8 percent of the members of the California General Assembly were members of ethnic minority groups, a level of representation that was less than a third of what would have been expected based on the minority composition of the state's population as a whole. Hispanics were especially underrepresented, with a representativeness ratio below 0.20 in 1990. Hispanic representation in the General Assembly increased dramatically in the watershed election of 1992, however, with Hispanic membership in the General Assembly tripling,

With the advent of term limits expulsions, Hispanic General Assembly representation jumped again from 12 members in 1994 to 16 in 1996. Thus term limits seem to have increased electoral opportunities for Hispanic candidates, bringing their proportion in the General Assembly to 20 percent and producing representativeness ratios in the 0.75–0.85 range by the late 1990s and early 2000s.

The number of Asian American Assembly members also increased in California from 1990 to 2002, even more than the increase in Asian Americans as a proportion of California's population. By 2002, while still underrepresented, the representation ratio for Asian Americans climbed dramatically to 0.62 from 0.12 a decade earlier.

In contrast to the situation for Hispanic or Asian American candidates, African American membership in the California Assembly declined over the course of the 1990s. Hence, as table 4.3 makes clear, by 2000 the number of African Americans serving in the General Assembly was only about 75 percent of what it would be expected to be based on the proportion of African Americans in the state's population. The trends in Michigan and California with respect to representation of members of ethnic groups during the period that term limits were being imposed suggest two important factors. First, term limits may provide differential electoral opportunities for various ethnic minority group members. Second, when veteran legislators retire ethnic minority group members are viable candidates in districts in which the majority of voters are not members of the same ethnic minority group. Thus, term limits not only increase electoral opportunities for ethnic minority candidates to win election in majority-minority districts, but they demonstrate the electoral viability in open seat contests of candidates whose ethnicity differs from most voters, at least in Michigan.[5]

Distribution of Institutional Power

Some scholars of state legislatures worried that term limits might reduce the number of ethnic minority group members in caucus leadership positions. Many ethnic minority state legislators come from safely partisan districts in which they are able to win reelection easily for decades. This meant that, before term limits, the seniority system provided opportunities for these veteran legislators to advance within the caucus and committee leadership structure, giving them more power to help their constituents than a simple tally of their number would suggest.

In the Michigan House throughout the period of our study there are five leadership positions that received an additional salary increment because they have clearly identifiable duties and responsibilities.[6] These are speaker, minority leader, majority and minority floor leaders, and

chair of the appropriations committee. There are various other designated positions, the number and names of which seem to fluctuate. It
appears that the duties attached to these positions vary from substantive
to symbolic and additional remuneration for these "extra" leadership
positions varies across the legislative terms we compared. Therefore, we
discuss in detail only the top five leadership positions in the Michigan
State House of Representatives.

Prior to term limits, Michigan's House Democratic caucus retained
the same leadership team from 1992 to 1997. Depending on the electoral fortunes of the party these three gentlemen served as speaker or
minority leader, majority or minority floor leader, and chair or minority
vice chair of appropriations. The appropriations committee leader was
an African American male. The other two leaders were white males. On
the Republican side of the aisle, the retirement of the caucus leader
during the three sessions between the passage of term limits and the
initial expulsion of veteran legislators led to more turnover in party leadership. However, the gender and ethnicity of the people holding top
leadership positions in the Republican caucus did not change. They
were all white males.

Immediately after term limits expulsions, the House Democratic
caucus in Michigan elected a white male as its minority leader and an
African American male as its minority floor leader. The Republican
caucus elected white males as speaker, majority floor leader, and chair of
the appropriations committee. In 2000, the Democratic caucus elected
an African American male as minority leader and a white woman as
minority floor leader. The Republican caucus again elected three white
males to its three top leadership positions. In 2002, a white woman who
was a former House member and termed-out state senator won a state
house seat and won election from her caucus colleagues to become the
minority leader. Additionally, the Democratic caucus chose an African
American woman to be minority floor leader. On the Republican side,
the three top positions, speaker, majority floor leader, and appropriations chair continued to be held by white males.

Term limits, by truncating the seniority system, have not undermined
ethnic minority group members' leadership prospects in the Democratic
caucus. African American members of the Democratic caucus continued
to hold positions on the leadership team during the period we studied,
both before and after term limits. Further, term limits appear to have
helped women assume leadership roles—provided they are Democrats.

On the other hand, even with seniority removed, no women have
been elected to any of the top five leadership positions in the Republican

caucus. There has only been one minority group member in the Republican caucus during the seven election cycles we examined. This lone minority group member did not serve in any of the top leadership roles or in any of the various additional titled positions. For Republicans, it appears that it will take more than the demise of the seniority system to improve women's prospects of breaking into the top five leadership positions, and until there is at least a small cohort of ethnic minority group members in the Republican caucus, there is no prospect for ethnic diversity in Republican leadership roles with or without term limits.

Age Distribution

Many prospective candidates who might be interested and willing to serve in the Michigan House of Representatives might think twice about giving up a career to run for a position that could lead to unemployment six years hence. Indeed, one rationale used to justify the 38 percent pay raise legislators provided for themselves shortly after term limits took effect was that people needed to be offered more money to entice them to give up or curtail their existing career and run for open state house seats. Indeed, one of our respondents told of being asked to run for office many years earlier, but said he couldn't afford to take the time away from his small business until his children were grown and through college (interview notes, 1999–2000). Term limits advocates argued on the other hand that by forcing veteran legislators out of office, fresh, energetic, newcomers would reinvigorate the legislature. This rhetoric hardly seems to suggest an image of retirees increasing their ranks in the chamber, but retirees might be among those most willing to embark on a short stint of service.

Looking at table 4.4, we see evidence that, prior to term limits, the Michigan House included a sizeable cohort of members older than 60. Although there was an occasional instance in which someone under 30 was elected to the chamber, this was fairly rare. As term limits expulsions approached, we see a slight increase in the number of people in their twenties winning elections. We also see a decline in the number of members serving after they reach age 60. After 1998, when term limits expulsions created 64 open seat elections, the number of representatives age 60 or over declined. This is hardly surprising. It reflects the forced retirement of some long-serving members who had reached 60 after serving several terms in office. This is consistent with the predictions about term limits' effects.

In the following two election cycles, the number of members over age 60 increased steadily until in 2002 it returned to its pre–term limits

Table 4.4 Members of Michigan House by age categories, 1986–2002

Year elected	Democrats, percent in caucus (number)		Republicans, percent in caucus (number)		All members, percent in chamber (number)	
	under 30	over 60	under 30	over 60	under 30	over 60
1988	1.6 (1)	6.5 (4)	1.6 (1)	13.6 (8)	1.8 (2)	10.9 (12)
1990	1.6 (1)	18.3 (11)	2.0 (1)	8.0 (4)	1.8 (2)	13.6 (15)
1992*	0.0 (0)	23.6 (13)	0.0 (0)	5.5 (3)	0.0 (0)	14.5 (16)
1994**	0.0 (0)	27.8 (15)	3.6 (2)	7.1 (4)	1.8 (2)	17.3 (19)
1996**	5.2 (2)	19.0 (10)	3.8 (2)	5.8 (3)	4.5 (4)	12.7 (13)
1998***	7.7 (4)	9.6 (5)	0.0 (0)	1.7 (1)	3.6 (4)	5.5 (6)
2000	9.6 (4)	15.4 (6)	0.0 (0)	6.9 (4)	4.5 (4)	10.9 (10)
2002*	19.1 (8)	17.0 (7)	6.4 (4)	12.7 (7)	11.8 (12)	12.7 (14)

Notes
* First post-reapportionment elections.
** Term limits in place, no one yet forced out.
*** Term limits implemented—64 incumbents termed out of office.

level. After three post–term limits election cycles, this reflects election of older representatives running for open seats. In other words, prior to term limits, representatives elected during their middle years often served until they were ready to retire in their sixties or seventies. After term limits, more people are winning election to the chamber for the first time as senior citizens or nearly so. If it continues, this trend might give new meaning to the phrase, "seniority system."

Additionally, the election of 2002 brought in a large cohort of twenty-year-olds, more than double the number serving at any other time during the past decade and a half. These representatives seem more likely to inject into the chamber the vim and vigor promised by term limits advocates. On the other hand, some of their colleagues express concern about whether people who have not yet paid property taxes or had children or held another full-time job can adequately represent the interests of constituents for whom these are overriding concerns. As one respondent noted, "Their life experiences are quite limited" (interview notes, 2001–2002).

Conclusions

Do term limits increase the diversity of the state legislature? In California the answer was yes, in Michigan, maybe. The difference appears to rest with the fate of the Democratic party. This suggests that there may be an interaction effect between term limits and partisan control of the chamber. With Democrats expanding the number of seats in the California General Assembly, the increased number of open seat elections yielded more women and more ethnic minority group members. In Michigan, as the Democratic Party lost seats coincident with the advent of term limits, ethnic and gender diversity declined. Republican women in both states are not recruited extensively to run in districts in which they might win seats, and term limits alone are unlikely to change this. Minority group members have benefitted from term limits in California—a state in which Hispanics were heavily underrepresented before term limits. In Michigan, which had a more representative proportion of ethnic minority legislators serving in the House of Representatives before term limits, it appears that term limits initially had some impact, but that that may have been ephemeral. Therefore, we find some support for the hypothesis that term limits releases "pent up" voting strength for ethnic minority group members. Additionally, the numerous open seats provided opportunities for ethnic minority group members to win elections in Michigan in which members of their ethnic group did not form a majority. We find this to be an optimistic affirmation of the ability of voters to judge candidates based on their qualifications instead of their skin color.

Petracca (1996) suggests that the full impact of term limits will not be realized until they are in place for several years. We whole-heartedly agree, but their initial effects indicate the trajectory of many of those changes. On the whole, the ethnic distribution of members in the Michigan House continues to closely approximate the proportion of ethnic group members in the state, although we should note that this is concentrated in the Democratic caucus. The number of women in the Democratic caucus as a proportion of the caucus rose, although the number of Democratic women serving has declined from its 1998 peak of 18. Republican women have seen a decade of progress unraveled by term limits. Overall the decline in Republican women helped produce a decline in the number of women in the chamber to levels below those in 1992. More seniors seem to be winning their first election to the state house at the same time that more 20-year-olds are doing so.

In California, ethnic minority group members were substantially underrepresented in the General Assembly prior to term limits. Although their numbers in the General Assembly continue to lag behind their proportion of the population, the gap has narrowed after term limits, primarily due to gains made by Hispanic and Asian American candidates. The number of Republican women, always well below the number in the Democratic caucus, remained relatively stable despite term limits. So, overall women made some incremental gains in the California General Assembly.

These differences between California and Michigan probably reflect the continued Democratic control of the chamber in California and the shift to Republican control of the chamber in Michigan. Gaddie and Bullock (2000) found nationally that partisan control of the legislature by Democrats was a positive force in increasing the number of women in office. The same can be said about ethnic minority group representation.

Thus, term limits seem to provide opportunities for women and ethnic minority group members within the Democratic Party, thus, enhancing descriptive and, possibly, substantive representation. But this is not so for the Republican Party, at least not currently, in California and Michigan. Republican women seem especially disadvantaged by term limits. If the trajectory established during the first several election cycles under term limits continues one might envision an increasingly diverse Democratic caucus and an increasingly homogeneous Republican caucus. Thus, the level of diversity in the chamber as a whole will then depend primarily on the electoral fortunes of the two major political parties.

CHAPTER 5

Career Paths of Term-Limited
State Legislators

Term limits advocates envisioned a legislature populated by elected officials who would look like "mom and pop from the corner grocery store," and would want to "put in a couple of years of public service and then return to the private sector" (California Journal, 1991, p. 490). These citizen legislators they reasoned would neither be driven by reelection concerns nor beholden to special interests. They would be a more representative cross-section of people (Detroit Free Press, October 12, 1992). Term limits opponents feared that instead of rectifying the ills of special interest influence and creating greater representation, high turnover and lack of experience would rob the legislature of expertise needed to counteract the power of the executive branch, lobbyists, and others in the political system (Detroit Free Press, April 2, 1992 and Milliken, 1992). So while both sides anticipated that term limits would attract amateur legislators, some saw this as an asset and others as a liability.

Some scholars, however, disputed the assumption that term limits would produce a different kind of legislature. Fowler (1992) for instance, pointed out that fundraising and other political resources would continue to be the province of career politicians. Although participation might expand as political parties and other intermediaries cultivated promising local politicians for higher office, the average citizen would still be unlikely to have the political resources or financial means to run for higher office let alone the political ambition to do so (Monerief, Squire, & Jewell, 2001).

Prior to term limits, professionalized legislatures, such as Michigan and California, offered many benefits to entice incumbents to stay in office (e.g., personal offices, staff, travel allowances, and reasonable salaries). Many of these politicians made a life-time career of legislative service, exhibiting what Schlesinger (1966) calls "static ambition." Term limits foreclose this. Some politicians, Schlesinger observes, have "progressive" political ambition. They seek ever higher office and use the lower chamber of the state legislature as a stepping stone or "springboard" (Squires, 1988). Others exhibit "discrete ambition" (Schlesinger, 1966), serving only for a limited time in a single office to pursue some narrow or limited objective. Term limits advocates exalted the virtues of elected officials who exhibit discrete ambition and hoped that term limits would increase their ranks in the state legislature. However, term limits may attract more candidates with progressive ambition because there will be more regular, predictable opportunities for local officials to move to the State House or General Assembly and for State House and Assembly members to move to the State Senate and beyond.[1]

In this chapter, we explore three related questions about the career paths of representatives in the Michigan State House. First, we explore the threshold question of whether term limits attract more citizen legislators to the state legislature. Second, we look at the reasons representatives give for running for office, including the people or groups that recruited them or at least encouraged them to run. Finally, we look at both their career plans and the jobs they find and seek after their terms in the Michigan House expire.

Their Roots: Citizen Legislators or Career Politicians?

Political experience is strongly associated with winning open seat elections (Gaddie and Bullock, 2000). Accordingly career politicians win most elections. One representative we interviewed explained that he had previously held a seat on the county commission, but that he and his predecessor in the State House had switched positions in the last election (interview notes, 1999–2000). This suggests that term limits simply initiate a game of musical chairs among local officials and state officials rather than a new era of "average" citizens serving in the Michigan State House of Representatives.

In our earlier investigation of the "new breed" of citizen legislators (Faletta et al., 2001; Rader, Elder & Elling, 2001), we discovered that most Michigan and California newcomers serving in the session immediately after the first term limits expulsions had held other political offices, primarily at the local level.[2] Has this pattern persisted now that more election cycles have unfolded or have the ranks of local politicians been depleted, leaving the field open for novices?

Using personal biographies of Michigan House members,[3] we gathered data about representatives' prior careers, as well as whether they had any prior political experience. After term limit expulsions began, the proportion of State Representatives who had some prior political experience increased dramatically. Only 41 percent of those elected during or before 1992, when voters passed Michigan's term limits law, had some prior political experience either at the local or state level or in some cases both.

Of those elected during the interim period (1994 and 1996) between passage of the law in 1992 and expulsions from the State House in 1998, 57 percent had prior political experience. These representatives were elected before the legal fate of term limits had been decided by the Michigan Courts, so their tenure in the House was uncertain. Most of them had prior political experience and most were politically ambitious, as we would have expected. If term limits were ruled unconstitutional, they could continue for multiple terms in the House. If the term limits law was ruled constitutional, they could serve in the House for six years and then run for the crop of open seats in the State Senate in 2002 when term limits first expelled 30 out of 38 State Senators. They are an ambiguous group. They cannot truly be considered "post–term limits" legislators. Neither can they be considered fully part of the pre–term limits cohort. Given their peculiar position, they may have made electoral decisions based on conditions that neither the pre–term limits veterans nor the "new breed" of post–term limits candidates faced.[4]

But what about those elected in 1998 or after? They would be expected to include a sizeable cohort of amateur citizen legislators if term limits are fulfilling their proponents' promises. Yet a whopping 74 percent of these post–term limits representatives—those first elected to the Michigan State House during 1998, 2000, or 2002—had prior local political experience![5]

Service as a county commissioner was and remains the most common form of prior political experience for State Representatives. Twenty percent of the post–term limits representatives had served on a county commission, while only 14 percent of those elected during or before 1992 were former county commissioners. Twenty-six percent of the representatives elected during or after 1998 had served in Lansing before, either as a legislative aide, often to their predecessors, or in some other branch of state government.[6] Again this is a sizeable increase over the cohort elected during or before 1992, only 14 percent of whom had political experience in Lansing prior to their election to the House.

In addition to the newcomers with prior political experience, in 2002, a few veterans termed out of the State Senate ran for seats in the lower chamber—often for the seat they held prior to serving in the State Senate. On balance there seems to be an increase of career politicians in the State House and political novices seem to have become a rare breed after term limits. After term limits, prior political experience seems to be an increasingly common prerequisite for service in the State House.

Why do They Decide to Run for a State House Seat?

Given that those elected to the post–term limits Michigan House were likely to have held a local political office, we wanted to explore why they decided to leave a career and/or their local political position to run for a State House seat that they could hold for no more than six years. Were they self-starters or people who were recruited or encouraged to run? We wondered why these people chose to run given the shortened tenure and the challenges financially and politically of a campaign for the State House. To explore this, we asked our respondents to tell us the reasons they decided to run. We also asked them specifically if anyone had asked them to run.

Recruiting candidates

Term limits, with its constant cycling of elected officials into and out of office, sustains a recurring demand for new candidates willing to run for a fairly short stint in the State House of Representatives. As we noted in chapter 2, it takes money to run a political campaign, especially if the election is likely to be competitive. Furthermore, in closely contested races that might decide which political party controls the chamber, current and former elected officials are likely to be involved in recruiting viable candidates to optimize their party's chances of victory. Thus we expected that a large number of the post–term limits representatives would have been recruited—possibly even groomed—by other political actors who would have a vested interest in enhancing their political parties' fortunes and could help a candidate tap into the financial largess of political patrons. We were not surprised to find fewer self-starters elected after term limits than before. Forty-six percent of those running before term limits were adopted—1992 or earlier—were self-starters, reporting that "no one" had asked them to run. Only 28 percent of the post–term limits cohorts—those running for the first time in 1998 or

2000—said this. Nearly three-fourths (71 percent) of those who were first elected in 1998 and 2000, after term limits, said that one or more people or groups asked or encouraged them to run.[7]

We also found, as expected, that compared to those elected in 1992 or earlier, more of the 1998 and 2000 newcomers reported that public officials were among those who had asked or encouraged them to run. Slightly more than half (54 percent) of those who were elected to the Michigan House during or prior to 1992 said someone asked or encouraged them to run for office. Former or current state legislators were the most commonly mentioned recruiters after term limits, asking or encouraging 26 percent of the 1998 and 2000 newcomers to run. Only 17 percent of our respondents elected in 1992 or earlier said that former or current state legislators were among those asking or encouraging them to run and fewer than 10 percent of them reported that any other government actors had asked them to run. One-third of our respondents who ran after term limits said that government actors other than former or current state legislators had asked them to run. In fact, those elected in 1998 and 2000 were more likely to mention that several different sources, including friends, family, and coworkers, had asked them to run. A few members elected in 1998 and 2000 noted that some people had discouraged them from running.

As we noted in chapter 3, interest groups were more involved in recruiting candidates who won election in 1998 and 2000 than they were in 1992 or earlier elections. Term limits seem to have escalated the involvement of political parties and interest groups in recruiting candidates. Self-starters have become less common instead of more common. In this more politically charged climate, "mom and pop from the corner grocery" are unlikely to make the short list of potential candidates.

Reasons for running

We now turn to the reasons representatives gave for running for the State House of Representatives. Politicians with discrete ambition—the type term limits advocates hope to attract—are motivated by a desire to work on specific issues or to advance a specific cause (Schlesinger, 1966). Professional politicians, on the other hand, are more likely to enjoy politics and the thrill of the campaign, treating elected office as both a vocation and avocation (Ehrenhalt, 1991). Some plan to move up the electoral chain to higher office, exhibiting what Schlesinger calls progressive ambition; others are content to stay where they are. Among those representatives elected during or before 1992, slightly more than half (54.5 percent) said that running for a seat in the State House was a logical next step in their political career. For those interviewed who were elected in 1998 or afterward, the proportion was virtually identical (57.5 percent). Thus, politicians who have progressive ambition appear to be equally common in the Michigan House of Representatives both before and after term limits.

Proponents of term limits often assume that the presence of incumbents deters potentially promising newcomers from even trying to run for office. Yet, we found that 20 percent of our respondents who were elected before term limits had run for the State House before, while only 7.5 percent of our respondents who were elected during or after 1998 had tried this. This supports our contention from chapter 1 that potential challengers in the term-limited electoral environment are likely to wait for an open seat instead of challenging an incumbent.

Approximately one-third of those elected during or before 1992 claimed that they had an active interest in politics prior to running for the House. Most noted that they had worked on political campaigns or considered themselves to be activists. This dropped to about one-quarter for who were first elected during or after 1998. The proportion who said they were running to help their political party (e.g., holding the seat for the party) decreased from 14.5 percent for the cohort elected during or before 1992 to around 5 percent for the cohort elected during or after 1998.

We assumed that the availability of open seats wrought by term limits would be a major reason representatives would give for running for office. It was indeed commonly mentioned. Forty-two percent of those first elected during or after 1998 mentioned it. But it was also a very common reason given before term limits, mentioned by 38.2 percent of our respondents elected during 1992 or earlier. As our respondents reminded us, redistricting and open seats have always provided opportunities for new candidates to run, even before term limits insured a predictable supply of open seats.

Those elected before or during 1992 appear to have been more "issue-driven" and more ideologically motivated. They were nearly twice as likely as those first elected in 1998 or 2000 to say that they ran because they wanted to work on a specific issue and nearly three times as likely to say that they ran to advance a particular ideology such as smaller government or cutting taxes or a particular position on abortion. They were approximately 2.5 times as likely as those elected in 1998 or 2000 to say that their frustration with the status quo was a motivating factor in their decision to run for office. Because respondents could list multiple reasons motivating them to run, many of the respondents who listed issue-based or ideological reasons for running also said that progress in their political career was also a factor in their decision to run.

To test whether there was any change in the number of representatives elected who exhibited "discrete" ambition, we examined the full set of reasons given by each respondent. We excluded any who gave career-based reasons for running. Only those who said that specific issues motivated them to run were classified as having discrete ambition. Using these admittedly stringent criteria, we found that discrete ambition was rare in the Michigan State House of Representatives regardless of the status of term limits. We also found that it became even less common rather than more common after term limits, dropping from 20.4 percent of those first elected before term limits implementation to 16.5 percent among those elected during 1998 and 2000.

Given that discrete ambition is generally associated with specific policy-making goals, we wondered whether there was any difference among those we classified as having discrete ambition in the amount of time they reported spending studying proposed legislation or developing their own legislation. We asked representatives about the time they spent on both of these activities, using a five-point scale ranging from none (0) to an enormous amount (4). We also compared the mean amount of time representatives said they spent on these activities to the average amount of time they spent on all 11 activities we asked about. We found that discrete ambition was not associated with spending more time studying proposed legislation. We found that newcomers to the House both before and after term limits spent more time doing this than did their more experienced colleagues, probably because veterans are already more knowledgeable about the issues and are more strategic in terms of their investment of time.

We did find that representatives who we classified as having discrete ambition reported spending more time developing their own legislation. They reported doing this at a mean level of 2.6 slightly more than halfway between "some" and "a lot" on our scale compared to their more politically ambitious colleagues who reported spending a bit less time on this (mean 2.4). Although this difference was small, it was statistically significant ($t = -1.7$ sign. $p < 0.09$). Additionally, respondents we classified as having discrete ambition placed a higher priority on this activity than did their colleagues. Those with discrete ambition spent more than their average amount of time on this activity while their more politically ambitious colleagues spent less than their average time developing proposed legislation (mean difference from the mean of 0.13 for those with discrete ambition and -0.23 for the other representatives,

$t = -2.68$, sign. at 0.008). The main effect of term limits has been to reduce the number of these policy-driven representatives, from 22 before term limits to 14 for the two sessions after term limits.

Life After the Legislature

Finally, what will incumbent legislators do after they are thrown out of office? Do they abandon further political activity and return to private life? Or do they exhibit "sustained ambition," seeking other political offices or some other form of public service, including nonelected roles in government? We asked our respondents what they planned to do when they were termed out of office. Given that the best laid plans often go awry, we also tracked their progress through various jobs and multiple runs for elected office to see what they actually did after they were termed out of office.[8]

Future career plans

Looking at table 5.1, it is strikingly apparent that progressive political ambition or at least sustained political ambition abounds in the Michigan House of Representatives, especially after term limits.[9] At all levels of "seniority"—newcomers, midterm representatives and lame ducks—a larger percentage of representatives serving after term limits planned to run for another political office than did before term limits expulsions.

The longer representatives served, the less likely they were to say they would return to the private sector. For the two cohorts whose members can be followed across a series of terms, we also find fewer planning to return to the private sector after their legislative service. Almost half of the people we interviewed who were elected in 1996 finished their first term of service with plans to return to the private sector. At the end of their second term in office, 12.5 percent planned to return to the private sector. It appears that the allure of political life becomes more enticing the longer elected officials serve, but this happens so quickly that even Michigan's highly truncated years of service cannot allay the call of the campaign trail.

Not surprisingly a sizeable number, approximately a quarter, of the veteran legislators who had served before term limits planned to become interest group advocates or lobbyists after they were termed out. Their knowledge of the political process and their contacts on issues on which they worked, often for more than a decade, were probably very valuable to advocacy groups and lobbying firms. Members of subsequent cohorts rarely mentioned this possibility, however. This may suggest that they do not amass the wealth of experience and connections that would make them valued advocates or lobbyists.

Table 5.1 Future career plans of Michigan State Representatives

Career planned after house service	Level of experience and status of term limits when respondent was interviewed and year first elected					
	Newcomers before term limits, 1996 (%)	Newcomers after term limits, 1998 & 2000 (%)	Serving second term before term limits, 1994 (%)	Serving second term after term limits, 1996 & 1998 (%)	Lame ducks before term limits, 1992 or earlier (%)	Lame ducks after term limits, 1994 & 1996 (%)
Run for some other political office	60.0 (12)	75.7 (53)	29.4 (5)	73.5 (50)	47.1 (24)	75.8 (25)
Work in the non-elected public sector	20.0 (4)	10.0 (7)	23.5 (4)	19.1 (13)	9.8 (5)	9.1 (3)
Work as an advocate or lobbyist	10.0 (2)	2.9 (2)	0.0 (0)	0.0 (0)	23.5 (12)	3.0 (1)
Return to the private sector	45.0 (9)	41.4 (29)	47.1 (8)	29.4 (20)	29.4 (15)	21.2 (7)
Retire	20.0 (4)	15.7 (11)	17.6 (3)	7.4 (5)	11.8 (6)	9.1 (3)
Don't know	25.0 (5)	37.1 (26)	47.1 (8)	20.6 (14)	33.3 (17)	18.2 (6)
Number of Respondents	20	70	17	68	51	33

Note: * Totals exceed 100% because many respondents listed several options for the future.

About one-third of the veteran legislators forced out of office in 1998 said that they didn't know what they were going to do, despite the fact that they would be out of work in a matter of a few months. Post–term limits lame ducks are less likely to profess that they didn't know what they'd be doing next. Most of them have plans for their future, and before and after term limits between 20 and 25 percent of their colleagues complain that the lame ducks are more interested in looking for their next job than in performing their current legislative duties (interview notes, 1997–1998, 1999–2000, 2000–2001).

Not only did many representatives plan to run for another elected office, half of them did so. Of the 195 different people holding a seat in the State House during the three sessions, 1997–1998, 1999–2000, and 2001–2002, we found that 98 had run for some other office.[10] Not surprisingly the proportion running for another office was highest among the lame ducks forced from office. Of the 109 lame ducks, 65 (or 60 percent) ran for another office. Twenty-eight representatives ran for another office at the end of their second term—45 percent of the number who served a second term in the House during these three sessions. Amazingly, 20 percent of those serving their first term in 2001–2002 ran for another office.

The early departure of first-and second-term representatives reflects opportunity provided by the first term-limits expulsions in the State Senate in 2002 combined with redistricting after the 2000 census. Of the 107 election contests in which these 98 representatives participated (yes, some ran more than once for another elected office), 78 were contests to win a seat in the State Senate. Given that the Michigan State Senate has only 38 seats, there were more losers than winners in these races. Despite the poor odds of victory, five representatives launched a Senate campaign after one term in the House and 26 others ran for the State Senate after serving for two terms in the State House. As several Democratic representatives told us,[11] their new House district included only a small slice of their old district, so a race against another incumbent House member in the newly drawn district would be hard to win and would only yield two more years in the legislature. Therefore, they reasoned, "Why not try an equally hard, but potentially more rewarding race for the State Senate that would provide at least four, possibly eight, more years in the legislature?" (interview notes, 2001–2002). Although this situation is likely to recur episodically as this large cohort of State Senators is termed out every eight years, the combination of redistricting and the first mass expulsion from the State Senate are likely to have accentuated the lure of a State Senate race for representatives who were not yet termed out of the

State House. This is consistent with the opportunity structure imperative identified by Schlesinger (1996).

Eight more representatives ran for a national- or state-level political office. These offices included Michigan Secretary of State, U.S. Senate, U.S. Congress, and judicial positions within the state. The four representatives running for judicial positions won their elections; those running for statewide or national office lost.

Only 44 of the 109 representatives forced from office have, so far, refrained from running for a higher political office. Of these 44, several ran for local elected positions in large cities and populous counties. Thus, the evidence overwhelmingly refutes the proposition that term limits will mean the end of career politicians in the state legislature. Those elected after term limits appear more likely to pursue opportunities to advance their political career than their predecessors were. This increase in campaigning may interfere with the work of the chamber. Among our respondents serving after term limits, 13.6 percent complained that the election contests were interfering with the work of the chamber, often as a result of competition between members of the same political party who would square off against each other in the primary for an open seat in the State Senate. Only 6.7 percent of our respondents serving before term limits made similar comments about the negative impact of impending elections for other offices.

Despite the large number of career politicians serving in the Michigan State House both before and after term limits, many representatives have other careers. The proportion of State Representatives who bring life and career experience from jobs in education (14 percent) and as lawyers (12 percent) remained unchanged by term limits. The number of representatives with backgrounds in business increased dramatically after term limits rising from 17.5 percent among those elected during or before 1992 to 38.3 percent for those elected in 1998 or after. Although only 5 percent of the representatives serving after term limits expulsions had background as health care professionals, there was only one health care professional serving in the House before 1998 (less than 1 percent). Local radio and television "celebrities" and religious leaders both increased their ranks among State Representatives after term limits, although their ranks remained small (3.2–8.8 percent). The number of farmers in the State House after term limits expulsions shrank from 16 percent to 5 percent. Likewise the number of workers in trades and construction shrank from 6 percent to 3 percent.

Are representatives with some occupational backgrounds more likely to return to their community and eschew further political service?

Lawyers were the most likely to pursue political careers after being termed out of the State House. Educators were nearly as likely to do so. Seven of nine or 78 percent of the chamber's former lawyers stayed in politics. Eleven of fifteen or 73 percent of the termed-out former educators stayed in political life. Businessmen and businesswomen were also likely to continue in political life. Fifteen of 22 or 68 percent of the former businessmen and businesswomen remained in politics. Farmers were the occupational group of termed-out legislators who were more likely to go back to private life than to continue their political career, but even four of the nine former farmers (44 percent) remained in politics after being termed out of office.

Conclusions

In the social sciences one usually needs to nuance one's findings because there are often conflicting and contradictory indications. Not so here. The wealth of evidence we examined about the backgrounds of representatives elected to the Michigan House of Representatives after term limits leaves little doubt that while the stream of newcomers flowing into Michigan's lower legislative chamber may be newcomers to the State House, they are not newcomers to politics. Representatives elected after term limits are less likely to be political novices than they were before term limits. Further, they are no more likely than their predecessors to be motivated by discrete political ambition. Indeed, they are more likely to say that running for the State House was the next logical step in their political career. Many of those who initially professed no future plan to run for another elected office, added this to their list of options by the end of their second term in the Michigan House. Finally, those elected after term limits are much more likely than their predecessors to leave after serving one or two terms if a political opportunity presents itself. Thus, we conclude that the idea that term limits would produce a new breed of citizen legislators is not fulfilled. Indeed the effect has been quite the opposite. Term limits in Michigan have so far increased the proportion of representatives who are politically ambitious career politicians.

Whether and how this influx of career politicians affects the work of the legislature is the subject that we address in the following chapters. Term limits critics worried that political novices would be putty in the hands of career bureaucrats and lobbyists and special interests. The dominance of career politicians serving in the Michigan House after term limits could mean that some of their more dire predictions are less likely to occur.

CHAPTER 6

Home Style Under Term Limits: Responding to Constituents

If elected officials do not act in the best interests of their constituents, they will be voted out of office—or at least that's a common assumption. This threat at the ballot box supposedly motivates legislators to respond to their constituents' needs and concerns. Special interests, however, may sabotage legislators' responsiveness to their constituents by providing the money that reelection-seeking legislators need to campaign for office. Some scholars argue that professional, career legislators are more susceptible to this financial temptation (Mitchell, 1991). Therefore, they argue that if term limits attract a "new breed" of citizen legislators, constituents' interests instead of special interests will dominate elected officials' agendas.

Other scholars disagree, arguing that because term-limited politicians will not be preoccupied with reelection, they will care less instead of more about their constituents' interests. For example, evidence provided by Herrick, Moore, & Hibbing (1994) documents that U.S. House members who were voluntarily retiring made fewer trips back to their districts and assigned fewer staff to their district offices. Term limits may mean that there will be a lot more people retiring from office every election cycle. If retiring legislators are less concerned about the wishes of their constituents, this could mean that under term limits legislators will become less responsive to their constituents. On the other hand, evidence shows that retiring U.S. House members are as responsive to their constituents' preferences as are those members who are not retiring (Dougan & Munger, 1989; Lott & Reed, 1989). So one of the questions about term limits is whether the responsiveness of legislators to their constituents is increased or decreased after limits are imposed.

This debate becomes even more complicated, however, because some people think that representatives should respond to their constituents, while others see this as a source of wasteful pork-barrel projects. For those who scorn what they describe as hypersensitivity to constituents' concerns exhibited by reelection-seeking, career politicians, reducing the responsiveness of legislators to constituents will allow the general welfare of the state as a whole to prevail over narrow, local interests (Petracca, 1991; Will, 1992). But even if elected officials are freed of these local demands, there is no guarantee that they will act in the public interest. For example, term limits could create more cohesive political parties by disconnecting legislators from the local demands of their constituencies (Glazer & Wattenberg, 1991). Or term-limited legislators could seek recognition outside of their district to curry favor with those who can provide rewards and opportunities after legislative service ends (Kesler, 1990; Montgomery, 1990; Benjamin & Malbin, 1992; Herrick & Nixon, 1994). Thus term limits might increase "shirking" and various forms of "nest-feathering" as those who are no longer eligible for reelection advance their own future career prospects instead of their constituents' interests. So even if term limits increase or decrease legislators' responsiveness to constituents, there are people who would continue debating whether this is a good or a bad impact of term limits.

Solid empirical evidence on legislators forced to retire under term limits is scarce. Based on a survey of nearly 3,000 state legislators in term limited and non–term limited states, Carey, Neimi, and Powell (1998 and 2000) found that newly elected legislators in states anticipating term limits spent less time on casework and constituent service than did their counterparts serving in state legislatures without term limits laws. This might suggest reduced concern for the needs and interests of constituents on the part of legislators elected in a term-limited milieu. On the other hand, it might suggest that there are fundamental differences between term-limited and non–term limited legislatures, such as the level of professionalization and associated staff resources needed to do extensive casework. Additionally, Carey, Niemi, and Powell's survey was conducted in 1995 before term limits had actually forced out any legislators.

There are two major problems with making inferences about term limits based upon the behavior of legislators who forego reelection voluntarily. First, they are rarely worried about subsequent career opportunities because they are often retiring or accepting another job offer. In contrast, many legislators whose tenure is curtailed by term limits may be maneuvering to extend their political careers in other offices or find another job, and such maneuvering may affect their legislative behavior. Second, unlike retiring legislators, with term limits legislators' eminent departure will be clear for their entire final term in office. This could lead other institutional actors, such as bureaucrats or other legislators, to treat legislators about to be turned out of office, those called lame ducks, differently (Trpovski, Sarbaugh-Thompson, & Strate 2001a).

John Carey's work (1996) is particularly illuminating with respect to these effects—albeit in a Latin American rather than North American context. Carey compares the behavior of members of the Costa Rican national assembly following the adoption of term limits with the behavior of national legislators prior to the adoption of such limits.[1] He also compares the behavior of the members of the term-limited Costa Rican national assembly with that of the members of the Venezuelan national assembly who are not subject to term limits. His basic argument is that term limits significantly weaken, if they do not entirely eliminate, the power of the electoral incentive (Rae, 1971; Mayhew, 1974; Cain, Ferejohn, & Fiorina, 1987) that supposedly prompts legislators to be attentive to the needs and desires of their constituents.

For our purposes, Carey's (1996) most important finding is that term-limited Costa Rican legislators tend to behave in ways that are likely to help them to secure their futures after their legislative service has ended. His findings "support unambiguously the premise that legislators under term limits will be responsive to the interests of prospective future employers, even at the expense of the interests of their current electoral constituency" (p. 193).

In this chapter we explore three competing factors related to term limits that could affect the relationship between legislators and their constituents: larger flocks of lame ducks, altered career paths and political ambitions, and new institutional norms and expectations. Specifically we address the following questions. First, do lame ducks shirk their responsibilities to their constituents? Second, do the activities lame ducks attend to most assiduously in their district suggest that they are "nest-feathering" as they look beyond their current legislative service to other career opportunities? And, finally, do term limits change legislators' responsiveness to their constituents, perhaps by attracting a "new breed" of legislators or by changing existing institutional norms?

Data and Methods

To explore the effects of term limits on the responsiveness of legislators to their constituents, we asked House members how much time they spent on constituent-related activities and also about the groups of people from their district on whom they relied for information and guidance on a difficult policy issue. Specifically, we analyzed four questions about time allocation that asked about the amount of time spent communicating with constituents, helping constituents with problems, attending meetings and events in their home district, and trying to get their district's "fair share" of government money and projects. These questions were part of the series of questions about time spent on 11 activities that we have revisited throughout the book. In the following discussion we also consider three sources of information and guidance from the representative's district: key local officials, advisors in the district, and other constituents. These questions were asked as part of the series of questions about the extent to which the representatives relied on several sources of information and guidance when trying to form a position on a specific issue considered in a committee on which they served.

We also asked respondents a third set of questions intended to explore the priority House members give to their constituents' views when they conflict with their own personal views and the priority they give the needs of their district compared to the needs of the state as a whole. These two indicators measure what is often called, respectively, the representational role orientation and the areal role orientation of legislators, based on a conception proposed years ago by Wahlke et al. (1962). Responses to these two role-orientation questions were recorded on a seven-point continuum. The question about representational role orientation asked, "If there were a conflict between what you feel is best and what the people in your district want, what would you do?" The continuum was anchored at one end with, "Always do what the people in the district want." The other end was anchored with, "Always do what you think best." The question to measure areal role orientation asked, "If there were a conflict between what is best for your district and best for the state as a whole, what would you do?" The seven-point continuum used for this question was anchored with the following two phases: "Always look after my district" and "Always look after the state."

Representatives are Generally Responsive to Constituents

To explore term limits' effects on relations between representatives and their constituents, we compared the 1997–1998 House (before term limits expelled any legislators) to both the 1999–2000 House and the 2001–2002 House (the first and second sessions after term limits expelled veteran legislators). First and foremost, we found that most legislators spent "a lot" or "an enormous amount" of time working with or on behalf of their constituents. This was true regardless of whether representatives were elected before or after term limits implementation, whether they could continue serving in the Michigan House, or whether they had plans to run for another elected office.

As we noted in the introduction, we calculated a difference between the average amount of time the legislator reported spending on all of his or her activities and the time spent on each of the four constituent-related activities. These differences between the mean and the amount of time spent on a specific activity tend to be fairly small, generally fractional amounts. Readers are reminded that negative numbers indicate that the representative reported spending less than an average amount of time on the activity; positive numbers indicate that he or she spent more than the average amount of time on the activity. We can think of these difference numbers as a measure of the priority given to the activity. We found that as a group our respondents placed a high priority on constituent-related activities. Thus, members of the Michigan State House of Representatives not only devote a lot of time to constituent-related activities but they place a high priority on these activities.

A Brief Explanation of Statistical Methods Used

Results presented in this chapter are based on a type of statistical analysis called three-way analysis of variance. As we discuss the first constituent-related activity, time spent communicating with constituents, we will describe the reasons we decided to use this technique. We ask for indulgence from readers with background in statistics while we clarify the necessity for multivariate analysis to others in our audience. Readers who want more details about the analyses can consult the endnotes and refer to our more technical treatment of these data in our other work (Wilson et al., 2001).

Analysis of variance answers questions about whether there are differences between groups. More specifically, it compares means for different groups of respondents to see whether the means vary more within the group or between the different groups. Three-way analysis of variance means that there are three factors used to place the respondents into groups. The factors are: (1) respondent is serving before or after term limits expelled veteran legislators (before or after term limits expulsions); (2) respondent is serving in his or her last permissible term in the

House (lame duck or not); (3) the respondent is considering running for another elected office (future political career aspirations or not). Because each factor we used has two values, we will be comparing eight categories of respondents. For example, one group would be representatives serving before term limits expulsions who are not lame ducks and do have future political aspirations. The results we discuss in this chapter compare time spent by these eight groups on constituent-related activities and consulting of district sources. We provide a summary of our findings in table 6.1.

For readers who are unfamiliar with multivariate statistics, we explain a few key concepts before beginning to discuss our findings. In three-way analysis of variance, it is possible to identify effects of a single factor or effects of combinations of two or three of the factors. When we talk about the main effects of one of the factors, for instance lame duck or not, we are talking about just grouping the respondents by that factor—into two categories while adjusting for the effects of the other factors. When we talk about the interaction of two of the factors (e.g., lame duck or not and planning to run for another elected office or not) we are comparing four groups created by just these two factors adjusting for the effect of the other factor. We will describe the advantages of using several variables simultaneously (multivariate analysis) as we report our findings about the first of the constituent-related activities.

Time Spent Communicating with Constituents

Representatives serving after term limits expulsions reported spending even more time communicating with their constituents than did their predecessors. Lame ducks, however, reported spending less time communicating with constituents. Given that our interview respondents in the pre–term limits expulsions group included more lame ducks (51 of 95) than did our respondents during the two post–term limits expulsions sessions combined (34 of 186), we wanted to see whether this finding about term limits simply reflected the larger number of lame ducks among the pre–term limits cohort. Thus, we need to consider simultaneously both lame duck status and term-limits expulsions. We can do this statistically by including two separate variables, one for pre- or post–term limits expulsions and another for whether the legislator responding was a lame duck or not.

We discovered that the change in the time spent on this activity was attributable to the numerous lame ducks who were spending less time communicating with voters and not directly to term limits implementation.

Table 6.1 Time spent on constituent-related activities

	Actual amount of time				Priority compared to other activities			
	After term limits expulsions	Serving last term (lame duck)	Future political aspirations	Interaction effects: none	After term limits expulsions	Serving last term (lame duck)	Future political aspirations	Interaction effects: Term limits expulsions & political aspirations
Communicating with constituents	—	Approx. 1/4 point decrease	—	—	—	—	—	—
Attending district functions	—	Approx. 1/4 point decrease	Approx. 1/4 point increase	—	—	Slight decrease	Approx. 2/3 point increase	—
Helping constituents with problems	—	—	—	—	Approx. 1/5 point increase	—	—	No political aspirations: approx. 2/3 point higher after term limits
Getting district gov't money & projects	—	Approx. 1/4 point decrease	—	—	—	—	—	—

District sources of information and guidance

	Extent of consulting				Relative importance compared to other sources			
	After term limits expulsions	Serving last term (lame duck)	Future political aspirations	Interaction effects: none	After term limits expulsions	Serving last term (lame duck)	Future political aspirations	Interaction effects: Term limits expulsions & political aspirations
Consults key local officials	Approx. 2/5 point increase	Approx. 1/3 point increase	—	—	Approx. 1/3 point increase	Approx. 2/5 point increase	—	No political aspirations: approx. 2/3 point higher after term; Limits expulsions than before

Table 6.1 Continued

District sources of information and guidance

	Extent of consulting				Relative importance compared to other sources			
	After term limits expulsions	*Serving last term (lame duck)*	*Future political aspirations*	*Interaction effects: none*	*After term limits expulsions*	*Serving last term (lame duck)*	*Future political aspirations*	*Interaction effects: Term limits expulsions & political aspirations*
Consults advisors in district	Approx. 1/3 point increase	—	—	—	Approx. 1/4 point decrease	—	—	—
Consults other constituents	Approx. 1/2 point increase	—	—	—	Approx. 1/3 point increase	—	—	—

Roles

	After term limits expulsions	*Serving last term (lame duck)*	*Future political aspirations*	Interaction effects: term limits, lame duck and future political aspirations	*After term limits expulsions*	*Serving last term (lame duck)*	*Future political aspirations*	Interaction effects: term limits expulsions with future political aspirations
Representational Areal role	—	—	—	—	—	—	—	Prior to term limits expulsions with future political aspirations: Lame ducks were slightly more than a point more state-oriented than those who could serve another term in the House.

The mean was 3.36 for those who could serve again (about halfway between "a lot" and "an enormous amount"), while the mean for lame ducks was 3.12 (slightly above "a lot") (sign. at $p < 0.02$). Even though lame ducks spent less time communicating with their constituents, they were still fairly attentive.

We also wanted to determine if future political aspirations affected the time legislators spent communicating with constituents. We investigated this by adding a third variable, future political aspirations, to the two variables that we just discussed. Using all three factors simultaneously we found that future political aspirations did *not* affect the amount of time representatives spent communicating with their constituents, when we control for the effects of being a lame duck and of term limits expulsions.[2]

Turning to the priority legislators place on communicating with constituents, we found no statistically significant effects from any of the three factors we considered: term-limits expulsions, lame duck status, and future political aspirations. Therefore, even though lame ducks spend less time on this activity, the decline is proportional to their overall reduction in time spent attending to their job. The relative amount of time they spent communicating with constituents did not change. This aptly demonstrates why we feel it is important to discuss the relative priority representatives give an activity as well as the quantity of time they report spending.

Time Spent Attending Events in Their District

We discovered that lame ducks spent less time attending events in their district. The mean was 3.17 (slightly more than "a lot") for those who could serve more terms compared to 2.89 (slightly less than "a lot") for the lame ducks (sign. at $p < 0.05$). On the other hand, we discovered that representatives with future political aspirations reported spending more time attending meetings and functions in their district. The mean was 3.15 for those planning to run for another office and 2.91 for those *not* planning to do so (sign. at $p < 0.05$).[3]

Lame ducks not only spent less time on this activity, but they placed a lower priority on it. The decline was small, however, from a mean of 0.58 (slightly more than a one-half point above average) for those who can serve in the House again to a mean of 0.42 for lame ducks (sign. at $0 < 0.1$). On the other hand, this activity had a higher priority for respondents with future political aspirations. They spent nearly two-thirds of a point more time on this than their average time for all 11 activities (mean= 0.62). Their colleagues who do not plan to run for another elected office report spending only about one-third of a point more time attending events in their district than the average amount of time they spent on all 11 activities (mean = 0.38) (sign. at $p < 0.01$).[4]

Time Spent Helping Constituents with Problems

Michigan House members spend a lot of time helping their constituents with their problems. We found no change in the time spent on this activity before and after the implementation of term limits. Further, many respondents reported that their staff members spent an enormous amount of their time doing this.

Although all groups of House members place a higher than average priority on helping constituents with problems, this priority increased for members serving after term limits expulsions. Respondents serving after term limits expulsions reported spending nearly two-thirds of a point more than their average time (mean = 0.63), compared to their predecessors, who reported spending a bit less than half a point above their average (mean = 0.46) (sign. at $p < 0.13$).

We found an interaction effect between the status of term limits and future political aspirations. The interaction effect means that term limits seem to have one effect on time helping constituents for those respondents with future political aspirations and a different effect for those without future political aspirations. Respondents with future political aspirations placed almost the same priority on helping constituents with problems before and after term limits (means of 0.57 and 0.54 respectively).[5] Respondents who had no future political aspirations give this activity a lower priority before term limits than they do after term limits (mean of 0.36 before term limits and 0.73 after. This interaction effect was sign. at $p < 0.08$).

Interestingly in the term-limits milieu, House members who were the least accountable at the ballot box (those who were lame ducks with no future political aspirations) reported spending the most time helping constituents with problems. Readers are reminded of the situation we described in chapter 5 in which a legislator's future constituents might have different interests than his or her current ones. One might speculate that attentiveness to future constituents could explain the tendency after term limits of those running for another office to spend less time helping their current constituents. Additionally, their imminent return to their local community might motivate representatives not running for another office to pursue constituent service for their neighbors. Alternatively, it is possible that these few representatives who "lack" political ambition may reflect the potential for citizen legislators to be more responsive to their constituents. Even if this explanation proves to be true, term limits seem to reduce instead of increase the number of these citizen legislators serving in the Michigan State House of Representatives. So this is not likely to have a major impact on legislative responsiveness overall.

Time Spent Getting the District's Share of Money and Projects

We discovered that the amount of time spent on getting the district its fair share of government money and projects differed, but only slightly, for those serving in their last term. The mean was 2.76 for those who could serve more terms in the Michigan State House, while for the lame ducks, it was 2.52 (sign. at $p < 0.12$).[6] There were no other statistically significant effects, and no statistically significant changes in the priority given to this activity. In other words, this decline in time spent was proportional to the overall decline lame ducks reported that they spent on average doing the 11 job activities we asked them about.

The diminished emphasis placed by last-term members on "seeing that the district gets its fair share of government money and projects" suggests that term limits might reduce pork-barrel spending. For some term limits advocates this would be evidence that term limits have accomplished one of their intended goals. On the other hand, the same data may be read as evidence of shirking and a diminished commitment to the needs and interests of the people who elected legislators to bring home the bacon.

We should stress that this is only a small decline in time spent and that it reflects only the overall tendency of lame ducks to spend less time on various aspects of their job. Spending less time on this activity may have little or no effect on the actual number of such projects statewide or on total amounts of money earmarked for pork-barrel projects. Practically speaking it may simply mean that individual districts can expect a "dry spell" every six years when their representative is termed out of office.

Summary of Time Spent on Constituent-Related Activities

We find substantial evidence that lame ducks spend less time on constituent-related activities. The one exception to this, helping constituents with problems, actually increased for some lame ducks—those without future political aspirations who were serving after term limits. Additionally, we discovered respondents with future political aspirations spent more time attending meetings and events in their district. This pattern suggests that the time spent on activities in the term-limited legislative environment is contingent on the representative's future career plans. Those planning to continue in the political arena cultivate groups and reach out to groups of voters. Those planning to return to the community, or possibly hoping to find a job in the community, concentrate on helping individuals with their problems. Therefore, we find that lame ducks engage in selective nest-feathering that offsets somewhat their more general tendency to shirk.

Consulting with District Sources About Difficult Issues

We turn now to another facet of legislator–constituent relations. For this part of our investigation, we asked House members about the extent to which they consulted various sources when trying to decide how to vote on a particularly difficult issue seriously considered by a committee on which they served. In this chapter we were interested in the extent to which representatives relied for information and guidance upon three sources of information in their district—key local officials, advisors in the district, and other constituents.

While legislators spend a lot of time on constituent-related service activities, they do not spend much time listening to or consulting with their constituents. Our respondents, both before and after term limits were implemented, relied only a little or not at all on sources of information and guidance in their districts. These levels are either at or below their average level of consulting with all sources. This suggests a fairly paternalistic relationship in which legislators communicate with and help their constituents, but do not listen to them very extensively. As we discuss in chapter 9, both before and after term limits the sources representatives listen to most are those in the capital, primarily in the House itself, and those representing organized groups.

Extent to Which Members of the House Rely on Key Local Officials

After term limits expulsions, respondents report relying on information and guidance from key local officials more than their predecessors did.

Further, lame ducks both before and after term limits expulsions report relying on key local officials more than do their colleagues who can continue to serve in the Michigan House. In both cases the increases are small, a shift from slightly above "a little" to about halfway between "a little" and "some," but statistically significant.[7]

As we noted earlier, respondents answered these questions by describing different committees and different issues. To adjust for the possibility that some issues involved extensive consulting with many sources of information and others involved little or no consulting, we compared the amount of consulting with key local officials to the respondents' average level of consulting for all 17 sources we asked them about. We found that prior to term limits expulsions, representatives consulted key local officials slightly less than their average level of consulting (mean = −0.21), while after term limits expulsions they consulted this source slightly more than their average level (mean = 0.15). We also found that respondents who could serve in the House again consulted this source of information and guidance slightly less than their average level of consulting (mean = −0.23), while lame ducks consulted this source slightly more than their average level of consulting (mean = 0.17).

In addition to these two main effects, we found an interaction between the status of term limits and future political aspirations (sign. at $p < 0.07$). We found that legislators who did not have future political aspirations consulted key local officials at different levels before and after term limits expulsions. Specifically those serving before term limits expulsions without political aspirations consulted key local officials at a level almost half a point below their average level (mean = −0.41), while those serving after term limits expulsions who also had no future political aspirations consulted key local officials at a level a quarter of a point above their average level of consulting (mean = 0.25). We found no difference between representatives with future political aspirations serving before or after term limits were implemented. Representatives with future political aspirations consulted key local officials at their average level of consulting regardless of term limits (means = 0.00 and 0.04 respectively).[8]

We interpret this finding as a reflection of representatives' concern about earning a living and supporting their families after they were termed out of office. Many legislators in the pre–term limits expulsion cohort who were not planning to run for future office were old enough to retire. As we noted earlier, 13 of them planned to do so. Many lame ducks serving after term-limits expulsions were too young to retire. Key local officials could be an important link to local jobs. We infer from this that consulting key local officials about difficult issues could be a way to maintain ties that term-limited representatives may need to find a job in their local community.

Extent to which Representatives Consult Advisors in Their District

Representatives rarely reported consulting advisors in their district, and those who did this at all did not do so extensively. In all cases, this source was consulted less than the average level. With that caveat, we found that representatives serving after term limits expulsions reported consulting advisors in their district more than did those serving prior to term limits expulsions. The increase was slight and only marginally statistically significant (sign. at $p < 0.15$). The mean difference from the average for those serving before term limits expulsions was -0.39 while after term limits expulsions, it rose to -0.13. In general consulting advisors in their district is an uncommon phenomenon that became slightly less rare after term limits.[9]

Extent to which Representatives Consult Other Constituents in Their District

Representatives serving after term limits expulsions reported consulting constituents more than their predecessors did. The mean extent of consulting reported by those serving after term limits expulsions was 1.59, slightly more than halfway between "a little" and "some," while the mean reported by those serving before term limits expulsions was 1.14, slightly more than "a little" (sign. at $p < 0.05$).[10] We found no other main effects and no interaction effects.

We also found an increase in the priority of constituents among those consulted. Those serving before term limits expulsions reported consulting their constituents slightly less than average (mean = -0.11), while those serving after term limits expulsions consulted their constituents about a quarter of a point more than their average level of consulting (mean = 0.26) (sign. at $p < 0.07$).[11] This could suggest stronger ties between constituents and those they elect to represent their views, although we remind readers again that the respondents reported consulting constituents only a little. We can only say that an uncommon phenomenon has become slightly more common, but it is still not a major source information and guidance.

Summary of Representatives' Consulting with Sources from the District

Although consulting with sources of information and guidance in the district is still not common, for respondents serving after term limits expulsions, it is slightly more common. Not only did the extent of this consulting increase, the priority given to these district sources increased too. Further, we found no evidence that lame ducks rely on these sources any less than their other colleagues do. Indeed lame ducks consulted with key local officials, more than did their colleagues who could continue serving in the House. This was especially true for lame ducks without future political aspirations suggesting that in the term-limited political environment, key local officials are an important link to future jobs outside the political arena near the legislator's home. This trend, although very slight, is a step in the direction that term limits advocates had hoped to trigger.

Term-Limit Effects on Legislators' Role Orientation

Our third set of variables focus on the role orientations espoused by members of the Michigan House; that is, how they conceived of their jobs as representatives. We asked members about what Walhke (1962) describes as their representational role and their areal role.

The representational role involves that trade-off between acting as a delegate, voting the way people in the district would vote, or voting as a trustee, based on one's own judgment or conscience. To measure respondents' representational role, we asked House members what they would do on an issue on which there was a conflict between "what people in the district want" and "what you think is best." They were asked to respond on a seven-point scale running from "always do what people in the district want" to "always do what you think best."

We found no relationship whatsoever between representational role orientation and the implementation of term limits, future political aspirations, or the lame duck status of the respondent. The mean for all groups was slightly more than four, which was the midpoint on the seven-point scale. The conception of legislative role orientations reflected in this question has been criticized by some students of legislative behavior as naive and overly simplistically (Jewell, 1982). Perhaps, not surprisingly then, we found that this question elicited considerable resistance among veteran legislators and enthusiasm among freshmen. Many veteran legislators found it hard to imagine such conflicts; others said,

"It depends on the issue." When pressed, most responded on our seven-point scale, albeit with some extended discussion and qualifications. Thus, resistance to the question reduced the response rates among veteran legislators well below those for most other questions we asked. Freshmen on the other hand often commented that this was a good question.

In another question, we explored what Wahlke (1962) called areal role orientation. This explores potential tension between the needs of the representative's district versus the needs of the state as a whole. Specifically we asked, "If there were a conflict between what is best for your district and best for the state as a whole, what would you do?" One end of the scale was anchored with "Always look after my district" and the other with "Always look after the state." The mean (3.4), for this question was tipped slightly toward looking after their district, although again this was close to the midpoint of four on the seven-point scale.

Interestingly we found a three-way interaction effect that was statistically significant at the $p = 0.1$ level. Among the eight groups created by classifying the respondents based on the status of term limits, lame duck status and future political aspirations, two groups responded at levels that were quite different from each other and from the overall mean. Those groups were both planning to run for another elected office and were serving prior to term limits expulsions, but one group consisted of lame ducks while members of the other group could run for the State House again. The mean for the former group, the lame ducks about to be termed out of office and planning to run for something else, indicated that they had a more "statewide" orientation, with a mean of 3.94 nearly the midpoint. The other group, those who could run for the House again, but planning to run for something else after their allowable terms in the House expired, reported a more district-centered orientation, with a mean of 2.89. Among those serving subsequent to term-limits expulsions, whether lame ducks or not, whether planning to run for another elected office or not, all had group means fluctuating very slightly from the overall mean of 3.4. We infer from this that respondents planning to run for higher office who had served for decades in the legislature were more likely to run for an office in which they needed to appeal to voters outside their district, hence their broader areal orientation. On the other hand, those who were not lame ducks, but planning to run for something else, possibly even a local government office, intensified their district orientation to secure their base and insure that they continued to have the option of building on that foundation. This suggests that role orientation may be fairly fluid and influenced by political expedience.

Finally, we asked representatives to grade the House as a whole on its ability to respond to the needs and concerns of the state's constituents. Because we assumed that legislative priorities would favor constituents represented by members of the majority political party in the chamber, we considered both the status of term limits and whether the respondent was a member of the majority or minority political party. We found that the average grade House members gave themselves was higher before term limits than afterward and that the average grade given by members of the majority political party in the chamber was higher than that given by the minority party. Additionally we found that the gap between the grades given by minority and majority party members was wider after term limits than it was before. Pre–term limits majority party members gave the chamber an average grade slightly above a B. Their minority party colleagues gave the chamber an average grade slightly below a B. After term limits the majority party awarded an average grade of a B+. Their minority party colleagues gave an average grade of C+. All of these differences are statistically significant.[12] Members of the minority political party complained after term limits that the needs and concerns of a large segment of the state's voters were not being adequately represented by the majority political party's legislative agenda.

This could suggest that the statewide orientation of representatives in the term-limits milieu has suffered, but could also reflect the possibility that before term limits, the Democratic majority would have anticipated some need to compromise with the Republican party to increase the likelihood that the Republican Governor and Republican-controlled State Senate would support bills the House passed. We hope, in future work, to disentangle the effects of single-party control of the legislative and executive branches of government from the effects of term limits. We mention these findings despite their limitations to remind readers and ourselves that representation has both district and statewide facets that need to be considered in assessing term limits' effects.

The New Versus the Old Breed

Role orientations afford us yet another opportunity to assess whether people elected to the Michigan House under a term limits regime represent a "new breed" of legislators or whether the institutional norms of appropriate conduct have changed legislators' beliefs about how they should do their job. As one veteran representative pointed out "Term limits could advantage local interests, but for some things statewide implications are important" (interview notes, 1997–1998).

The group that most unambiguously represents any "new breed" in the Michigan House consists of those elected after term limits were implemented in 1998, leaving no uncertainty about issues of constitutionality and enforcement. Conversely, respondents who most unambiguously represent the "old breed" are those who were elected before 1992, before term limits was even on the agenda in Michigan. We found no difference between these two groups in their orientation toward their representational role or their areal role. We did, however, gain additional insight into the effect of plans to run for another elected office on the areal role orientation of representatives. Members of the old and new breed who had future political aspirations gave more weight to the welfare of the state as a whole than did their colleagues. Thus we found little to suggest that the post–term limit group brought anything approaching a fundamentally different set of role orientations. The intervening group, those elected after term limits were adopted, but before they were implemented show some slight differences in their areal role orientation, but this was an ephemeral phenomenon. In other words, for better or for worse, in terms of role orientation, the "new breed" looks a lot like the "old breed" with future political aspirations continuing to affect areal role orientation.

Conclusions

Term limits not only insure a steady influx of newcomers to legislative chambers, they produce intermittent flocks of lame ducks leaving. We find that these lame ducks tend to be less attentive to their job duties in general, including constituent-related activities. They spend less time communicating with constituents, attending meetings and functions in the district, and trying to assure that their district gets its fair share of government money and projects. In some instances, however, we found that their political ambitions offset their tendency to shirk more generally.

We found that representatives serving after term limits expulsions relied more on the three district sources of information and guidance than their predecessors did. We note, however, that this still meant that they consulted these sources only "a little" or slightly more. We found that lame ducks consulted local officials more, but, again we stress, still not very much. This was especially true for those serving after term limits were implemented and also for those without future political aspirations. This suggests that ties to people in the district are a valuable resource for future jobs, but that different groups of people are differentially valuable for reelection campaigns or nonelected jobs in the district.

The day that Michigan House members are elected to their third term, they know that in a little more than two years they will be out of a job. After they are forced out of office, most will not return to private life. Rather the vast majority seeks another elective office—possibly in the State Senate or in any one of a number of local offices, such as mayor or county commissioner, or for the few seats in the U.S. House or Senate. They may also seek an administrative or staff position in federal, state or local government or join an advocacy or policy-oriented group as a lobbyist or work for a multiclient lobbying firm. In any case, House members' current electoral constituencies only partially determine their futures. Those not planning to continue elected political careers spent more time helping constituents, while those planning to continue running for other elected offices spent more time attending meetings and events in their district. This suggests that the mix of constituent-related activities pursued by a "lame duck" is contingent on his or her future career plans. Thus, there seem to be last-term effects that motivate term-limited legislators to be highly selective in their relationships with constituents and their attention to their districts. From this we infer that nest-feathering is a major influence on the choices these lame ducks make about their relationships with constituents and the time they spend on constituent-related activities.

We might infer from their slightly greater reliance on district sources of information that legislators are increasingly inclined to act as delegates instead of trustees toward their constituents. This is possible. We would be more comfortable making this inference if the amount of this consulting exceeded "a little" and if we had found any changes at all in their representational role orientation. We found no such evidence. Therefore, we hesitate to read too much into this. Absent more compelling evidence, we are not convinced that the role orientations of the "new breed" of post–term limited legislators differ from the "old breed." The major change attributable to term limits seems to be the greater focus on a future job and the relative importance or unimportance of constituents in gaining that job.

For the upwardly mobile career politicians in the House, the relevant question may be which constituents are the most valuable for their future campaign? For example, the authors know of a district represented by a House member who might run for a State Senate seat that will be vacant in 2006. One corner of that district is heavily Democratic, and voters in the district as a whole are closely divided between the two parties. The Senate District for which the legislator could run does not include this bastion of Democrats. Despite the fact that the representative is a somewhat moderate Republican, it would not help his future primary contest for the Senate seat if he were to be responsive to his Democratic constituents. Indeed he is no longer accountable to them at the ballot box, needing instead to appeal to future voters who are much more conservative than his current constituents. Given the number of representatives who will be termed out of the House during the next four years, he is likely to have at least one, possibly more, opponents in the Republican primary, and many of them are likely to be more conservative than he is. If he decides to compete he will need to be able to run on a fairly conservative voting record. Thus, in some circumstances political ambition has the potential to undermine the electoral accountability of legislators to their current constituents.

This situation, in which current constituents are only partially included among future constituents, varies from state to state. In California for instance, the 80 General Assembly districts are nested pairs that each comprise half of one of the 40 State Senate districts. All current constituents form half of a politically ambitious General Assembly member's future constituents. Thus, the increased political ambition that seems to accompany term limits could increase electoral accountability in California, and other states with "nested districts." It has the potential to have the opposite effect in Michigan and other states that require little overlap between lower and upper chamber districts.

PART THREE

---

*Term Limits and the Michigan House
as an Institution*

The Seven Types of People in The World

CHAPTER 7

Networking in the House: Winning Friends and Influencing People

All organizations, including state legislatures, operate through formal and informal relationships among their members. The formal side of an organization consists of the official roles and responsibilities of its members and the written rules or procedures. The informal side consists of norms and social or interpersonal relationships. Evidence suggests that social interaction in the informal organization affects the behaviors and attitudes of actors as they perform their formal roles and duties (Barnard, 1938; Marsden & Friedkin, 1993) and that legislatures are no exception to this (Patterson, 1959; Caldeira et al., 1993). Furthermore, changes in the formal rules and roles typically affect informal relationships and the expectations people have about the ways they should interact with each other. Therefore, the formal and informal facets of the organization interact.

Term limits changed the operational rules of the legislature by setting a fixed maximum length of service instead of letting voters and political parties choose the legislator's length of service. This severely truncates seniority and produces less experienced, transient committee chairs, speakers, floor leaders, and other formal leaders. Prior to term limits, legislators often served in these roles for several sessions. Top leaders rose through the ranks based on their performance in less powerful leadership positions (e.g., as chairs of minor committees). Without longevity to insure a fairly stable coterie of top leaders, the competition for these positions will expand while the opportunities for colleagues to assess the leadership ability of candidates will contract. Additionally, people holding leadership positions will occupy those roles for brief periods, which may decrease their need to appease their followers and may decrease the loyalty of their supporters as everyone looks toward the future and the inevitable changing of the guard. Thus, a change in the formal rules will affect the informal processes and dynamics of the legislature. Furthermore, we agree with other scholars (Carey et al., 1998) that these effects are likely to be among the most profound impacts of term limits. In this chapter and the ones that follow, we turn our attention to the ways in which changes in the formal structure interact with informal facets of the legislature.

By shortening the time legislators serve together, term limits may alter the development of interpersonal relationships. These relationships can affect the development of trust and respect among legislators. According to members of the Michigan House, trust affects who is seen as an honest broker in negotiations and who is chosen to hear a nascent idea and give an honest reaction. As one legislator put it, you can take some risks with a friend that you can't take with a stranger (interview notes, 1997–1998).

In a legislature, friends don't necessarily agree with each other. Indeed many of the legislators described friendships in which they could strongly disagree and then walk out of the chamber together and have a beer, dinner, and conversation. As one veteran legislator put it, if you haven't developed a friendship, you could still be mad two days later after that kind of disagreement (interview notes, 1997–1998). Trust and respect between legislators who disagree facilitates compromises on key issues. Therefore, changes in interpersonal relationships among legislators can profoundly affect the work of the legislature. As one House member explained, "it's easier to communicate with friends because you need fewer words and they'll use their right brain and try to see intuitively what you're trying to say or do. A non-friend has to stick with the hard facts on paper. So friends keep things moving" (interview notes, 1997–1998).

In this chapter, we look at two relationships between members of the Michigan House of Representatives, friendship and influence. First, we wanted to know who the legislators considered to be their especially good friends within the chamber. We also wanted to explore the role played by friendships in the legislative process. Therefore, we asked legislators whether they thought their friendships affected the work of the House and why this was or was not so. Second, we wanted to know who among their colleagues legislators thought were highly influential and why. If respondents named only people in formal leadership positions, we asked whether there were any highly influential members other than formal leaders.

Legislative Friendships

There are many reasons that friendships are important to the smooth functioning of a legislature. Patterson (1959, p. 109) found that friendships in the Wisconsin Assembly seemed "to mitigate against the development of potential conflicts, to provide channels of communication and understanding among members who share goals, and to facilitate logrolling." The ability to compromise and build coalitions within one's own party and across party lines is often essential to passing legislation. This may be facilitated by interpersonal relationships between legislators based on mutual trust and personal respect despite different positions on issues. The importance of the informal organization in facilitating communication within an organization (Barnard, 1938) suggests that interpersonal relationships such as friendships among legislators support crucial activities in the formal organization. These relationships may take extensive time and repeated contact to develop, particularly with members of the opposite party. Carson (1998) noted that long-term relationships among legislators increase their ability to negotiate solutions and settle disputes. As she pointed out, term limits are likely to affect the ability of legislators to reach consensus, especially if it involves bipartisan negotiations without cross-party friends who help broker these deals. Therefore, if term limits affect the number or pattern of friendships that develop between legislators, the ramifications for the work of the legislature could be profound.

Even after the massive turnover precipitated by term limits, the Michigan House of Representatives appears to be a friendly place. Turning to table 7.1, we see that almost everyone in all three sessions reported having friends and is named by someone as a friend. In the 1997–98 session, 89 representatives named one or more of 106 of their colleagues as an especially good friend. This produced 478 friendship dyads. In the 1999–2000 House, 105 representatives were befriended by one or more of 86 representatives, producing 497 friendship dyads. In the 2001–2002 House 104 representatives were befriended by one or more of 91 representatives leading to 498 friendship dyads.

Especially given the surprising prevalence of friendships after term limits, we wondered how so many newcomers became friends so quickly. We found several noteworthy differences in the ways friendships formed after term limits. These are summarized in table 7.2. First, after term limits more representatives reported that they knew their friends in the chamber from their time working together prior to serving in the Michigan House of Representatives (12 percent said this after term

Table 7.1 Effect of term limits on friendship and influence networks in the Michigan House of Representatives

	Friendship networks			Influence networks		
	1997	1999	2001	1997	1999	2001
Total number of colleagues named (*Multiple mentions were accepted*)	478	497	498	667	428	508
Number of different representatives named	106	105	104	90	68	91
Number of respondents who named colleagues as friends or influential	89	86	91	92	89	91
Number of times leaders were named as friends or influential	48	40	47	210	170	195
Leader mentions as % of total	10.04	8.04	9.44	31.50	39.70	38.40
Colleagues named by members of the other party as friends or influential	97	85	85	235	139	147
Percentage of friends or influentials named across party lines	20.29	17.10	17.06	35.20	32.50	28.90
Times leaders were named as friends or influential across party lines	42	27	36	71	62	69
Leader mentions by members of the opposite party as % of total mentions	43.30	31.76	42.35	30.21	44.60	46.94
Average connectedness within the network (alters within two steps of ego)	39.02	42.45	42.44	77	56.26	70.59
Maximum connectedness within the network (alters within two steps of ego)	79.82	76.15	86.24	96.33	86.24	97.25

Note: Calculated using UCINET VI.

limits compared to 8 percent before term limits). Some had worked together in local politics, as county commissioners or city council members, or had been active in the local political party or were from politically connected families active in local, state, and national politics. As one representative commented about a much younger colleague whom he listed as a friend, "I've known him since he was a gleam in his father's eye" (interview notes, 2001–2002).

Second, we found that propinquity mattered much more after term limits than before. Approximately 20 percent of our respondents serving

Table 7.2 Reasons friendships form and affect the work of the House

	Before term limits (percent (number))	After term limits (percent (number))
Ways friendships form and nature of friendships		
Shared characteristics	16.0 (15)	17.4 (32)
Work on same issues	13.8 (13)	9.8 (18)
Propinquity	11.7 (11)	20.1 (37)
Same views	4.3 (4)	11.4 (21)
Different views	21.3 (20)	15.8 (29)
Knew before	8.5 (8)	12.5 (23)
Relationships not friends	12.8 (12)	4.9 (9)
Too few friends	10.6 (10)	12.0 (22)
Less diverse with term limits	0 (0)	4.3 (8)
No time with term limits	5.3 (5)	10.3 (19)
Ways friendships affect work of the House		
Comfort level	53.2 (50)	58.2 (107)
Facilitates negotiation	25.5 (24)	20.1 (37)
Keeps conflict issue-based	22.3 (21)	12.0 (22)
Help & support	19.1 (18)	17.4 (32)
Bipartisanship	16.0 (15)	17.9 (33)
Quid pro quo with friends	9.6 (9)	7.6 (14)
Number of respondents	94	184

after term limits mentioned that they had become friends with proximate people, such as seatmates. Only 11.7 percent of our pre–term limits respondents said this. Prior to term limits, representatives drew lots by order of seniority to choose their seats. Therefore, it is likely that friends chose to sit next to each other, and generally members of the same party were segregated sitting on "their own side of the aisle." After term limits, with seniority truncated and most representatives having the same level of seniority, the drawing for seats more closely approximated a lottery, making it more difficult for friends to sit together. Therefore, after term limits we were told more frequently about representatives who had become acquainted through the contact they had as seatmates. This again underscores the extent to which term limits interact with institutional rules and practices.

In some states legislators are assigned seats based on their district, with members of the opposite political party often sitting next to one another. In those states the decline in friendships between members of the opposite party that occurred in Michigan, which we describe below, might be ameliorated by the contact between members of the two major political parties who might be sitting near each other on the floor of the chamber.

Before term limits representatives were more likely to say that they had become friends with a colleague by working together on issues. Nearly 14 percent of the pre–term limits respondents mentioned this compared to slightly less than 10 percent of the post–term limits respondents.

Prior to term limits slightly more than one-fifth of our respondents noted that friends often held very different views on issues. After term limits a little less than one-sixth of our respondents mentioned this. Conversely, before term limits only 4 percent of our respondents said that they had formed a friendship because a colleague shared their views. After term limits 11 percent of our respondents said that this was a reason they had become friends with a colleague. Both before and after term limits, shared personal characteristics provided the basis for many friendships. For example, groups of women or minority group members met informally and became friends. Also, groups of representatives from the same county or the same geographic region became friends, some-times riding back and forth to their district together or sharing hotel rooms when they needed to stay overnight in Lansing. After term limits, several of the "vulnerables," [1] who often need to vote against their caucus in order to defend themselves in the next election cycle, mentioned befriending each other. Before term limits 16 percent of our respondents mentioned these shared characteristics as a source of their friendships. After term limits this proportion rose, but only slightly, to 17.4 percent. [2] These comments are summarized in table 7.2.

In addition to the open-ended comments about friendships, we mapped a network of friendships based on whom each respondent iden-tified as his or her friends. Information about this network is summa-rized in table 7.1. We found that after term limits the House was statistically significantly more connected than it was before term limits. We can measure this by moving out from each representative to include his or her friends and also the friends' friends. In the jargon of network analysis, this is called going two steps out from "ego." The average number of representatives in the friendship network that are within "two steps of an ego" increases from 39 in 1997–1998 to 42.5 in 1999–2000 and nearly 46 in 2001–2002. This means that the average number of representatives that were either a friend or a friend of a friend of each representative increased by an average of seven colleagues per representative across the three sessions we studied.

Although friendships across party lines were less common, they have not disappeared with term limits. Referring again to table 7.1, there were 97 friendships between members of the opposite party reported prior to term limits, and 85 cross-party friendships in 1999–2000 and in 2001–2002. Not only were there fewer cross-party friendships, but fewer representatives reported having any cross-party friends. In 1997–1998, 42 representatives considered one or more members of the opposite party to be an especially good friend. In 1999–2000, this number fell to 36; and in 2001–2002 it declined to 27. This is consistent with other indications of increased homogeneity in the friendship network. It is also consistent with the open-ended comments indicating that after term limits more friendships formed among representatives who shared the same views, circumstances, or characteristics. If this is the case, it may affect the work of the House because friendships that transcend parochial boundaries and broaden one's perspective are the ones that facilitate compromises and negotiations over public policies that address the concerns of diverse constituencies in the state.

Effects of Legislative Friendships on the Work of the House

The primary value of friendships among legislators, according to our respondents, is to increase the comfort level, soften the rough edges, and build trust and respect among colleagues. Fifty-three percent of our respondents before term limits and 58 percent after term limits made comments to that effect. Especially among the post–term limits respondents, building a sense of trust was an important by-product of friendship. Before term limits 21.1 percent of our respondents mentioned trust specifically, while after term limits this rose to 37.6 percent. As we explore in chapter 8, it is difficult for newcomers in any organization to figure out whose advice to trust, and legislatures are no exception to this. We found it interesting that among post–term limits respondents, friendship became more important in deciding whose advice to trust and with whom one could candidly discuss issues. Even more interestingly, more respondents before term limits clarified that they were talking about relationships instead of friendships. They distinguished between people with whom they felt they had close working relationships and friends—those with whom they interacted socially. Nearly 13 percent of our pre–term limits respondents made this distinction compared to a little less than 5 percent of our post–term limits respondents.

A second major value of friendships, according to our respondents, was that they facilitate negotiation and help the legislature function more efficiently or effectively. This response was more common before term limits (25.5 percent), but approximately 20 percent of our respondents said this even after term limits. An additional benefit of friendships was their role in keeping conflict over issues from becoming personalized. More than 22 percent of our respondents mentioned this before term limits, but after term limits only 12 percent made similar comments. Many of our respondents acknowledge that they would help a friend or at least not attack their issue or bill if at all possible. They acknowledged, however, that there would be some issues on which they wouldn't be able to help because of the effect on their constituents. Before term limits 20 percent of our respondents said this, while after term limits 18 percent did.

Many term limits advocates worried that deals were cut between blocs of veteran legislators. Less than 10 percent of either cohort of legislators mentioned that they knew of instances in which friends traded favors or friendships that operated on a quid pro quo basis (9.6 percent before term limits and 7.6 percent after term limits). This suggests that there is less risk of this than some term limits advocates believe.

Patterns of Influence

In the following discussion, we explore changes in the patterns of influence within the Michigan State House of Representatives before and after term limits. The ability to acquire and use influence is important in many professions, but especially so in a legislature. Although both formal and informal influence are important, the former is easier to recognize. As Porter and Leuthold (1970, p. 79) observed in their study of state legislatures, "[b]ecoming an 'insider' in part means becoming familiar with the informal distributions of power and authority in the legislative body ..." Therefore, we predicted that after term limits representatives would tend to identify primarily occupants of formal leadership as influential, whereas pre–term limits representatives, who were more likely to have acquired "insider" knowledge, would include more informal leaders among those they named. We expected this to be particularly true for colleagues of the opposite political party.

As table 7.1 summarizes, there were 667 designations of influential colleagues in the 1997–1998 term. Ninety different influential actors were named by 92 representatives. (Respondents could name as many colleagues as they wanted.) In the 1999–2000 House, 89 representatives identified one or more of only 68 of their colleagues whom they considered influential. This produced 428 designations of influence (a decline of approximately one-third in the number of influentials mentioned). In the 2001–2002 cohort, 91 respondents said one or more of their House colleagues was influential. Despite the dramatic drop during the first session after term limits, the number of influence mentions rebounded to 508 in the second post–term limits session, although that is still 25 percent lower than the number of influential colleagues named by the pre–term limits representatives. Hence it appears that fewer representatives are recognized as influential after term limits. This suggests that there are fewer competing sources of influence to which representatives are exposed, but we caution readers that, based on information we discuss in coming chapters, it is probably not accurate to infer that this makes representatives more independent. Indeed, based on findings that we present in other chapters, it would appear that the smaller cohort of influential actors may have more power to exert influence over their colleagues than the larger pool of more disparate actors did in the past.

The fact that the five top formal leaders (speaker, majority floor leader, minority party leader, minority floor leader, and chair of appropriations) were a higher proportion of the total number of influential colleagues mentioned after term limits suggests a concentration of power. The proportion of party leaders mentioned as influential was 31.5 percent in 1997–1998, 40 percent in 1999–2000, and 38 percent in 2001–2002. This trend suggests that not only are fewer colleagues seen as influential after term limits, but influence in the post–term limits legislature is more narrowly distributed and increasingly concentrated in the hands of the top leaders. Commenting on lack of power of representatives outside the top leadership, one representative described the House as a dictatorial place, explaining that the "rest of us [those not in leadership] are equally impotent" (interviews, 2001–2002).

We also asked members the reasons why people were identified as influential. There are several noteworthy differences between the reasons given by those serving before term limits expulsions and those serving afterward. Table 7.3 compares these reasons. While both before and after term limits, holding one of the top formal leadership positions was the most common reason someone was seen to be influential, there was an 11 percent increase in the number of respondents serving after term limits who gave this reason. After term limits, there was a decline of more than ten percentage points in the influence attributed to committee chairs, a phenomenon that we discuss in great detail in chapter 8.

Table 7.3 Sources of influence in the Michigan House

	Before term limits, (percent (number))	After term limits, (percent (number))
Influence of formal roles		
Top leaders	76.4 (68)	87.5 (161)
Chairs & key committees	25.8 (23)	14.7 (27)
Appropriations	49.4 (44)	36.4 (67)
Attributes or actions producing influence		
Knowledge or experience	38.2 (34)	26.1 (48)
Issue specific	33.7 (30)	22.3 (41)
Effort & commitment	12.4 (11)	16.3 (30)
Relationships	11.2 (10)	31.0 (57)
Get things done	15.7 (14)	15.8 (29)
Moderating force	28.1 (25)	14.7 (27)
Intimidation	2.2 (2)	10.9 (20)
Political resources	3.4 (3)	6.5 (12)
Positive personal attributes	33.7 (30)	28.8 (53)
Governor outside	5.6 (5)	18.5 (34)
Combined other outside	3.4 (3)	16.8 (31)
Party caucus view	33.7 (30)	47.3 (87)
Number of respondents	89	184

Respondents serving before term limits were more likely than those serving afterward to say that colleagues serving on the Appropriations Committee were influential (49 percent before term limits compared to 36 percent after). Looking at the two post–term limits sessions separately reveals that the decline in influence attributed to members of the Appropriations Committee is especially pronounced in the 2001–2002 session. While 44 percent of the 1999–2000 respondents attributed influence to serving on the Appropriations Committee, only 29 percent made this same claim in the 2001–2002 session. Indeed one respondent described the committee as a "turkey farm" to which members were sent to keep them from causing mischief in the policy committees. This was a startling assessment given the importance typically attached to the legislative power of the purse. We also suspected that the precipitous decline in state revenue robbed service on appropriations of its usual influence. Given that the cupboard was bare, there was no "pork" to distribute, and hence no influence to be gained.

Other respondents commented that inexperienced speakers found the power of the Appropriations Committee threatening, so they tried to keep that committee weaker than it had been historically. This is consistent with responses to a question we asked about the extent to which representatives consulted the speaker about a difficult issue considered by a committee on which they served. Appropriations Committee members relied on the speaker less than did members of other committees, and after term limits this tendency became more pronounced.[3]

Another noteworthy difference is the decline in knowledge, expertise, or experience as a basis for influence. We used two separate categories to explore the effect of knowledge on influence: general knowledge and issue-specific knowledge. General knowledge was based on life experience, background in a career or prior government, including legislative, experience. Issue-specific knowledge included both expertise based on career and professional training as well as legislative work on an issue or committee in a specific area. Here again we found a decline of more than ten percentage points in the number of respondents who used either of these types of knowledge to explain a colleague's influence. Although this is consistent with the loss of experience in the post–term limits chamber, the failure of life or non-legislative career experience to compensate for experience in the legislature suggests that the merits of "real world" experience touted by term limits advocates are not fully appreciated by one's legislative colleagues—even those elected after term limits.

There are often questions about whether influence flows from what one does or whom one knows (Francis, 1962). After term limits expulsions, one's personal relationships were seen as a major reason that representatives had influence. These relationships included being friends with the top leaders and having valuable connections outside the legislature, such as who one's spouse knew or worked for. These relationships were rarely listed as a source of influence prior to term limits expulsions (11 percent), but after term limits 31 percent of our respondents mentioned one's personal relationships as a source of influence. After term limits expulsions, hard work and commitment were also slightly more likely to contribute to influence than they were before term limits, although this was rarely mentioned regardless of the status of term limits (3 percent before term limits and 6 percent afterward). The ability to "get things done" contributed to House members' influence according to an equal proportion of respondents (nearly 16 percent) both before and after term limits. After term limits expulsions, both how hard one works and what one accomplishes remain important, but who one knows becomes more important. Representatives' personal connections were mentioned much more often than their personal effort after term limits as a source of influence.

The ways in which some colleagues interacted with others contributed to their influence, too. Prior to term limits expulsions the ability to moderate disputes or to help find the middle ground was mentioned as a source of influence twice as often as it was after term limits expulsions. As one veteran representative put it, "people might be amazed that [we] could make a deal with such different philosophies, but I always thought that's the genius of politics. You have to move the state forward. . . . There was that zone to work in" (interview notes, 1997–1998). We noted with some surprise that after term limits nearly 11 percent of our respondents said that colleagues became influential through intimidation, which included aggression, bullying, and suppressing dissent. Only 2 percent made comments of this sort before term limits.

Although still a minor source of influence, having political resources, such as money, was linked with influence more often after term limits expulsions. One representative, expressing outrage about being "charged" $10,000 to chair a committee, said "today it's $10,000 to the Republican Committee, next it could be $10,000 to (both) the Republican Committee and $10,000 to the House Republican Caucus Committee" (interview notes, 2001–2002). This finding is consistent with the power of money discussed in chapters 2 and 3.

Many term limits opponents worried that an inexperienced legislative chamber would be a pawn at the mercy of other more powerful actors. Prior to term limits expulsions only 6 percent of our respondents mentioned the governor as an influential "member of the House." After term limits 19 percent of the representatives named the governor when asked to name the most influential members of the Michigan House. When we clarified that we meant members of the House, several of them reiterated that the governor was the most influential member. As one representative pointed out, the governor had 31 years of experience and was dealing with 64 new representatives (interview notes, 1999–2000). Other outside actors, including lobbyists, were also mentioned much more frequently after term limits expulsions than they were before. Prior to term limits expulsions only three (3 percent) of our respondents mentioned outside actors as influential "members of the House," while after term limits expulsions, this rose to 17 percent. This would suggest that the fears of those who argued that term limits would weaken the legislature with respect to other governmental and nongovernmental actors were justified. We discuss these intragovernmental relationships in more detail in chapter 10.

Finally, many of our respondents thought of influence in terms of their own party caucus instead of the chamber as a whole, despite the wording of our question. This tendency to adopt a caucus frame of reference increased by nearly fifteen percentage points after term limits. This seems consistent with the overall increase in partisanship noted throughout our interviews. Returning to table 7.1, we see that for the most part our respondents named members of their own party as highly influential, although approximately a third of the influential actors they designated were members of the opposite political party. Here again, the tendency to name members of the other political party decreased after term limits. As a percentage of the total number of colleagues named, the influential people named by someone of the opposite party dropped from 35 percent in 1997–1998 to 33 percent and 29 percent in the two post–term limits sessions. After term limits, the five top leaders are named more often when members of the opposite party are named as influential. Before term limits just over 30 percent of the colleagues named by members of the opposite party as influential were among the top five leaders. This increased to nearly 45 percent and 47 percent respectively in the first and second post–term limits sessions.

Furthermore, in the series of closed-ended questions that asked legislators about use of their time, they were asked how much time they spent building coalitions to pass legislation. We asked first about building coalitions within the legislator's party and second about building coalitions across party lines. We found no difference in the amount of time pre–term limits and post–term limits representatives spent building coalitions within their own political party. Both groups reported spending half-way between some and a lot of time on this. Time spent building coalitions across party lines declined, however, after term limits took effect. The time spent building coalitions across party lines was nearly identical before term limits to that spent building coalitions within one's own party. After term limits this dropped by a quarter of a point on our five-point scale.[4] Once again this reinforces the image of influence concentrated within the political party or caucus instead of the House as a whole. It further suggests a decline in bipartisan negotiation.

Summary

The number of representatives seen by their colleagues as influential declined with the advent of term limits and the importance of formal roles in gaining influence increased. Additionally, informal influence, especially across party lines, decreased dramatically. These findings suggest that after term limits influence is more concentrated among a few individuals within one's own political party. Relationships, knowing the right people, became more important and expertise and knowledge were less likely to produce influence. Without time to establish a reputation based on merit, term-limited legislators seem to rely more on visible clues about whom to follow.

There is ample evidence that the quality and structure of leadership affect the work of a legislature (Francis, 1989; Hamm, 1982; Jewell & Whicker, 1994). Therefore, we anticipate that changes in the structure of influence that we found after term limits are likely to have far-reaching impacts. We continue to explore this as we turn our attention toward vote cuing and committee work and finally toward the capacity of the House to influence other branches of government in the following chapters.

Conclusions

We continue to find that term limits affect the Michigan House in both anticipated and unanticipated ways. Overall, the number of legislators seen as influential declined, as we expected it would. The magnitude of the decline was more dramatic than we had expected, especially for informal influence—that which occurs without a formal role or formal powers. The prominence of the formal roles in determining who is seen as influential was hardly surprising, but the effect was larger and more persistent than we thought it would be. In the 1999–2000 session, given the immense size of the freshman class, we expected these effects, but the trend continued into the 2001–2002 session, which had only 21 newcomers. Increased reliance on formal influence suggests an institutional change in the structure of leadership in the term-limited House. This is an important finding because it suggests that the officials of party caucuses may have increasing influence over term-limited legislators that may be linked with their increased involvement in funding political campaigns—a phenomenon we noted in chapters 2 and 3. With increasingly large pots of caucus and leadership PAC campaign money to distribute, House legislative leaders have greater power to punish or reward members of their caucus—giving their concentrated power some teeth. Prior to term limits, McAnaw and Schiffer (1995) describe power in Michigan's legislature as hierarchical, but distributed. They say that "Power is shared extensively: 'It's like fine old wine, nobody gets very much'" (pp. 114–115). After term limits, we find that this is no longer true. Power is concentrated and far less distributed, with caucus leaders and the governor giving committee chairs and fellow partisans their marching orders. We return to this theme again in chapter 10.

We did not expect the continued high levels of friendship across all three legislative sessions. Rather with the influx of 64 newcomers, we expected friendships, particularly especially good friendships, to become rare. We discovered that many of the representatives knew each other from positions held in local government. This produced a network in which the representatives who were co-members of cliques often came from the same geographic area and friends tended to be relatively homogeneous. Many respondents in the post–term limits House identified their friends by geographical categories, such the "Downriver Caucus," or all the others from Detroit, or by ethnic designations, such as the Dutch Mafia or the Black Caucus or the Fab Five (from northern Michigan). This suggests that many of the reported friendships developed outside the legislature, and the in-group clustering may contribute to regional, ethnic, and partisan fracturing of the legislature because of the declining number of friendships across these traditional boundaries. If these prior friendships mean that the friendship networks consist of more homogeneous groups of legislators, this could profoundly affect the work of term-limited legislatures. Some evidence suggests that more contact among actors who share personal characteristics leads to greater homogeneity of attitude and reinforces one's perceptions (Bienenstock, Bonacich, & Oliver, 1990). In homogeneous networks, people tend to assume that group norms are shared more widely than they are (Bienenstock, 1990). In our continuing analyses, we plan to explore the composition of the friendship cliques more systematically and will continue to pay particularly close attention to changes in relationships that cross party lines and to the regional component of friendship groups.

Looking at the number of friendship ties, one might assume that the House was a highly collegial body. However, according to our respondents who served both under term limits and prior to them, the level of partisanship is now much higher than it was prior to term limits. The decline in cross-party friendship in the post–term limits sessions is consistent with this and might accelerate this trend. The decline in cross-party friendship was not ameliorated by the smaller freshman class in the 2001–2002 session, suggesting that it is a systemic feature of the post–term limits legislature. Fewer cross-party friendships may lead to more fractious debate and less civility between the parties. Anecdotal evidence from our face-to-face interviews confirms that this is happening, and we have provided evidence of this trend throughout this book.

The few legislators remaining who served in the last pre–term limits session find this to be a shocking and stark contrast. The persistent decrease in cross-party friendship ties and in cross-party designations of influential colleagues suggests that partisanship is likely to become more entrenched without brokers who can bridge the gulf between factions in the legislature.

The high level of friendship masks another post–term limits change. During our interviews with some post–term limits legislators, the person would comment that he or she would consult with a chair or minority vice chair of such and such committee, and then, parenthetically, give the name of the person in addition to the formal title. When we coded several of these responses, we realized that the person named was not always the occupant of that position, and sometimes was not now on nor had ever served on that committee. In some of the more extremes instances, respondents incorrectly identified the chair and/or minority vice chair of a committee on which they had served for at least eighteen months and sometimes more than two years. We never encountered these kinds of errors in the pre–term limits interviews.

These mistakes suggest that while the number of especially good friends remained consistent before and after term limits, the overall level of familiarity in the legislature has declined. Many of these acquaintances are "weak ties" in a network, meaning that the actor knows another actor well enough to contact the person, but not well enough to report regular interaction. The importance of weak ties has been established in other contexts such as job searches (Granovetter, 1973 and 1974). Indeed Granovetter finds that the presence of weak ties is a better predictor of whether an unemployed person can find another job than are the job seeker's strong ties (e.g., friends and relatives). If the term-limited legislator has fewer weak ties, it could mean that he or she would not know who to ask outside his or her compatriots to find information about the other side of an issue. Thus, one wonders whether legislators' lack of knowledge about colleagues outside his or her friendship group might thwart the work of the House, despite or perhaps even because of continued strong friendship ties. We continue to explore these legislative relationships and their impacts on policy making in the following chapters.

CHAPTER 8

Conflict, Compromise, and Partisanship: Committees Under Term Limits[1]

Committees play an important role in policymaking (Francis, 1985), especially in states like Michigan where committee chairs and caucus leaders control the flow of bills through the committees (Hamm et al., 1999). In addition to the formal power committees have in policymaking, committee members influence policy through their expertise, experience, and their network of contacts. Often members' occupational background and other pre-legislative experience and expertise are considered when leaders assign them to a committee. In legislatures with high levels of continuity in committee assignments across sessions, committee members become experts through training by interest groups and staff and by listening to testimony and working on a wide range of issues in the policy area (Porter, 1974). Committee members' expertise leads other legislators to rely on them for information about complex issues sent to the floor by their committee. Finally, legislators frequently ask to serve on committees with jurisdiction over policy issues crucial to their district or to key constituents, making them a conduit for knowledgeable, interested local actors to influence policymaking. Thus, not surprisingly, some people, including interest groups (Sarbaugh-Thompson et al., 2002), consider committees to be where the action is in a legislature. And committee chairs in the Michigan House have historically played a central role in that action.

The 64 Michigan State House members "termed" out of office in 1998 included 27 of the 34 chairs of standing committees. To explore the effect of this on the Michigan State House, we focus on three related roles played by committee chairs: (1) *a gatekeeper*, using formal institutional powers to control the work of their committee; (2) *a manager*, moderating committee members' conflicting interests and goals; and (3) *a substantive expert* serving as a key source of information for committee members. Although we concentrate primarily on the roles played by committee chairs, committee members also play important roles in the work of the Michigan State House. Representatives might look to committee members for information and guidance to decide how to vote on bills that reach the chamber from that committee. We focus briefly here on changes in the role played by committee members, returning to this in later chapters in greater detail.

As the experience level of committee chairs and members decreased with term limits, did committee chairs continue to play a central policy-making role through their committees? Were chairs able to manage members' diverse views and interests as well as they did in the past? Were they seen as a source of expertise in the substantive area of their committee's work? We explore these and similar questions in this chapter.

Methodology

The following analyses rely on three sets of questions from our interviews with members of the Michigan State House of Representatives. First, we examine an open-ended question and a scaled-response question about the chair's control over a committee's work. Second, we investigate a scaled-response question about the level of conflict on the committee and a pair of open-ended questions that asked about the chair's conflict management strategies and the sources of conflict on the committee. Third, we analyze a series of scaled-response questions about the extent to which respondents relied on a variety of sources for information and guidance about a difficult issue seriously considered by a specific committee on which they served.[2]

We hypothesized that there would be both institutional- and individual-level effects on the performance of chairs and the work of committees in a term-limited House. The institutional effects could arise from changing relationships among party leaders, the caucus, committees, and members in a term-limited House. Individual effects could arise from the limited legislative and committee experience that chairs and committee members have in a term-limited House. It is difficult to disentangle the institutional effects of the term-limited House from the effects of less seasoned members and chairs because there were so few inexperienced chairs before term limits and so few experienced chairs after term limits. However, we explore both effects whenever possible in our analyses.

Institutional Context

In the Michigan State House of Representatives, committees have extensive formal powers. This was true before and after term limits. The full chamber cannot consider a bill unless a majority of the committee members support it. In other states, Maine for example, all bills are sent to the floor with a positive, neutral, or negative recommendation from the committee. In Michigan not only does the committee's vote determine whether a bill reaches the floor of the chamber for consideration, but a committee chair can decide whether or not to have the committee consider a bill assigned to his or her committee. Committee chairs use this agenda control to act as gatekeepers with respect to the committee and, through the committee, as gatekeepers with respect to the full chamber. Additionally, the speaker has complete discretion in deciding which bills to assign to which committees. If the speaker wants to insure that a bill does not reach the House floor, he or she can choose to assign it to a committee chair who will never bring the bill up in committee. Conversely, if the speaker wants to insure that the bill will reach the floor, he or she can assign it to a friendly chair of a committee composed of faithful partisans. Finally, if a committee is not acting on a bill the speaker wants to have sent to the floor, the bill is likely to be reassigned to another committee. Thus, the work of committees in the Michigan House is a major facet of the influence exercised by the speaker and also the influence exercised by the chairs of the most powerful committees.

Term Limits Effects on Chairs' Experience

If committee chairs are less experienced, what impact will that have on the work of committees? To discern impacts of term limits that arise from the lack of experience of committee chairs in a term-limited legislature, we first address a threshold question. Do term limits reduce the legislative experience of committee chairs and by how much?

Prior to term limits most chairs were experienced veterans of the House. Committee chairs in the 1997–1998 Democratically controlled House had an average of 8.9 years of prior service (approximately 4.5 sessions) and the most experienced chair had served for 13 previous sessions. In 1995–1996, when Republicans controlled the House, chairs averaged 7.5 years of experience (almost 4 sessions) and the most seasoned chair had served for 9 previous sessions. In 1999–2000, with the advent of term limits, committee chairs had an average of 1.7 years of prior service.[3] Under term limits, even the most veteran chairs will typically have served only 4 years or 2 previous sessions. In 1995–1996 there were no freshman representatives chairing committees; in 1997–1998 one freshman chaired a committee. In 1999–2000, under term limits, 12 freshmen representatives chaired committees. Interestingly, in 2001–2002 no freshmen chaired committees, and chair experience rose to an average of 2.6 years. Clearly the legislative experience of committee chairs dropped dramatically in the Michigan House with the advent of term limits, but it appears that having experimented with freshmen as chairs in 1999–2000, the 2001–2002 House leadership chose more experienced chairs. Thus freshman committee chairs may continue to be rare even in the term-limited House, and chair experience seems likely to stabilize at slightly more than two years of experience—a relatively long tenure in the term limits milieu.[4]

In the pre–term limits House, surrounded by colleagues with decades of experience, an inexperienced chair could be working at a severe disadvantage. But would limited experience have a similar effect on a committee chair in the post–term limits House with an overall decline in tenure among all the members? Would committee members still rely on the chair to the same extent? Or, given the control that the speaker could potentially exercise in the Michigan House, would the speaker instead of the chair control the committee agenda? Even in the anti-seniority atmosphere of the post–term limits House, would some of the more experienced members on the committee, even in the chair's own party, challenge his or her authority?

We hypothesized that an inexperienced chair would be less able to control the work of his or her committee and would be more likely to be swayed by the speaker or other party leaders. To investigate this, we asked the representative to tell us about the amount of control the chair exercised over the work of a specific committee on which he or she served. We asked specifically "How much control would you say that the current Chair of the ———— Committee has over the work of the Committee?" Respondents were given a five-point scale ranging from "none (coded as 0)" to "an enormous amount (coded as 4)." Respondents were also asked to explain their response.

Chairs as Gatekeepers

Experience does have an effect on the amount of control chairs exert over the work of their committees. Committee members reported that first-term chairs exerted between "some" and "a lot" of control over the work of their committee, a mean of 2.7 on our five-point scale. Committee members said that second-term chairs and veteran chairs exercised more control, 3.2 and 3.3 respectively, which translates into more than "a lot" on our five-point scale.[5] Additionally, chairs exerted more control over the work of their committees before term limits. Some of this appears to be the result of the greater experience of pre–term limits chairs, but we also find some limited evidence that after term limits chairs with comparable levels of experience exerted less power over their committees. Second-term chairs are the only cohort for which we have enough cases before and after term limits to compare groups based on length of service.[6] There were no third-term chairs and only one first-term chair before term limits. There were eight second-term chairs serving before term limits and twenty-five second-term chairs serving after term limits. Comparing chairs in their second term of service, before and after term limits, we found that before term limits committee members said that second-term chairs exerted almost "an enormous amount" of control (mean of 3.7), while after term limits committee members said that chairs in their second term exerted only "a lot" of control (mean of 3.1). These findings suggest that committee chairs may be less influential actors in the term-limited House because of institutional changes, such as a shift in the balance of power, as well as because of their lack of experience. However, we would be more confident of this institutional effect if we had more cohorts with the same levels of experience to compare. Yet as we discuss later, other evidence is highly consistent with this limited finding.

If committee chairs exert less control over their committees, it could mean that control has become more widely distributed among committee members or it could mean that control of the work of the committee has become more concentrated at higher levels in the House leadership hierarchy or that committees have become more chaotic. Open-ended responses summarized in table 8.1 show that, both before and after term limits, most chairs exercised control over the work of the committee based on the institutional rules, such as agenda control. Table 8.1 also shows that the role played by the party leadership changed under term limits. In the term-limited House more than one-third of our respondents indicated that the party leaders or caucus exerted influence over the chair's agenda compared to less than one-sixth of the pre–term limits respondents. This further supports our finding that for second-term chairs both institutional changes as well as their lack of experience contribute to their decline in control over their committees.

Even more startling were comments about the governor's influence over the chair's control of the work of the committee after term limits. No respondent mentioned the governor's control over committee chairs

Table 8.1 The work of the committees before and after term limits

	Before term limits (percent (number))	After term limits (percent (number))
Sources of control over work of committee		
Institutional rules	58.2 (32)	55.9 (90)
Party leaders	14.5 (8)	34.2 (55)
Governor influences	0.0 (0)	21.7 (35)
Number of respondents	55	161
Sources of conflict on committees		
Region and geography	7.8 (7)	11.0 (19)
Ideology	6.7 (6)	9.2 (16)
Groups divided on issues	1.1 (1)	8.1 (14)
Intra-party conflict	6.7 (6)	9.2 (16)
Budget constraints	4.4 (4)	7.5 (13)
Political posturing	9.7 (7)	4.0 (6)
Number of respondents	90	173
Conflict management by the chair		
Bipartisanship	20.0 (18)	11.0 (19)
Routine issues	5.6 (5)	4.0 (7)
Deliberate & negotiate	45.6 (41)	49.1 (85)
Majority voting	28.9 (26)	28.3 (49)
Gather & use knowledge	12.2 (11)	11.6 (20)
Autocratic chair	14.4 (13)	16.8 (29)
Silenced opposition	3.3 (3)	15.0 (26)
Rammed through	4.4 (4)	14.5 (25)
Comity, courtesy	24.4 (22)	12.7 (22)
Personality clashes	3.3 (3)	6.9 (12)
Good management by chair	40.0 (36)	22.0 (38)
Lack of chair control	4.4	17.9
Number of respondents	90	173

prior to term limits. After term limits 22 percent of our respondents said that the governor exerted control over the chair. As one respondent told us, [the Chair] "has some control, but he does what he's told. He's told me so. He's not a fan of charter schools but votes for it in committee. The Governor has the control. The Chair says, 'I'm a team player.'" (interview notes, 1999–2000). Another respondent said that the committee chair had a lot of control, explaining that while [the chair] "was taking orders from the governor, [the chair] still controlled the actions of the committee. Not acting independently, though" (interview notes, 1999–2000). Comments like these suggest that the influence of both party leaders and the governor increased after term limits, although part of the increased influence of the governor might be related to the change in partisan control of the House.[7] The governor was a Republican during all six years of our investigation, while the pre–term limits chairs were Democrats and the post–term limits chairs (1999–2000 and 2001–2002) were Republicans.

One would expect some committee members, especially members of the minority party, to find the committee chair's control to be frustrating. Yet the proportion of respondents who made negative comments about the committee chair remained virtually unchanged before and after term limits (14.5 and 13 percent respectively). On the other hand, the proportion praising the committee chair decreased by half after term limits, from 14.5 percent before term limits to 7.5 percent afterward. To explore this, we turn to the sources of disagreements that inevitably arise in legislative committees and to the way chairs manage this conflict.

Effects of Term Limits on Committee Conflict

There are many reasons that committee members are likely to disagree. In Michigan, regions of the state compete with each other for money, government projects, and other benefits; and budget constraints can intensify the competition between regions. Even within the same political party, ideology divides legislators. Most conflict is issue-based, but occasionally committee members personalize the conflict, even though there are fairly strong institutional norms discouraging this. Finally, and most obviously, there is partisan conflict and political posturing to get media coverage for electoral advantage.

Looking again at table 8.1, we see that the percentage of respondents mentioning most of these sources of conflict increased after term limits. The one exception to this pattern was political posturing. By this we mean taking a position so that someone could run on an issue in a future electoral competition. A higher proportion of the respondents serving before term limits said this was a source of conflict than did respondents serving after term limits. Even so, this may be the result of term limits, as termed-out veteran legislators prepared to run against each other for another elected office.

One might assume that the minority party would report more conflict on committees. As one respondent said, "when you're in the minority, there's always conflict, you can't get your issues to go forward" (interview notes, 1999–2000). We found more evidence of this difference in perceptions between the minority and majority party after term limits. After term limits, the mean level of committee conflict reported by members of the majority party was 1.9 (a little less than some) while the minority party reported a mean level of conflict of 2.2 (a little more than some). Although this is not a major difference, it was statistically significant.[8] Prior to term limits, by contrast, both parties reported almost identical levels of conflict on committee—a mean of 2.15 for the majority party and 2.14 for the minority party. This suggests that prior to term limits, committee chairs may have been more willing to engage in bipartisan negotiations. Twenty percent of the respondents serving before term limits said that there was little or no partisan conflict on their committee. This response became much more rare after term limits, dropping to 11 percent of the respondents.

Levels of conflict vary not only with the skill and temperament of the chair and the committee members, but also with the nature of the issues assigned to the committee. Approximately 5 percent of our respondents both before and after term limits said that was no conflict on a specific committee because that committee only dealt with routine issues. The Appropriations Committee is more prone toward conflict, both before and after term limits. As one respondent pointed out, "On appropriations we don't have the luxury of going year after year without resolving issues" (interview notes, 1997–1998).

Additionally, there are differences of opinion on the role of conflict in committees. One veteran legislator who claimed that there was an enormous amount of conflict on one committee described the conflict as "fun—not open [conflict] but scrimmaging" (interview notes, 1997–1998). Another veteran legislator told us about a committee that dealt with issues that tended to "run the gamut" from one extreme to the other, saying that there's a lot of conflict on the committee, and "I'm not saying that in a negative way" (interview notes, 1997–1998). These positive interpretations of conflict suggest that, in the pre–term limits House, it was sometimes a constructive part of working out differences on issues among people representing diverse constituencies. We found no comparable comments about the value or positive nature of conflict made by our post–term limits respondents.

Committee Chairs as Conflict Managers

The way that a committee conducts its work depends on the formal powers of the chair and the informal norms and work habits of its members. One of the functions of legislative norms is to help manage conflict (Wahlke et al., 1962). Hedlund (1984), summarizing research on legislative norms, finds that norms of interpersonal behavior surface consistently in these studies (e.g., respecting colleagues and keeping one's word). With fewer veteran legislators to socialize newcomers and to enforce and reinforce norms governing working relationships, these norms are less likely to persist (Axelrod, 1984). Thus we hypothesized that less experienced chairs might be less skilled in managing conflict and less able to negotiate compromises as well as less thoroughly socialized into norms governing legislative work relationships. We hypothesized that this could lead to a loss of civility on committees and elsewhere in the legislature.

Comparing the work of committees before and after term limits, we found several similarities in the ways committee chairs managed conflict. Approximately half of our respondents before and after term limits, mentioned negotiation and deliberation as a way their committee chairs resolved conflict. Also approximately 28 percent of our respondents both before and after term limits said that conflict was resolved by voting or majority rule. Often respondents pointed out that this was a last resort after the chair had tried to negotiate consensus. In other instances this was the only strategy the respondent mentioned. Additionally, almost equal, but relatively small proportions of our respondents said that the chair conducted hearings or otherwise used or gathered information to help resolve conflict over an issue considered by the committee.

Differences between the pre–term limits and the post–term limits committee environment became apparent as the respondents described various techniques used to overcome opposition, however. Chairs were seen as autocratic by only a slightly higher proportion of the post–term limits respondents (16.8 percent after term limits compared to 14.4 percent before). Yet, as we noted earlier, 15 percent of post–term limits respondents said that the chair silenced opposition in committee meetings compared to 3 percent of the pre–term limits respondents who mentioned this. In fact before term limits, some respondents noted that the chair always let the minority party members have their say before calling for a vote. Prior to term limits very few (4.4 percent) of our respondents reported that chairs limited debate, refused to allow committee members to ask questions during hearings, withheld the bill from minority party members or otherwise, as one respondent put it, "ramrodded" the bill through without letting people know what they were voting on (interview notes, 2001–2002). After term limits, 14.5 percent of our respondents mentioned these tactics. Additionally, a slightly higher percentage of the post–term limits respondents

(12.1 percent compared to 7.8 percent before term limits) said that the chairs were receiving their marching orders from the party leadership.

The institutional norms of civility seem to have suffered with the advent of term limits. The level of mutual respect and courtesy among members and accorded to members by the committee chair seems to have decreased substantially after term limits. Before term limits a quarter of the respondents said that positive personal relationships, such as courtesy, respect, and civility, helped resolve conflict on the committees. After term limits this decreased by half, to an eighth of the respondents. Although still not commonly reported, personality clashes or personal conflict doubled—mentioned by 3.3 percent of our respondents prior to term limits and by 6.9 percent after term limits. One member said that he believed that new members were "obnoxious" to him because he would be termed out soon. He claimed that one problem with term limits was that new members asserted themselves in "disrespectful and inappropriate ways" (interview notes, 1997–1998).

Additionally, in the Michigan House, which has had frequent shifts in partisan control during the 1990s, both parties appreciated the plight of the minority party and knew that if they severely suppressed the opposition, they might be in the minority after the next election and be subjected to similar treatment. Therefore, one veteran representative claimed that "part of [the civility and courtesy] is the fact that we've had frequent partisan shifts so the current chair was once working under the minority vice chair, and there's a healthy respect. That chair was probably even-handed. There's a respect for the minority party, and we've tried to do things on a bipartisan basis" (interview notes, 1997–1998).

Comments during the 1999–2000 session suggest an entirely different tone in many committee meetings and a different interpretation of conflict. When asked how the chair resolved conflict, one respondent said that members of the committee "yell, scream, holler and criticize, hope it gets in the newspaper and then walk out" (interview notes, 1999–2000). Other respondents said that committee members were "gaveled down" by the chair and might get to ask only one question (interview notes, 1999–2000).

Given that with one exception the proportion of respondents mentioning that various sources of conflict increased after term limits and given the general tenor of the situations our respondents described, we expected to find that the amount of conflict committee members reported experiencing in committees after term limits would have increased—perhaps even dramatically.

We were surprised to discover that responses to the scaled question about the amount of conflict on committees showed a slight, though not statistically significant, decrease in the amount of conflict respondents perceived on committees after term limits. This seems inconsistent with the open-ended comments about the sources of conflict, but on closer examination, it appears that the lower level of conflict reported may reflect chairs' efforts to suppress conflict instead of a congenial atmosphere reflecting an absence of conflict among committee members. This interpretation would be consistent with the fivefold increase after term limits, reported earlier, in the proportion of respondents who said that the chair silenced dissent.

Open-ended comments summarized in table 8.1 indicate that term-limited chairs may be less capable of managing conflict than were pre–term limits chairs, regardless of the level of the conflict. Forty percent of our respondents before term limits said that committee chairs managed conflict well or provided us with examples of good conflict management. After term limits the proportion praising the chair's management or describing good conflict management techniques dropped to 22 percent. Additionally the proportion of respondents who said that the chair could not manage the conflict on the committee rose from 4.4 percent before term limits to 17.9 percent after term limits. Several respondents serving after term limits described poor conflict management techniques, such as highly personalized conflict, especially directed by some chairs toward members of the minority party. A few members of the majority party as well as several members of the minority described some of the same incidents. Thus, we are not convinced that the lower levels of conflict reflect harmonious, smooth-running committee meetings in the post–term limits political environment of the Michigan State House of Representatives. In fairness we should note that there were fewer of these incidents described during the second post–term limits session (2000–2001)—perhaps reflecting the value of serving for at least one term as a committee member before chairing a committee.

Chairs as Substantive Experts

In addition to formal rules of the institution and experience running a committee, the chair is often an expert in the issue area(s) over which his or her committee has jurisdiction. In the pre–term limits legislature the chair would often be one of the more senior members on the committee. However, in the term-limited House, especially if freshman legislators chair committees, most members of the committee may be more experienced and believe they have as much or more expertise than the chair has. If this were the case, one would not expect committee members to rely heavily on the chair for information or guidance about difficult issues considered by the committee. On the other hand, given that members and chairs are typically assigned to committees in which they are interested and presumably have expertise, newer committee chairs may bring a wealth of career and life experience to their positions. This could lead committee members to trust the chair's judgment and rely on him or her heavily.

To explore this we compared the extent to which committee members reported consulting chairs who were either less experienced or more experienced than the respondent. To do this we used data from the series of questions in which we asked respondents to tell us about a difficult issue seriously considered by a specific committee on which they served. We then asked them a series of questions using our five-point scale, running from "none" to "an enormous amount." We asked about the extent to which they relied on each of 16 to 18 different sources of information and guidance. These sources included the committee chair, subcommittee chair if the person served on the appropriations committee, and the other members of the committee. Because the issues and committees varied from respondent to respondent, we created an average level of consulting for each member and calculated the difference between the amount of consulting for each source and the overall average level of consulting about the issue. We described this in greater detail in the introduction to the book.

Committee members reported in general that they consulted committee chairs at levels slightly above their average level of consulting, as indicated by the positive values for consulting with the chair. The overall mean difference between average consulting and consulting with the committee chair was 0.33 units. This was slightly higher before term limits than afterward, but the difference was not statistically significant. We discovered, not surprisingly, that committee members were more likely to rely on the chair for information and guidance in deciding what to do *if* the chair was more experienced than the member. As noted throughout this chapter, we do not have a sufficiently large number of junior chairs in the pre–term limits cohort to disentangle the institutional effects of term limits from the experience level of the committee chair. We simply find that less experienced chairs are not a preferred source of information and guidance—a factor that may have influenced the 2001–2002 House leaders' decision not to appoint freshmen as committee chairs.

We also assumed that minority party members would be less likely to rely on the committee chair than would members of the chair's own political party. To further understand the role played by committee chairs in providing information and guidance on committee issues, we excluded members of the appropriations committee, with its heavy reliance on subcommittees and subcommittee chairs, and analyzed the policy committees separately.[9] We found that prior to term limits the extent to which majority and minority party members relied on policy committee chairs for information and guidance differed less than it did after term limits. Prior to term limits both majority and minority party members of the policy committees relied on the committee chair slightly more than average (means of 0.86 for the majority party members and 0.45 for the minority party members, significant at 0.03). After term limits, the extent to which majority party members relied on the policy committee chairs increased to a mean of 1.02 while the mean for the minority party members dropped below their average level of consulting to −0.11.[10] This affirms the more partisan tone of the policy committee deliberations we found in the open-ended comments we described earlier.

Committee Members' Experience and Expertise

The role played by committee chairs is important, but many committee members are influential too. Before term limits, many representatives integrated their occupational experience, district and constituent interests, and committee work to become experts in specific policy areas. As long-term committee members, they studied specific policies in depth. Under term limits, we hypothesized that the opportunities to develop expertise through committee work would be truncated, but that career or life experience might compensate for legislative expertise.

To explore whether term limits affected committee members' role providing information or guidance to their colleagues, we needed first to determine whether the level of continuity of committee service changed in the Michigan House of Representatives with the advent of term limits. This is a threshold question. Often when discussing the shorter term-limited tenure in the institution, we assume that shorter tenure is correlated with fewer years of continuous service on a particular committee, but legislatures vary widely in the percentage of members who serve repeatedly on the same committee across multiple legislative sessions (Hamm & Hedlund, 1990).

With a three-term limit on service in the House, we were especially interested in determining the number of pre–term limits representatives who had served more than three consecutive terms on the same committee. If the pre–term limits House lacked continuity on committee service, term limits might not change committee experience dramatically. To explore the continuity of committee membership, we examined committee service of House members in six pre–term limits legislative sessions between 1987–1988 and 1997–1998.

When a legislative chamber changes partisan control, committees are often renamed and reconfigured to reflect the priorities of the two political parties. Given that partisan control of the Michigan House changed often during the years we examined, we first needed to find committees that continued across multiple sessions of the legislature. We found 12 committees that, in one form or another, persisted from 1987 to 1998. We then calculated the average number of years members served on these committees. We did not calculate means for the 1987–1988 session or the 1989–1990 sessions because we wanted to include at least three years of potential service (the maximum under term limits) in calculating these averages. The 1991–1992 session averages are based on three possible sessions of service experience (1987–1988, 1989–1990, and 1991–1992), which corresponds to the mandatory constraint on committee service under term limits. The 1993–1994 session is based on four possible sessions of experience on the committees and so on. The means across the 12 committees appear in the notes for this chapter.[11]

Prior terms of service on these 12 committees remains remarkably stable, ranging between 2.02 and 2.23, across the four pre–term limits sessions, despite the difference in the number of possible prior terms of service used to calculate each mean. The maximum possible service for 1997–1998 was six terms, double the maximum possible—three terms—for 1991–1992. Yet the average service in 1997–1998 was barely higher than the average for committee members in 1991–1992. This suggests that even prior to term limits, committee members' service continuity was limited by various factors, such as change in partisan control of the legislature, changing interests of committee members, retirements and electoral defeats, or changing needs and interests of leadership.[12]

In 1999–2000 and 2001–2002, after term limits, the average terms of service on committees was 1.24 and 1.51 respectively. Clearly the experience of committee members in the term-limited House is lower than that prior to term limits. It is interesting to note, however, that *if* members were assigned to the same committee for all three of their terms of service, the average experience of committee members could rise under term limits to three terms, a level higher than the average before term limits.

Although the average length of service on the same committee could increase under term limits to reach or exceed the pre–term limits level, there is no way for individual members to serve more than three sessions on the same committee. Prior to term limits many of the longest serving members on each of the twelve committees we examined had served for all six of the sessions we examined. Therefore, under term limits committees will no longer have the handful of members whose institutional memory and experience spans more than a decade of service and who are often considered experts by their colleagues of both political parties and by external actors.

Information Gathering by Committee Members

One way committee members develop expertise is through information provided by lobbyists and interest groups (Porter, 1974). To explore differences and similarities between the information gathered by pre– and post–term limits representatives, we asked them to tell us the extent to which they relied on each of several different sources of information or guidance on a difficult issue before a specific committee on which they served.[13] Table 8.2 presents the mean difference from the average amount of consulting for the sources of information before and after term limits. We will discuss the top five of these sources here. First and foremost, there is surprisingly little difference between these top sources of information and guidance. The five sources of information and guidance that representatives relied on more than others are identical before and after term limits, although their rankings differ. All these sources of information have a positive mean difference indicating that, on average, they are consulted more than average.

Representatives in both sessions relied most heavily on subcommittee chairs—but this is relevant only for members of the Appropriations Committee. Representatives serving after term limits relied next most heavily on lobbyists. Lobbyists were an important source of information and guidance for pre–term limits respondents also, but they ranked fourth instead of second. Prior to term limits committee chairs ranked second among members of the majority party. The committee chair was also an important source of information to the post–term limits legislators who were members of the majority party—holding third place in their rankings, just barely ahead of consulting with other committee members. Other committee members ranked fifth for the pre–term limits respondents. Partisan staff received the third highest priority in the pre–term limits cohort's sources of information and guidance, but ranked fifth among the post–term limits cohort's sources.

Table 8.2 Sources of information and guidance for committee decisions

Rank	Source of information about a difficult committee issue (Mean difference above average level of consulting)	
	Before term limits expulsions 1997–1998 session	After term limits expulsions 1999–2000 and 2001–2002 sessions
1	Subcommittee chairs (1.75)	Subcommittee chairs (1.32)
2	Committee chair by majority party (0.77)	Lobbyists (0.69)
3	Partisan staff (0.71)	Committee chairs by majority party (0.66)
4	Lobbyists (0.71)	Other committee members (0.66)
5	Other committee members (0.58)	Partisan staff (0.54)
6	Nonpartisan staff (0.26)	House fiscal agency (0.24)
7	House fiscal agency (0.20)	State agencies (0.20)
8	State agencies (0.20)	Party caucus (0.19)
9	Committee chairs for minority party (0.11)	Nonpartisan staff (0.17)
10	Party caucus (0.08)	Constituents (0.15)
11	Constituents (−10.11)	Key local officials (0.04)
12	The Speaker, majority party only (−0.13)	Minority leader by minority party (0.01)
13	Minority leader by minority party (−0.13)	Advisors in the district (−0.08)
14	Key local officials (−0.16)	Committee chair by minority party (−0.14)
15	Advisors in the district (−0.34)	The speaker, majority party only (−0.49)
16	Senators (−0.44)	Senators (−0.56)
17	The governor (−0.48)	The governor (−0.60)
18	National conference of state legislators (−0.87)	National conference of state legislators (−0.84)
	Newcomers relied more on nonpartisan staff	Newcomers relied more on committee members
Number of respondents	91 with missing data for some questions	182 with missing data for some questions

We also wondered whether newcomers to the House would be more or less likely to rely on the committee chair for information and guidance. Although newcomers were neither more nor less likely to rely on the committee chair, we discovered that they were more likely to rely on their fellow committee members than were their more experienced colleagues on the committee. The mean difference for consulting with other policy committee members was above the average level of consulting. It was 0.57 for experienced members and 0.74 for newcomers. This was a weakly statistically significant difference.[14]

Conclusions

With the advent of term limits, committee chairs are less experienced and committee members have less continuity of service on their committees. These changes are associated with a decrease in the amount of control chairs exercise over the work of their committees and an increase in the influence of party leaders and the Governor's Office over committee agendas. Thus, committee chairs appear to be less autonomous actors and less skilled at managing conflict and are often seen as having less substantive policy expertise than the more senior members of their committees. The term-limited House in general and committee work in particular evinces greater concentration of control in party leadership and more partisan policymaking.

It is unclear whether conflict on committees has increased in the term-limited House, but norms of civility and respect for dissenting opinions seem to have declined. Prior to term limits the House changed partisan control regularly,[15] and members seem to have realized that intense partisanship could be repaid with a vengeance.

Although term-limited representatives still see their committee chairs as influential in general, they are less likely than their pre–term limits counterparts to rely on them as sources of information and guidance about a difficult issue before the committee or the chamber. Under term limits, representatives report that they rely on senior chairs for information and guidance about difficult issues considered in their committees. They do not rely as heavily on chairs when they are their junior colleagues. This suggests that House members still seek information from those they see as more knowledgeable than themselves, but committee chairs in a term-limited House often fail to meet this criterion. This difference surfaces more prominently among minority party members, who before term limits consulted committee chairs more than their average level of consulting, despite their partisan differences. After term limits minority party members consulted committee chairs less than their average level of consulting.

If the chair is a less important source of information and guidance on issues considered by a committee, where do term-limited representatives turn? Newcomers seem to turn to their colleagues on the committee. Lobbyists and partisan staff also are two sources the representatives relied on extensively both before and after term limits, but especially after term limits. The top five sources of information and guidance used by committee members remained remarkably constant before and after term limits. We explore the effect of term limits on information gathering and vote cuing more extensively in chapter 9.

CHAPTER 9

Deciding How to Vote: Sources Legislators Rely On

Legislators cannot be experts on everything, so they rely on each other or on sources outside the chamber for information and guidance about legislation (Porter, 1974; Kingdon, 1989). Knowing when to do this and who to rely on is a crucial part of a legislator's job. With term limits, there are so many new colleagues that it may be more difficult to know which of them to turn for advice or to ask questions. With less time and fewer opportunities to establish one's reputation for candor and honesty, colleagues, especially those seeking different viewpoints, may not know whom to trust. Hence, we speculated that term limits would affect the sources of information that representatives rely on to learn about issues. Specifically we expected that after term limits, newly elected representatives would consult fewer colleagues within the legislative chamber. We further speculated that term limits would affect the level of consulting and the range of sources consulted outside the chamber. Here we assumed that newly elected representatives would turn to familiar local sources whose opinions they trusted, but those sources might also be less likely to represent the broad range of interests affected by a bill. Newly elected representatives may have a difficult time learning when and how to rely on information from lobbyists and representatives of organized groups. Therefore, we expected that they would be reluctant to rely on this source of information.

In this chapter, we expand our discussion from chapter 8 about the sources of information and guidance consulted when representatives confront a difficult issue at the committee level to an investigation of the sources of information and guidance representatives rely on when an issue reaches the floor of the chamber. To investigate this latter form of consulting, or as it is sometimes called, vote cuing, we asked representatives two sets of questions about specific issues that might reach the House floor: (1) school choice and (2) licensing and regulating health care professionals.[1]

We modeled these questions after those used in John Kingdon's (1989) investigation of voting decisions in the U.S. House of Representatives. We concur with his assessment that it is important to ask legislators about specific issues to provide a referent to facilitate recall and encourage concrete responses. These two specific issue areas were chosen because they are matters that arise regularly and predictably in virtually all sessions of the Michigan House of Representatives. Additionally we chose issues for which we assumed that the pattern of consultation would differ in predictable ways. Political salience and public attention are characteristics that are likely to produce different patterns of consulting by elected officials (Price, 1978), and the role played by interest groups and other external sources of information tend to vary with the public salience and scope of the issue (Thurber, 1991; and Haider-Markel, 1999).

School choice is a politically salient issue in Michigan, and many representatives stake a position on this during their campaign for office. Issues involving the licensing and regulating health care professionals are rarely noticed by anyone except the professional groups affected, and the pros and cons tend to be fairly technical. It is extremely unlikely that candidates for the legislature would stake out a clear position for or against licensing massage therapists, for example, during their political campaign. The professionals involved and possibly a small band of consumer advocates are likely to be the only actors who notice debates about licensing or regulating health care professionals, even when action is eminent.

To analyze the consulting network within the House on these two issues, we formed a network of relationships of who consulted with whom and used network analysis techniques similar to those we used to analyze networks of influence and the friendship networks in chapter 7. To investigate the sources of information that representatives rely on outside the chamber and to determine which of all the sources mentioned, inside and outside the chamber, were the most important, we analyzed the open-ended responses to the questions about school choice bills and about bills licensing and regulating health care professionals.

Most Important Sources of Information and Guidance on School Choice

We organized the open-ended comments of our respondents about their consulting into six broad categories: (1) constituents and other individuals in the member's district including local teachers and parents; (2) local officials, including school board members, superintendents, and other administrators in the local intermediate school districts within the member's district; (3) organized groups and lobbyists, including the Michigan Education Association, unions, charter school advocacy groups, and other lobbyists; (4) actors in state government and in state agencies, including legislative staff, the Michigan Department of Education, the Governor's Office, and State Senators; (5) colleagues currently serving in the House; and finally, (6) "myself alone."

We examined effects of the number of terms a legislator had served as well as the institutional effects of term limits with their potential to alter collective expertise and limit long-term relationships. We also return briefly to the prospect that representatives elected after term limits might be a "new breed," who would be more self-reliant and less inclined to consult any other sources for information on this issues. The rank order of sources consulted by representatives serving before and after term limits appears in table 9.1. We see that these are almost a mirror image of one another. House colleagues were named as the most important source of information by the largest proportion of pre–term limits respondents while those serving after term limits ranked this source fifth out of the six possible categories. The percentage of respondents serving before term limits who said that House colleagues were their most important source of information (29.3 percent) was substantially higher than the percentage (18.5 percent) of representatives serving after term limits who said they would rely on their colleagues the most. One pre–term limits respondent justified his greater reliance on fellow House members by saying, "I have a personal relationship with them. I see them daily. If they mislead me, they'll suffer. The lobbyists' allegiance is to the client not to me" (interview notes, 1997–1998).

The most important source of information on school choice issues named by the highest proportion of those serving after term limits was "myself alone."[2] Responses we classified in this category were made by respondents who would not consult other sources because they already had made up their mind on this issue or that they wouldn't need any additional information. These legislators said they might listen to other actors, but it would not make any difference in their position. In other words, we reserved this classification for those whose answers indicated at least some clear element of self-referential consulting. Interestingly, lame ducks serving after term limits were more likely to say that they would rely only on themselves than were their less experienced colleagues.

Organized groups and lobbyists seemed to be a more important source after term limits than they were before. This source was ranked

Table 9.1 Most important source of information and guidance*

Rank	School choice			Licensing or regulating health professionals		
	Before term limits	After term limits	Affect of experience after term limits	Before term limits	After term limits	Affect of experience after term limits
1	House colleagues (29.3%)	Myself alone (24.1%)	1st term (23%) 2nd term (19%) 3rd term (37%)	House colleagues (34.8%)	House colleagues (32.9%)	1st term (32%) 2nd term (41%) 3rd term (17%)
2	Individuals in the district (22.7%)	Organized groups & lobbyists (23.5%)	1st term (20%) 2nd term (27%) 3rd term (23%)	Individuals in the district (29.0%)	Individuals in the district (27.7%)	1st term (30%) 2nd term (29%) 3rd term (21%)
3	Myself alone (20.0%)	Local officials (22.2%)	1st term (23%) 2nd term (24%) 3rd term (17%)	Organized groups & lobbyists (26.1%)	Organized groups & lobbyists (27.1%)	1st term (21%) 2nd term (27%) 3rd term (41%)
4	Organized groups & lobbyists (13.3%)	Individuals in the district (21.6%)	1st term (29%) 2nd term (13%) 3rd term (23%)	House staff (8.7%)	House staff (9.7%)	Too few cases to subdivide
5	Local officials (12.0%)	House colleagues (18.5%)	1st term (22%) 2nd term (18%) 3rd term (13%)	Myself alone (8.7%%)	State government officials & agencies (7.7%)	Too few cases to subdivide
6	House staff (5.3%)	House staff (6.8%)	Too few cases to subdivide	State government officials & agencies (7.2%)	Myself alone (6.5%)	Too few cases to subdivide
N	75	162		70	156	

Note: * Totals exceed 100% because a few respondents said two or three sources were tied for most important.

as most important by the second highest proportion of those serving after term limits. By contrast this was named by the fourth highest proportion of those serving before term limits. Those naming this as their most important source of information was approximately ten percentage points higher after term limits (23.5 percent for those serving after term limits compared to 13.3 percent of those serving before term limits). Given the high hopes term limits advocates had for severing the connection between special interests and elected officials, we suspect this is highly disappointing to them. Additionally, we note that representatives after term limits serving their second and third terms were more likely than newcomers to say this was their most important source of information.

Local people were named as the most important source less frequently after term limits. For legislators serving before term limits, local people were the second most commonly mentioned source of information and guidance. This included parents, teachers, and others in their district. Term limits advocates had hoped this source would gain prominence, but it fell to fourth among the most important sources mentioned by those serving after term limits. We hesitate to make too much of this difference in the rankings, however, because there is only a 1 percent difference between the proportions of respondents serving before and after term limits saying that these actors would be their most important source of information. Yet, we note here too that experience affects the importance attached to local officials as a source of information. Those serving after term limits who were in their third term were much less likely to say that local officials, such as their intermediate school superintendent, were a valuable source of information for a bill on school choice.

Consulting Within the Chamber on School Choice Issues

High public salience often motivates legislators to develop expertise on an issue (Porter, 1974). Given that education issues typically have high public salience and that school choice has received extensive media and political attention, we expected that many legislators would be experts in this area. Yet developing this expertise might take time, and so the number of experts might decline after term limits. So we speculated that after term limits there would be fewer experts within the chamber with whom representatives would consult, especially given the relatively small proportion of representatives after term limits who said that colleagues were their most important source of information.

We see in table 9.2 that slightly fewer representatives reported consulting their House colleagues on school choice issues after term limits than they did before. Seventy representatives serving in the 1997–1998 session reported asking for information and guidance on school choice issues from their colleagues. After term limits the number of representatives who reported consulting with colleagues on school choice issues remained virtually unchanged, 69 in 1999–2000 and 65 in 2001–2002. However, the number of colleagues consulted increased from 40 before term limits to 59 and 48 in the 1999–2000 and 2001–2002 sessions, respectively. This produced 175 consulting ties between House colleagues before term limits and 194 and 181 ties, respectively, in the two post–term limits sessions. Thus, after term limits we found slightly fewer representatives consulting their colleagues, but those who consulted their colleagues consulted with more of them.

Table 9.2 Effect of term limits on consulting networks in the Michigan House of Representatives

	Consulting about a bill on school choice			Consulting about licensing or regulating health care professionals		
	1997	1999	2001	1997	1999	2001
Total Instances of Consulting	175	194	181	119	160	195
Number of representatives consulted by their colleagues	40	59	48	35	35	28
Respondents who said they would consult colleagues	70	69	65	76	72	79
Instances of consulting with committee members	141	136	133	94	139	144
Percent of consulting that was with committee members	80.60	70.10	73.50	79	86.90	73.80
Number of colleagues consulted across party lines	30	18	34	11	22	30
Percent of consulting that was across party lines	17.14	9.27	18.78	9	13.80	15.40
Committee members consulted by member of other party	25	17	26	9	21	23
Number of cliques (each member consults all the others)	38	46	50	13	45	59
Four-member cliques	5	5	10	0	0	22
Five-member cliques	0	0	1	0	0	3
Choke points or information dissemination hubs (maximum betweenness)	28.5	155.5	406.3	49	188.5	104.5

Note: Calculated using UCINET VI.

As we saw in chapter 8, one's colleagues on the committee are an important source of information for committee members. So too are the committee members for others in their caucus and in the chamber, although committee members became a slightly less "popular" source of information and guidance after term limits. Before term limits 80 percent of the House members who were consulted about school choice by their colleagues were members of the K-12 Education Committee. After term limits, this fell slightly to 70 percent in 1999–2000 and 73.5 percent in 2001–2002.

Consulting across party lines was rare both before and after term limits, representing less than 20 percent of the consulting that occurred. This is perhaps not surprising given the partisan and politically salient nature of this issue area. Where cross-party consulting occurred, an even higher percentage involved consulting with committee members (between 83.3 and 94.4 percent). Much of the cross-party consulting in the pre–term limits session arose from a formally scheduled round-table discussion of education issues that included members of both parties (interview notes, 1997–1998). More than half of the 2001–2002 cross-party consulting on school choice involved ties between four moderate Republicans who regularly voted with the Democratic minority to block their party's agenda to increase the number of charter schools operating in Michigan (interview notes, 1999–2000 and 2001–2002).

Network analysis measures can tell us about the ways information flows through a group of people. Using these techniques we found that the post–term limits consulting network is less likely to facilitate the flow of information across groups of actors from different political parties, different geographic regions of the state, and districts with different demographic characteristics.

In the pre–term limits House, we identified 38 fully connected groups or cliques, in which each member of the group consults with or is consulted by every other member. Of these 33 were of the smallest possible size (3 members) and only 5 cliques had four members. Prior to term limits, three of the five four-member cliques included members of both political parties, and these three cliques were diverse based on gender, ethnicity, geographical location and urban, suburban, and rural composition of the members' district.

In the 1999–2000 session of the Michigan House, we found 46 cliques. Again these are primarily small three-member cliques, and as in the pre–term limits House, there were only five four-member cliques. In 1999–2000, three moderate Republicans who were the swing votes on a charter school expansion bill linked four of the five four-member cliques.

Additionally, some three-member cliques included only representatives of the same ethnicity from urban districts. In the 2001–2002 House we found 50 cliques, one with five members and ten with four members. Again, moderates who cast deciding votes on school choice issues were comembers of many of the four-member cliques, and separate cliques of representatives from large urban areas became even more common.

The number of cliques increased in the post–term limits House, yet they were not as connected as the cliques in the pre–term limits House were. Although some sets of these post–term limits cliques are connected, they appear to be fragmented into several relatively homogeneous factions with few actors to link the factions together. With so many small subgroups, people who are members of several of these small groups play an important role in linking groups together and facilitating communication between the groups. This can be measured systematically by something called the "betweenness" of actors in a network. We provide technical details about betweenness in the chapter notes.[3] One can think of low betweenness as an indication of many redundant paths connecting two or more groups. High betweenness means that there are very few, maybe only one pathway.

Using betweenness we can measure the ease with which information flows within a network, and we can identify and measure the importance of choke points or hubs in a network. Betweenness of key actors in the two post–term limits sessions was much higher than it was in the pre–term limits session (155.5 units in 1999–2000 and a whopping 406.3 units in 2001–2002 compared to 28.5 units in the 1997–1998 pre–term limits session). This means that one could think of the post–term limits school choice consulting network as a system with more centralized points of information control. The network as a whole has more key hubs, who are the only actors connecting otherwise decoupled clusters of actors, especially in the 2001–2002 network. This could centralize or concentrate information dissemination or introduce choke points into the flow of information. In the pre–term limits House the lower betweenness of the school choice consulting network speaks of more overlapping relationships and multiple paths along which information could flow to reach the same actors.

Most Important Sources of Information—Licensing and Regulating Health Care Professionals

There are remarkable similarities before and after term limits in the sources of information and guidance that representatives relied on regarding licensing and regulating health care professionals. Returning to table 9.1, we see that there were three sources that a large percentage of representatives said that they considered to be the most important source of information and guidance on health care issues. Not only were these the same three sources before and after term limits, but their rank order was the same, too. Both before and after term limits, the largest proportion of representatives (approximately one-third) listed their colleagues in the chamber as their most important source of information on this type of issue. The second most commonly mentioned source of information was individuals in the district, including local health care providers and friends or relatives in the health care field. Twenty-nine percent of our respondents before term limits and nearly 28 percent afterward said these local actors were their most important source of information. Organized groups and lobbyists were nearly tied for second place, with 26.1 percent and 27.1 percent of our respondents before and after term limits respectively naming this as their most important source of information and guidance. The remaining sources were all listed by fewer than 10 percent of either cohort of respondents. Compared to the differences in most important sources that we found in consulting on school choice, we were struck by the similarities before and after term limits in the preferred sources of information and guidance on this more technical, less politically salient issue.

Although we did finding striking similarities overall between the pre– and the post–term limits sources of information, we discovered that the number of terms of experience representatives have served affected their choice of important sources of information on this issue. In the post–term limits House, lame ducks were less likely than their less experienced colleagues to say that other House members were their most important source of information.[4] Not surprisingly, it appears that these more experienced legislators felt that their junior colleagues were less valuable sources of information. What is more interesting is that this difference did not surface in the pre–term limits House, perhaps reflecting the large flock of lame ducks in that cohort who could have consulted with each other instead of their junior colleagues.

Post–term limits lame ducks were more likely than their less seasoned colleagues to say that organized groups or lobbyists were their most important source of information.[5] It appears that with experience more House members recognized that groups representing the professionals affected had valuable information to help them understand the pros and cons of the specific proposal. More experienced representatives may also feel that they know which lobbyists and representatives of organized groups they can trust and rely on for accurate information.

Consulting Within the Chamber About Licensing
Health Care Professionals

A particular bill licensing or regulating health professionals might target a small numbers of actors and be unknown to the general public, despite its potential importance to the general welfare. Therefore, it is rare for a position on this subject to be mentioned in an election campaign. It is also unlikely that legislators arrived in the State House with a pre-conceived position on bills in this area, except for those with a general aversion to regulating anything. Therefore, we expected many representatives would seek help deciding what to do in this area, but they would find relatively few experts among their colleagues especially after term limits. Still committee members or other experts within the House could play a major role in advising colleagues and providing information about the issue. So we expected the amount of consulting to increase after term limits, but to be directed toward fewer sources of information and guidance. We report our findings in table 9.2 to facilitate comparison with the more politically salient issue, school choice.

The amount of consulting about licensing or regulating health care professionals increased within the chamber after term limits, and information from colleagues was the most important source of information for approximately a third of our respondents serving either before or after term limits. In the 1997–1998 House, 76 representatives reported that they would consult with one or more of 35 of their colleagues for information and guidance on a bill licensing or regulating health care professionals. This produced 119 health care consulting ties of which 94 were directed toward members serving on committees with jurisdiction over health care issues. In the 1999–2000 and 2001–2002 sessions, the number of these ties increased to 160 and 195 respectively. The number of representatives involved in the consulting decreased slightly in the 1999–2000 to 72 representatives, who consulted with one or more of 35 colleagues. In the 2001–2002 House, the number consulting increased above the pre–term limits level to 79. But the number of representatives consulted decreased to 28 representatives.

The number of colleagues consulted in the chamber did decline after term limits, but only for the 2001–2002 session. This probably reflects the forced retirement after the 1999–2000 session of several legislators with expertise in health care, including an experienced committee chair, who had served in the legislature previously for a short time in the 1980s and was the most experienced member of the entire House during the 1999–2000 session. The number of representatives seeking information and guidance fluctuated, decreasing slightly in 1999–2000 and increasing to slightly above the pre–term limits level in 2001–2002. We suspect the decline in 1999–2000 may reflect the large cohort of newcomers in that session, who would have been more familiar with their "expert" colleagues in their second term (2001–2002). Returning to table 9.1, we note that second-term representatives were the most likely to consult their colleagues.

A large proportion of the consulting within the chamber was directed toward members of committees with jurisdiction over health care issues. In 1999–2000, 139 of the reported consulting ties (or 86.9 percent) involved committee members. As a proportion of all consulting on this issue, consulting with committee members declined in 2001–2002 somewhat, to 74 percent, but still remained close to the level we found before term limits (79 percent).

Prior to term limits representatives rarely reported that they would consult with members of the opposite party on licensing health care professionals. In the pre–term limits session, there were only 11 cross-party consulting ties about licensing or regulating health care professionals. Contrary to our expectations, cross-party consulting about licensing health care professionals increased after term limits, to 22 ties and 30 ties respectively. In 1999–2000, 17 representatives reported that they would consult with one or more of seven of their colleagues in the opposite party. In 2001–2002 this remained virtually unchanged with 16 representatives saying that they would consult with one or more of seven members of the opposite party. This increase reflected Democrats' reports that they would consult with a handful of Republicans with prior careers in health care (e.g., doctors, nurses) and with the committee chair in 1999–2000. Almost no Republicans reported that they would consult with Democrats on this issue. For example, of the cross-party ties in the 2001–2002 House, two Republicans reported that they would consult one Democrat each about a bill licensing or regulating health care professionals. All 28 other cross-party consulting ties reported in 2001–2002 involved Democrats consulting with Republicans, who were in the majority. The medical career expertise of a handful of Republican representatives and the extensive experience of the 1999–2000 Health Policy Committee chair is likely to explain this increased consulting among colleagues after term limits—especially the consulting across party lines.

In 1997–1998 there were 13 cliques of representatives who consulted each other about licensing or regulating health care professionals. All 13 cliques had three members. A small number of committee members were key actors involved in linking these cliques as comembers of two or four cliques each. Only one of the thirteen cliques included members of both political parties.

The number of cliques increased after term limits, and in 2000–2001 the size of the cliques increased. In 1999–2000, the number of cliques more than tripled to 45, yet all of these were small three-member cliques. Committee members and former medical professionals appeared prominently in these cliques and linked several of them. Two Republicans with career experience in medicine shared 14 clique comemberships. In 2001–2002 the number of cliques in the health licensing consulting network rose further to 59. Of these, 3 had 5 members, 22 had 4 members, and 34 had 3 members. Again, two medical professionals connected several cliques, sharing 20 clique comemberships.

Not surprisingly given the increased level of consulting with committee members and the increased size and number of cliques, the betweenness measures for the post–term limits House exceeded their pre–term limits levels, although after it spiked in 1999–2000, mean and maximum betweenness subsided in 2001–2002.[6] Committee members played an increasingly important role in disseminating information, regardless of their party affiliation. But there were multiple sources of expertise and we see fewer choke points or hubs in these consulting networks compared to the networks for school choice consulting. One reason this might be is that a highly technical issue such as this leaves inexperienced legislators without heuristics to decide what to do. Party ideology provides little help. Thus, representatives, especially Democrats, sought information from experts within the chamber, regardless of political affiliation.

Relationships Among the Relationships

In this chapter and in chapter 7, we have discussed two sets of relationships: influence and friendship and the two vote-cuing networks. Often networks of relationships in organizations are not independent of each other. One may tend to reply on one's friends for information and guidance, or people may seek out influential people as friends. We turn our attention now to the impact term limits may have had on the relationships among the various types of networks. To explore the system-level correlation between these networks, we compared the influence network to the other three sets of relationships (i.e., friendship and the two issue-based networks). Further, we correlated the friendship matrix with the two vote-cuing matrices to see whether there was a relationship between sources of substantive expertise and friendship.[7]

There are many bases of influence in a legislature. Recognized expertise, a position of legitimate authority (e.g., speaker), resources that can be used to reward (e.g., political caucus campaign money), and the ability to coerce or punish, referent power based on personal characteristics such as charisma, esteem, or identification (French and Raven, 1959) make each legislator more or less able to influence other legislators. Given that these are not independent, one might hope that legislators with greater expertise would establish more "referent" power (based on esteem) with other representatives who might seek information or guidance from them. This might mean that substantive experts would be elected to formal leadership positions (gaining legitimate authority) within the legislature. Further, it seems plausible that honest, trustworthy legislators would also tend to be sought out as friends. These members might build on these friendships to move into positions of formal authority. Although there is no guarantee that this will occur, it is more likely that these informal relationships with other members would evolve over time. Additionally, it is likely that members with access to needed resources, such as campaign fundraising ability, might be able to expand their network of relationships more quickly than those relying on their reputation as trustworthy friends. Therefore, we assumed that the relationship between the networks of relationships might change with large influxes of newcomers. Readers are reminded that we interviewed representatives after they had served at least 18 months of their two-year legislative term. Therefore, there was some time, although it was limited, for relationships to evolve even for newcomers.

As shown in table 9.3, we found that large influxes of freshmen seemed to attenuate the correlation between friendship and influence, but the association rebounded by the end of two terms of service—possibly because "friendly" representatives have a larger group of fellow representatives to influence. Alternatively the resurgence of this correlation could occur because influential people are often seen as desirable friends. In either case, as representatives become better acquainted with each other, friendships and perceived influence become more highly correlated—indeed more highly correlated than it was prior to term limits.

Both vote-cuing networks were also correlated with the influence network in all three sessions we examined. As shown in table 9.3 prior to term limits, the relationship between the health licensing vote-cuing

Table 9.3 Relationships between the networks

	1997–1998	1999–2000	2001–2002
Influence matrix correlations			
With especially good friends			
Pearson correlation	0.35	0.26	0.45
significance p <	0.001	0.001	0.001
With school choice vote cuing			
Pearson correlation	0.27	0.25	0.20
significance p <	0.001	0.001	0.001
With health licensing vote cuing			
Pearson correlation	0.18	0.25	0.25
significance p <	0.003	0.001	0.003
Friendship matrix correlations			
With school choice vote cuing			
Pearson correlation	0.30	0.36	0.29
Significance p <	0.001	0.001	0.001
With health licensing vote cuing			
Pearson correlation	0.13	0.16	0.09
Significance p <	0.191	0.01	0.133

Note: Calculated using UCINET VI.

network and the influence network was lower than the relationship between the influence and school choice vote-cuing networks prior to term limits. This pattern reversed by the second post–term limits session, but the differences are not large. Therefore, we infer that there is still an association between substantive expertise and influence after term limits—although influxes of newcomers may attenuate this relationship for the politically salient issue—school choice—and intensify it for the more technical issue—licensing health professional.

The school choice vote-cuing network is even more highly correlated with the friendship network than it is with the influence network, especially in the first post–term limits session with its 64 freshman representatives. The health licensing network is only slightly correlated with the friendship network before term limits and even less so after term limits. Vote cuing on this more technical issue is much less highly correlated with the friendship network after term limits than it is with the influence network. This suggests to us that on a politically salient issue when uncertainty is higher (due to the limited time to learn whom to trust), representatives are more likely to turn to friends for advice than they are to turn to influential colleagues. On the other hand, on more technical issues, such as licensing health care professionals, post–term limits representatives consult people with influence more than they did before term limits and more than they consult with friends on this type of issue.

Conclusions

In his classic study of congressional voting behavior, Kingdon (1989) discovered that members of Congress suffer not so much from a dearth of information as from a surfeit of information in deciding how to vote. What they need is usable information; that is, reliable information, readily acquired, and easily digested about the choices they must make.

Overall, we find evidence that term limited, representatives are choosing more homogeneous sources of information, which may limit their ability to explore the impacts of legislation on their own constituents and to make policy that will serve the welfare of diverse groups across the state. At its most extreme we find that self-referential consulting, which seems to us to be an oxymoron, is the most prominent source of information and guidance for post–term limits representatives considering a bill on school choice. Additionally, we found a dramatic increase in the key hubs or potential choke points in the consulting networks. This could make the flow of information more sensitive to influences that might be exerted on these key actors—a system that would be more vulnerable to "special interests" or one-sided information. It could also provide an efficient system to disseminate information to representatives who are short on time and climbing a steep learning curve. Given the potential for influence that this provides, one hopes that these hubs are exposed to diverse views and are trustworthy and accurate conduits for information.

One's colleagues are a readily available source of information that is likely to be reliable, particularly if one knows and trusts them. As we noted in chapter 7, friendship groups after term limits are often based on prior acquaintances from the local political scene. Thus, the post–term limits legislature is more likely to be populated by clusters of friends from the same city or county and from the same political party—a more homogeneous group than pre–term limits friendship groups. The school choice vote-cuing network and the friendship network are correlated both before and after term limits, but the relationship is especially strong in the first post–term limits session with its influx of 64 newcomers. So, it appears that on this politically salient issue, friends also tend to be the colleagues consulted for information and guidance when there is little time to develop other sources of information. Given that consulting networks based on friendship are likely to be more homogeneous in the post–term limits milieu, this could constrict the range of viewpoints considered in policy deliberations on this and perhaps other politically salient issues.

On the other hand, the consulting network on bills licensing or regulating health professionals is only weakly correlated with the friendship network and only during the first post–term limits session. This suggests that for more technical, less politically salient issues, representatives tend to consult those with expertise or influence instead of relying as heavily on their friends.

Familiar people at home in the district are an important source of information that legislators feel they can rely on. This is especially true for first-term representatives serving after term limits. However, the views of and information provided by one's own physician or a relative who teaches school may not represent the diverse constituencies affected by an issue. Friends and relatives are a much larger proportion of the individuals consulted in the district after term limits than before, suggesting once again the potential for a more homogeneous consulting network after term limits.

Other research suggests that more contact among actors who share personal characteristics leads to greater homogeneity of attitude and reinforces one's perceptions (Bienenstock, Bonacich, & Oliver, 1990). In homogeneous networks, people tend to assume that group norms are shared more widely than they are (Bienenstock, 1990). Thus, consulting among one's friends heavily, especially given the decrease in cross-party consulting and the decrease more generally of cross-party friendships, may limit the breadth of views term-limited legislators consider as they deliberate about legislation.

After term limits, the number of consulting ties between House colleagues increased for the vote-cuing networks on both issues that we investigated. More interestingly, however, both develop some key information hubs (key experts) that could either facilitate or constrict the flow of information. Further, the higher levels of the betweenness, especially on school choice issues, suggest that the consulting networks within the chamber after term limits are more centralized around a few key actors. A consulting network that is more centralized is likely to be more sensitive to and more easily influenced by a narrower range of information. It might also become less representative of the concerns of the broad range of constituents in the state. Lobbyists often cultivate key experts in an issue area (Porter, 1974). Without the time to train and develop their own legislative insiders from among the members of the House to help them pass or block legislation their clients care about, it is likely that lobbyists have identified and sought out these key actors so that they can target their time and attention on them. If lobbyists can sway the opinions of these key actors, they can indirectly influence the other legislators who rely on these key House colleagues for advice. If this is indeed the pattern that the lobbyist–legislator relationship approximates in the post–term limits milieu, one would hope that organized groups on both sides of the issues are equally adept at identifying and lobbying these key actors.

As representatives become more experienced, they discover that "good lobbyists" will present accurate information and will be candid about the "bad side" of their position. Thus they appear to be more willing to listen to lobbyists or other spokespeople for organized groups after they have served for awhile in the House. Organized groups and lobbyists seem to become more important as newcomers learn which spokespersons for these groups they can trust to provide honest information. As one post–term limits representative told us, "A good lobbyist will tell you what the opposing side would say . . . They'll tell you the bad side . . . Before I came to Lansing I thought that lobbyists were evil crooks and villains, but now there are many that I look to for information" (interview notes, 2001–2002).

Prior to term limits, representatives told us about inviting the best lobbyists from both sides of an issue to debate the pros and cons of a bill in front of them (interview notes, 1997–1998). After term limits, we did not hear about this happening, although perhaps it was simply not mentioned. Prior to term limits, veteran representatives repeatedly said that a lobbyist's reputation for honesty was something the lobbyist would preserve at all cost, because once lost it could never be regained. The same was also mentioned repeatedly about one's colleagues (interview notes, 1997–1998). It takes time to learn whose reputation is good, however, and time is one thing that is in short supply in a term-limited legislature.

22. Learn an Afrakan language, Mdw Ntchr, Kiswahili, Twi, Yoruba, Wolof, etc. You must learn to think in a language outside of your oppressor's thinking.

23. Sit in Afraka at least once in your lifetime, take your relatives because it is our Holy Land.

24. Keep and live Afrakan festivals, holidays, and spiritual systems like the Nguzo Saba and the Law of MAAT.

25. Sing and dance with Positive Afrakan music, art, and dance. Afrikan. Because your nobles are part of you... dance and put in constructing our New Afrakan rituals.

26. Organized housing... urgent... build... Nation building.

27. Develop and use Afrika... your resources and build your own...

28. Do not spend your money any place... Do not everything in society. Travel to Afrakan countries and spend your money in Afrakan... festivals.

29. Develop and delight in other Afrakan women... lovers and the... your personal relationship.

30. Develop discipline and control... save... for wellness, etc. to build

184

CHAPTER 10

Checks and Balances:
Intragovernmental Relationships
and Outside Influences

The notion of "checks and balance" is a fundamental tenet of American democracy that assumes that each branch of our government has powers that allow it to limit—check—the power of the other two branches. This system is based on the assumption that power is balanced between the three branches of government, and this balance prevents one branch from dominating policymaking. In part because of its highly professionalized legislature, Michigan's government closely resembles the national system based on three co-equal branches of government. But under term limits, its highly professionalized legislature could be overshadowed by its professional bureaucracy headed by a strong governor.

The "Yes on B" campaign, which led to the passage of Michigan's term limits law, promised Michigan voters a more independent legislature (State Archives of Michigan, 1992), seemingly reflecting a concern that this branch was falling under the sway of other factions active in Michigan government. Bureaucrats and lobbyists were two sources of outside influence that term limits advocates nationally claimed unduly influenced legislators (Niven, 2000).

Many observers of politics believe that legislatures nationally are losing power to the executive branch of government. Contrary to the claims of term limits advocates, term limits opponents worried that state legislatures would be weakened further by limiting the length of service. They feared that the steady stream of newcomers that inevitably accompany term limits would lack the experience needed to exercise the powers of the legislature effectively. This would cede power to other branches of government, especially the executive branch, which includes both the governor and officials working in the state agencies. The Michigan Legislature, particularly the lower chamber, was designed to be the part of the government most responsive to the "popular will." Therefore, weakening the legislature was seen by term limits' opponents as a prescription to create an "imperial governor," who could, aided by a phalanx of bureaucrats, dominate policymaking.

To explore changes in the balance of power between the Michigan House of Representatives and other actors, we rely on three questions that asked our interview respondents to give the House as a whole a letter grade (A to F with pluses and minuses permitted) on (1) its ability to work with the State Senate, (2) its ability to work with the Governor's Office, and (3) monitoring the implementation of programs. The latter activity is part of a legislature's responsibility to oversee the work of the executive branch of government—one of the checks and balances included in the Michigan Constitution. To explore whether the legislature was carrying out this duty as vigorously after term limits, we also asked legislators how much time they spent monitoring state agencies as one activity among the series of eleven activities we have discussed repeatedly throughout this book. Additionally, in the series of questions about the sources of information and guidance legislators relied on when confronted by a difficult issues considered in one of their committees, we asked about the extent to which they relied on Officials from State Agencies, the Governor's Office, and State Senators. Finally, toward the end of our interviews we asked an open-ended question about the most important impacts of term limits. In response to that question, respondents frequently mentioned changes in the balance of power between the House and the other branches of government. We incorporate these responses into our discussion of outside influences on the House after term limits.

The veteran legislators termed out in 1998 sometimes speculated about the potential for relationships between major actors to change. Some of them noted that as term limits drew nearer they were seeing signs of things to come, but they were not present during the post–term limits sessions to explicitly make these comparisons. Although the post–term limits cohort includes some former staffers and other actors who would have known what the balance of power was before term limits, most of those elected for the first time in 1998 or after are less able to judge the changes in the relationships between the House and the various groups of actors. Therefore, when we analyzed the open-ended question about the most important impacts of term limits, we relied heavily on the perceptions of those representatives who served both before and after term limits—those elected in 1994 and 1996.

The Relationship with Bureaucrats

The relationship between bureaucrats and legislators is a complex one that includes collaboration, cooptation, delegation, and monitoring. Legislators often rely on bureaucrats to develop as well as carry out policy. Bureaucrats seek to achieve their ends through legislators using information management, advocacy by clients who are often constituents, and by collaborating with interest groups to define and frame issues (Nakamura & Smallwood, 1980). As part of its constitutionally provided oversight powers, legislators can use hearings, audits, and budget appropriations to gain bureaucratic compliance to legislative intent. Thus, the relationship between bureaucrats and legislators can be both collaborative and adversarial. These relationships can take a variety of forms including iron triangles, issue networks, bureaucratic entrepreneurship, and legislative oversight.

Iron triangles, which are highly resilient policy-making subsystems composed of three groups of actors (legislators serving on the committee in the policy area, interest groups and their lobbyists representing actors affected by the policy, and bureaucratic agencies that implement the policy), remind us that the cozy relationships with elected officials are not limited to lobbyists, but include bureaucrats too. Term limits advocates believe that these relationships with bureaucrats undermine the independent judgment of legislators and assert that term limits will sever these ties (Niven, 2000). Yet, as we have noted repeatedly legislators cannot be experts on all subjects (Porter, 1974), so they rely on a variety of sources for information and guidance when trying to develop policy or decide how to vote. Less experienced and knowledgeable legislators, unsure of whose information to trust, may turn to bureaucrats, giving them more influence. Additionally, when it is difficult to monitor compliance, game theorists have demonstrated that partners in exchange relationships have an incentive to defect (Williamson, 1975; Axelrod, 1984). Therefore, bureaucrats have less reason to be forthcoming with novice legislators who have limited control over the ways bureaucrats use the state's funds appropriated to operate programs.

In instances where state agency officials seek to thwart legislators, term limits seem to help them do so. In response to our question about the most important impacts of term limits, many representatives serving before term limits noted that state agency officials ignored their requests because term-limited representatives would be gone soon. In anticipation of term limits expulsions, 11 percent of our pre–term limits representatives noted an increase in the power of state agencies. After term limits even more representatives said that an important impact of term limits was an increase in the power of the bureaucracy. For those who had served both before and after term limits, 27 percent made this comment. Twenty-two percent of those who had only served after term limits made this comment.

Shortening the tenure of legislators clearly decreases their collective level of experience and creates flocks of lame ducks. As we discussed in chapter 5, it also appears to be related to a higher chance that they will run for another elected office. Monitoring the performance of state agencies is unlikely to advance a legislator's reputation either within the chamber, in his or her caucus, or with large numbers of voters in the district. Thus, monitoring state agencies is often a low priority for reelection-seeking legislators confronted by myriad pressing demands. Additionally, inexperienced legislators with limited time to develop expertise may not be able to penetrate the complexities of state agencies to effectively monitor their performance. This expert knowledge is one of the sources of power bureaucrats have to "check" the legislature, but it needs to be balanced by the capacity of the legislature to scrutinize the agencies' performance. This takes knowledge that is primarily available from the civil servants working in the state agency—many of whom want their agency directors to be held accountable and want the mission of the agency carried out effectively. This means that legislators need to learn quickly what and who to ask about public programs. But, as one representative pointed out, "It's difficult for state agencies to educate members and provide information. It slows down the implementation of policies" (interview notes, 2001–2002).

Both before and after term limits representatives ranked Michigan's state agency officials slightly above average as a source of information and guidance on a difficult issue considered at the committee level. The ranking for state agency officials given by those serving before term limits was eighth out of eighteen. After term limits, the rank given was seventh out of eighteen. Therefore we conclude that, in general, term-limited legislators are just as willing as their predecessors to consult state agency officials.

On the politically salient issue of school choice, representatives did not rely heavily on state agency officials either before or after term limits, but this was especially true after term limits. Before term limits approximately 6 percent of our respondents said they consulted state agency officials about bills concerning school choice. After term limits, less than 1 percent said this. On the more technical issue of licensing or regulating health care professionals, representatives did consult state agency officials, but fewer did so after term limits. Before term limits 14 percent of our respondents said they would consult state agency officials about bills concerning these issues. After term limits slightly more than 11 percent said this.

These changes in information gathering hardly seem consistent with our respondents' claims that bureaucrats have gained power. Indeed, given that legislators are relying either at the same level or less heavily on state agency officials for information, this would suggest that they are more independent of the bureaucracy. Legislators' use of their oversight powers, while never outstanding, seems to have suffered a serious setback under term limits, however. And this appears more likely to contribute to the change in the relationship that our respondents reported.

Prior to term limits, representatives reported that they spent slightly more than some time (mean 2.0 on a zero to four scale) monitoring state agencies. After term limits this fell (mean 1.7) (sign. at $p < 0.02$). Both before and after term limits legislators reported spending less than their average amount of time on monitoring state agencies. However, the priority they placed on this activity, based on the difference between the average amount of time they spent on all their activities, decreased after term limits. Thus an activity that was already being somewhat neglected became even more neglected after term limits took effect.

Prior to term limits, respondents gave themselves an average grade of C for their ability to monitor the implementation of programs. After term limits, the average grade for this dropped to a C−. But those who served before and after term limits, that is those who could compare performance of this activity after term limits to its performance before, gave the House a grade halfway between C− and D+ for this activity after term limits. This suggests that the shift in power toward the bureaucracy may partially result from the legislature's inability or unwillingness to exercise its oversight powers.

To explore the reasons why monitoring of state agencies received these low grades, we asked respondents to explain the grades they gave. These comments are summarized in table 10.1. The reason respondents most often gave for the low grades for monitoring the implementation of programs was a lack of time and effort devoted to this. Before term limits 36.6 percent of our respondents said this compared to 42.2 percent

Table 10.1 Impediments to monitoring implementation of programs

Representatives' Comments	Before term limits (percent (number))	After term limits (percent (number))
Lack of time or effort	36.6 (26)	42.2 (57)
No systematic way to monitor	19.7 (14)	31.1 (42)
Lack of knowledge	23.9 (17)	28.9 (39)
Lack of authority or power	21.1 (15)	24.4 (33)
Ties with agency too cozy	14.1 (10)	17.0 (23)
Subgroup in house does this	28.2 (20)	15.6 (21)
Some individuals do this	16.9 (12)	1.5 (2)
Partisan politics affect this	18.3 (13)	10.4 (14)
Bureaucrats are more powerful	11.1 (10)	23.7 (42)
Respondents	n = 71	n = 135

after term limits. In addition to less time and effort spent on this activity, respondents seemed uncertain about how to assess agency performance comprehensively. Those serving after term limits were more likely to complain that there was no systematic way to monitor agencies. Approximately 31 percent of the post–term limits respondents said this compared to slight fewer than 20 percent before term limits. Prior to term limits respondents were more likely to say that a subgroup within the legislature, such as the Appropriations Committee or the chair of the committee with jurisdiction over the agency was responsible for bureaucratic oversight. Twenty-eight percent of respondents serving before term limits said this compared to 15.6 percent serving after term limits. We also encountered some respondents after term limits who expressed surprise at our questions about legislative oversight of the bureaucracy and in one instance asked "Do we do that?" (interview notes, 1999–2000). This suggests to us that after term limits legislators are less aware or sometimes unaware of the mechanisms that exist for carrying out this activity.

Respondents also frequently mentioned that they lacked the knowledge and expertise needed to monitor agencies. Approximately 24 percent of respondents serving before term limits and 29 percent of those serving after term limits mentioned this. Before term limits, our respondents told us about some of their colleagues who were effective in monitoring agencies. After term limits only 1.5 percent of our respondents mentioned that some colleagues were adept at monitoring agencies—a sizeable drop from the 17 percent who said this before term limits. These pre–term limits respondents told us about committee chairs whose former staff members worked in some of the agencies, and that these former employees would give the representative information needed to monitor those agencies. Also, pre–term limits representatives identified specific committee chairs who knew enough about the work of agencies under the jurisdiction of their committee to be able to question agency staff effectively. These expert chairs were rare even before term limits, according to our respondents.

Many respondents felt that the House lacked the power to exercise oversight over the bureaucratic agencies. This was only slightly more frequently mentioned after term limits. Twenty-one percent of respondents before term limits and 24.4 percent after term limits complained that the executive branch thwarted their efforts and that civil servants did not cooperate with their requests for information. Some felt that those responsible for exercising oversight had too "cozy" a relationship with the agency they monitored. This was mentioned by 14 percent of our respondents before term limits and 17 percent after term limits. After term limits some state agency employees we knew of told us that the directors of their agencies had forbidden anyone from talking directly to legislators without permission. Therefore, without the informal relationships between legislators and bureaucrats that would facilitate "leaks" of information and with a formal prohibition on responding to legislators' requests for information, it is not surprising that our respondents felt unable to assess the performance and program implementation of the agencies they oversaw.

Respondents serving before term limits were more likely than those serving afterward to say that subgroups of their colleagues in the House were responsible for bureaucratic oversight. Twenty-eight percent of respondents serving before term limits claimed this compared to 15.6 percent after term limits. The Appropriations Committee was frequently mentioned as a locus of bureaucratic oversight. This is consistent with the amount of time representatives both before and after term limits reported spending monitoring state agencies.

Respondents who served on the Appropriations Committee were statistically significantly more likely to spend more time on this activity than were their colleagues who served on policy committees. The mean time spent on this activity by Appropriations Committee members was 2.3 (slight more than some) on our five-point scale. Those on the policy committees reported spending about two-thirds of the way between a little and some time monitoring state agencies (1.7). Compared to the average amount of time spent on all activities, representatives serving on the Appropriations Committee said they spent only a little less on this (−0.22) than the average amount of time they spent on all activities.

Representatives not on the Appropriations Committee reported spending much less than their average amount of time on this activity (-0.89). Both these differences are statistically significant at $p < 0.001$.[1] Additionally, before term limits, respondents who served on the Appropriations Committee gave this an even higher priority, reporting that they spent slightly more than their average amount of time monitoring state agencies.[2]

Partisan politics permeate the relationship between the executive and legislative branches, and monitoring state agencies is no exception to this rule. Before term limits, with the Democratic Party in control of the House and chairing its committees, partisan politics was mentioned to explain difficulties monitoring state agencies much more often than after term limits when the executive branch and the House were both controlled by the Republican Party. Before term limits 18.3 percent of our respondents mentioned this and after term limits 10.4 percent made comments about this. Given the importance of committee chairs in performing oversight activities, it is likely that the majority and minority party members view this activity differently. This is likely to be especially true when the minority party also does not control the Governor's Office. We found evidence of this in the grades our respondents gave the House for its ability to perform oversight. The majority party tended to give itself higher marks on the quality of bureaucratic oversight both before and after term limits, but the difference was much larger after term limits when the Republicans controlled the House and chaired its committees and the governor, John Engler, was a Republican.[3] The amount of time representatives reported spending on this activity reflects greater scrutiny by the political party that does not control the executive branch. Democrats, especially before term limits, reported spending statistically significantly more time monitoring state agencies than Republicans did.[4] Without further data, it is difficult for us to disentangle fully the effects of term limits from the effects of Republican control of both the House and the executive branch.[5]

Overall it appears that the increased power of bureaucratic agencies reported by our respondents reflects the ability of state agencies to resist efforts, albeit limited, by legislators to monitor their performance. This arises both from the lack of knowledge and expertise of novice legislators compared to career bureaucrats and from the limited time legislators feel they have to devote to this activity. It may also, however, partially reflect the differences in partisan control of the chamber that coincided with term limits and the efforts of the executive branch to thwart legislative oversight. There is little political advantage to be gained from criticizing appointees of a governor of your own political party. Indeed, as a few of our respondents noted, there is some risk of retaliation from the governor if legislators within the same party monitored state agency directors too vigorously—and this seemed to apply both before and after term limits. It also appears that the executive branch used its powers to thwart legislative access to information that might have been used to monitor agency performance and that legislative novices lacked the relationships with lower-level bureaucrats that could have helped them circumvent this.

House–Senate Relationships Under Term Limits

We found no mention by either term limits proponents or opponents of the potential for the State Senate to become the repository of experienced legislators and for the House to become their "little siblings" (interview notes, 2001–2002). It appears that under term limits legislators will likely serve in the House before running for the Senate, turning the House into a training ground for the Senate. In response to our question about the most important impacts of term limits, approximately 3 percent of the veterans expelled from the legislature in 1998 anticipated that the Senate would gain power over the novice House. Only 8 percent of those serving only after term limits expulsions made this comment—possibly based on their experience as staffers or others with familiarity with House–Senate relationships before term limits expulsions. On the other hand, 27 percent of those who had served both prior to and after term limits commented that this had occurred. Given that more than a quarter of the representatives who saw and experienced the relationship between the House and Senate before and after term limits mentioned this as an important impact of term limits, we find this a fairly convincing indication that the relationship has indeed changed.

Within legislatures generally, there is competition between the "upper" chamber—the Senate—and the "lower" chamber—the House of Representatives or General Assembly. Several of our interview respondents referred derisively to the Michigan State Senate as the "House of Lords" (interview notes, 2001–2002). Term limits seems to have exacerbated Michigan's State Representatives' resentment of their Senate colleagues, and so when we interviewed members of the 1999–2000 and 2001–2002 House sessions, we added a question asking them to grade their ability to work with the State Senate. Because we did not ask this question during our first round of interviews, we cannot compare the post–term limits responses directed to the pre–term limits responses. We can, however, compare the responses of those who served during both the pre– and post–term limits session to those who served only after term limits. We found that those who had served during the 1997–1998 session gave working with the Senate lower grades than those who had served only after term limits. The cohort that had served both prior to and after term limits said that during the sessions after term limits expulsions the House deserved an average grade of slight above a C for its ability to work with the Senate. Those who had served only after term limits gave this an average grade just slightly below a B minus.

We also discovered that among our respondents serving after term limits expulsions 14.7 percent commented on the tension between the House and the Senate as one of the most important effects of term limits. This comment was made more often by those who had only served after term limits (15.6 percent) compared to those who had served both before and after term limits (10.9 percent). This tension was never mentioned by respondents who served only prior to term limits expulsions. After term limits it appears that this level of tension increased, given the proportion of our respondents who had served before and after term limits who mentioned this.

One source of tension between the House and the Senate in the post–term limits milieu is electoral competition between termed out House members challenging an incumbent senator. Given that most of the State Senators were termed out in 2002, only a few of the House members running for a State Senate seat were challenging an incumbent. As the 2006 election draws closer, there will be 30 incumbent State Senators, and challenges from termed out House members would seem to be more likely. This is likely to exacerbate an increasingly tense relationship between the House and the Senate. Jockeying for position in future electoral contests may affect policymaking and the willing-ness of the Senate to take positions that House members from the same political party could use to run against them.

Relationship Between the House and the Governor's Office

We also asked about the ability of the House to work with the Governor's Office. Michigan's governor during all three legislative terms we studied was John Engler, a very adept politician with decades of uninterrupted experience in Lansing. His political career began with his election to the Michigan House of Representatives in 1970 and continued with his election as a State Senator in 1978 and Governor in 1990, 1994, and 1998. Thus when 64 freshman representatives confronted this master politician, there was a vast discrepancy in the political experience each side brought to the table. Admittedly that situation may have been a unique by-product of the staggered implementation of term limits in Michigan. Yet even under a fully implemented set of term limits, it will be possible for a politician to serve six years in the House and eight years in the Senate—only six years less than the legislative service John Engler brought to his governorship—and then serve eight more years as governor. Therefore, it is reasonable to assume that in Michigan a master politician in the Governor's Office may periodically be pitted against a novice House.

A few veteran legislators (4.4 percent) serving before term limits foresaw the governor becoming more powerful after term limits. However, for those who served both before and after term limits, increased gubernatorial power was a big change. Nearly 44 percent of them commented that this was among the most important consequences of term limits. A substantial proportion of those serving only after term limits (26.2 percent) agreed with this assessment. This is consistent with the increase in the number of respondents who said that the governor was the most influential member of the House in the sessions after term limits—findings that we presented in chapter 7.

In chapter 8 we presented an ordered list of the sources that representatives reported relying on for information and guidance on a difficult issue considered in a committee. Both before and after term limits representatives report that the Governor's Office is the source they would rely on next to the least. Thus, the power of the Governor's Office as a source of information or guidance for individual representatives remains unchanged. So, it appears that information is not the way that the governor is exercising more power over the House.

During our interviews with several members of the top House leadership from both political parties, we asked where the most important decisions were made about bills concerning school choice and bills licensing or regulating health care professionals. Additionally we asked in general who determined when and if a bill reached the floor of the chamber. Based on their responses to these questions, it appears that the source of the governor's influence is control over whether action is taken on an issue—agenda control. The responses of these House leaders are summarized in table 10.2. After term limits, the Governor's Office was either the first or second most frequently mentioned locus of agenda

Table 10.2 Loci of most important decisions about an issue

Rank	School choice		Licensing or regulating health care professionals		Who determines when & if a bill reaches the floor	
	Before term limits	After term limits	Before term limits	After term limits	Before term limits	After term limits
1	Committee chair	Governor's office	Committee chair	House leadership	House leadership	House leadership
2	Committee meeting	House leadership	Governor's office	Governor's office	Committee chairs	Governor's office
3	House leadership	Majority party caucus	Regular committee meetings	Regular committee meetings	Majority party caucus	Lobbyists

control for both of the two specific issues and for the more general question about who decided when and if something reached the floor for a vote. Prior to term limits there is only one of the three situations in which the Governor's Office is one of the top three loci of agenda control for the House. That issue is the more technical of the two, and the members of the leadership noted that Governor Engler was generally opposed to additional regulation so it would be important to find out if he would simply veto whatever was being proposed.

Looking at table 10.2, it also can be noted that prior to term limits, committee chairs were the most frequently mentioned actors with agenda control for the two specific issue areas we asked about. They also ranked second in general in determining whether bills reached the floor of the House. After term limits, the committee chairs are not included among the top three actors with agenda control over either of the two specific issues: school choice or licensing or regulating health care professionals. Additionally, after term limits committee chairs were not included among the groups of actors determining when and if a bill reached the floor of the chamber. This change is consistent with comments of respondents about the diminished power of committee chairs, which we discussed in chapter 8. Readers are reminded that after term limits several respondents commented that committee chairs were pressured by the governor and the caucus leadership to bring up legislation that they did not support. We infer from this that some of the power formerly wielded by committee chairs over the agenda of the House has shifted to the Governor's office after term limits.

Finally, we asked our respondents during the two post–term limits sessions to award the House a grade for its ability to work with the governor. Our respondents gave themselves fairly high marks for their ability to work with the governor, between a B− and a B for the 1999–2000 session with its 64 freshmen and between a B and a B+ for the 2001–2002 session with its 21 freshmen. It is difficult to assess what these grades mean, however. Some members commented on their grades explaining that the high grade they gave reflected the fact that the House carried out the governor's agenda. Others gave an extremely low grade, saying that the House was merely following orders from the governor—carrying out his agenda instead of developing their own. Hence the same activity seemed to elicit contradictory grades, especially from members of the minority political party—the Democrats. This contradiction in the meaning of the grades given by the Democrats seems to be reflected in the bimodal distribution of their grades, which ranged from A+ to F but cluster at both ends of the distribution. Twenty-five Democrats gave the House an A or A+ for its ability to work with the governor. The median grade given by Democrats was a B. But 10 Democrats gave the House a D or F for its ability to work with the governor. The Republicans' grades ranged from C− to A+, normally distributed around the median grade of B.

As we noted earlier, the analyses we present here reflect the relationship between a vastly more experienced governor and a House comprised of possibly the largest cohort of newcomers likely to be seen even under term limits. Therefore, our findings may represent an extreme instance of the experienced governor—inexperienced legislature scenario. Yet, this scenario is likely to recur regularly and citizens need to be aware of its potential to undermine the checks and balances between the executive and the legislative branches of government. It would appear that the governor controlled the agenda of the House and that especially committee chairs lost power to the Governor's office and also to the House leadership

Conclusions

In the survey conducted by Wayne State University's Center for Urban Studies in 2003, respondents were asked about several of the relationships that we have discussed in this chapter. Specifically, three separate questions asked, "Some people say that term limits have increased the power of [the governor or bureaucrats or lobbyists] and decreased the power of legislators. If this is true, do you think that this is a good thing, a bad thing or are you uncertain?" Most respondents were uncertain about whether this was a good or bad thing. We are much less sanguine about this and agree with the substantial percentages of the survey respondents who said that these changes would be a bad thing.[6] As we noted in the introduction to this chapter, the American system of democracy is predicated on the ability of each branch of government to balance the other. Michigan's state government is based on these same principles of divided power. Therefore, changing the balance of power is something we see as striking at the foundation of Michigan's system of government.

We suspect that these relationships between the branches of government may vary depending on the qualifications of the actors involved. For example, in 2002 with term limits fully implemented, Michigan's new governor, Jennifer Granholm, had only limited state-level political experience—one four-year term as attorney general. The scramble for 30 open State Senate seats led to another mass exodus from the Michigan House. Therefore, nearly half the representatives in the Michigan House are newly elected. In terms of experience, Governor Granholm and the Michigan House of Representatives are more evenly matched, with probably a slight advantage toward the six-year veterans in the House. This match-up is likely to produce different dynamics that the one between veteran Governor John Engler and novice, newly term-limited House that we describe here. Thus we suspect that there is a set of scenarios based on the experience levels of the branches of government that will vary depending on which one is stronger. The problem for the Michigan House is that it is likely to be rather consistently on the weaker side.

Overwhelmingly, legislators say that these shifts in the balance of power have occurred. Other evidence from our interviews support their assertions and suggest that the House has become less powerful and that other actors within government have become more powerful. Additionally, Michigan has a strong tradition of bipartisan compromise within the legislature that has historically permitted that state to balance multiple strong competing interests (Kobrak in Rosenthal & Moakley, 1984). With the current empowerment of the Governor's Office and the political party caucuses and their leadership within the chamber, we are concerned about the state's ability to continue balancing these economic and regional interests effectively.

CHAPTER 11

Conclusions: Term Limits' Report Card

Term limits illustrate the potential for seemingly simple changes in a political system to have far-reaching, unintended, and unanticipated impacts. Hence our discussion of their impacts has ranged over many facets of state politics. Before we begin to synthesize and integrate these findings, we summarize them briefly.

In chapter 1 we found that term limits increased the number of open seat elections for the Michigan House of Representatives and the California General Assembly, a completely predictable outcome. Surprisingly, however, we found that this increase in open seats did not increase voter turnout, as usually happens in open seat elections. Additionally, having more open seat elections did not reduce the tendency for victors to win the general election by a landslide—that is, they did not produce more competitive elections. Both these potentially positive impacts (in our opinion) of term limits did not materialize in large part because most of Michigan's State House districts are drawn to insure that one or the other political party has a clear advantage. We found that primary competition sometimes increased for open seats, but not necessarily. Particularly if the district is a competitive one, political parties have an incentive to suppress primary competition to save scarce financial resources for the general election. In California competition declined even more than it did in Michigan after term limits. Even more surprisingly, we found that the power of incumbency increased after term limits because challengers appear to wait for an open seat race. Indeed, we speculate that the shorter the term limits, the more likely it is that candidates will wait to run in an open seat race. Thus, the promise of electoral competition in the State House has not been realized, and precisely because term limits in California and Michigan are so short, there are at best punctuated bouts of competition for open seats in primaries in districts that are not competitive.

In chapter 2 we found evidence that "economic" attention has shifted away from open seats now that they are so numerous and focused instead on the handful of competitive House districts that will determine the partisan control of the chamber. Whether these districts had open seat races or not, they attracted hundreds of thousands of dollars in campaign contributions. Many organized interests do not have deep enough pockets to participate at the level of the wealthiest contributors—a factor likely to influence the electoral outcome in these competitive districts. In fact we found that only five groups of donors were able to maintain their proportion of the money given to House candidates and still maintain their previous level of giving to State Senate candidates. These five groups were: individual donors, the candidate and his or her family, political parties, lawyers and lobbyists (the multiclient firms), and the government sector (such as the Township Association and other similar entities).

The higher costs of elections may disadvantage some groups of candidates, especially those who lack family or personal wealth. Additionally, as the costs of competitive elections have increased, the fundraising disparity between the two political parties has widened. Democratic House candidates raised only about half as much as the Republican candidates in the 2002 election. This probably reflects national trends and the advantages that partisan control of chamber offer instead of term limits. But the increased importance of money in winning House seats in the handful of competitive districts—an effect of term limits—may facilitate single-party domination of Michigan's legislature. This would be a dramatic reduction in electoral competition, especially given Michigan's long history as a two-party political system.

In chapter 3, we described the continuing ties between interest groups and legislators. After term limits, interest groups seem to give more money to legislators after they win their election than they did before term limits. The amount of money given seems to be based on the potential value of the legislators to the goals of the interest group based on the committees the legislators serve on and whether they are in the majority party. Additionally after term limits we found many indications that legislators rely more heavily on lobbyists for information about key issues. Thus, we find that term limits do not sever the ties between special interests and legislators. In fact these ties seem to have become stronger.

In chapter 4 we described the impact of term limits on the composition of the Michigan State House and the California General Assembly. In Michigan we found that more representatives are winning their first House election as senior citizens.

We also found that more candidates in their twenties are winning election to the State House. This is consistent with predictions that many prospective candidates in their thirties and forties and even in their fifties would not want to leave their careers for a short tenure in the legislature.

In Michigan, with a House membership that already nearly matched the ethnic diversity of the state, term limits initially increased ethnic representativeness. But the impact does not appear to have been permanent. In California, ethnic minority group members made substantial gains in the General Assembly, giving some support to the hypothesis that term limits release "pent up" ethnic voting strength. Most of the gains made by ethnic minority group members were within the Democratic caucus, therefore, the fortunes of the Democratic Party interact with the effects of term limits on ethnic group representation.

Similarly, we found that term limits provide opportunities for Democratic women, but not for Republican women. Given the increased number of Democrats elected to the California General Assembly, women in California are represented at nearly two-thirds of their proportion in the population. In Michigan, with Democrats losing seats in the House, women's representation dropped to 43 percent of their proportion of the population—a level not seen since 1992. Indeed, term limits turned back the clock for Republican women to 1990 in California too.

The trend that seems to be taking shape after term limits in Michigan and California is one of an increasingly homogeneous Republican Party and an increasingly diverse Democratic Party. With respect to gender diversity, the Republican Party recruits women to run for office in districts where they have no reasonable chance of winning. The Democratic Party on the other hand almost never engages in this practice of running women candidates as "sacrificial lambs." This practice predates term limits, and term limits are only responsible for changing the gender composition of the lower chamber of these two states legislature to the extent that they may have given the two major political parties differential opportunities to win elections.

In chapter 5 we found that far from attracting citizen legislators, Michigan House members after term limits are more politically ambitious and more likely to have had prior political jobs than were their predecessors. This bodes well for electoral competition in the State

Senate, but it poses problems for the work of the House when jockeying for political advantage in future campaigns interferes with getting the work of the chamber done. Even those legislators who initially planned to eschew a political career catch the "bug" and by the end of their second term in office are more likely to say they're considering running for some other elected office. Given the limited overlap between State House and State Senate districts in the districts drawn after the 2000 census, the future electoral plans of representatives may compromise their desire to represent some of their current constituents. This is likely to be particularly true for those whose views differ dramatically from those of the majority in the office for which the House member plans to run next.

In chapter 6 we discuss the effect "flocks" of lame ducks may have on accountability. In electoral politics one's lame duck status is often not known publicly until the term in office is nearly over. Not so with term limits. One's lame duck status is known for the entire two years of the final term in office. We presented evidence that sometimes this leads to shirking by lame ducks and leads other actors in the political system to treat them differently. Sometimes representatives' plans to run for another elected office seemed to ameliorate the more general tendency of lame ducks to shirk. Other times we found that representatives who planned to run for another elected office allocated their time and attention based on the potential for future electoral payoff.

We found in general, however, that representatives spend a lot of their time on the constituent-related parts of their job—a finding that should reassure voters of the generally high level of responsiveness of their state representatives both before and after term limits. Yet lame ducks use their time differently, and we found that they feather their nests by focusing on activities that are likely to help them get a future job.

In chapter 7 we discovered that the number of House colleagues who are seen as influential has declined and that those in top leadership positions are more frequently named as influential. This suggests that influence is more concentrated or centralized in the post–term limits House. Additionally it suggests that informal influence has declined. On the other hand, friendships seem to flourish in the post–term limits House, especially those based on prior political associations and regional ties established before service in the legislature. Friendships that cross party lines and friendships among people with "different views" became less common, however. This raises questions about the ability of friendships to help legislators understand the needs and interests of constituents of their colleagues. In a state with as much variety in regional and economic interests as Michigan has, it is difficult to bridge these differences. This is one of the functions friendships performed prior to term limits. Prior to term limits, friendships among those who held different views also helped keep conflict issue-based instead of personalized.

In chapter 8 we explored the role played by committee chairs after term limits. They are seen as less experienced, less informed, less capable of managing conflict and as less autonomous actors. The limited experience committee chairs bring to their role seems to reduce the amount of control they have over the work of their committees. The governor and the House leadership both seem to be able to dictate the chair's agenda, and we heard of instances in which legislation was taken from one committee and given to another if the chair didn't comply with the wishes of the governor or the House leadership. Civility and courtesy in committee meetings seem to have declined and many post–term limits committee chairs seem to suppress conflict instead of managing it. Finally after term limits, committee chairs are not consulted as extensively by members of their committees about difficult issues. To compensate for this, term-limited legislators turned to their colleagues on the committee and to lobbyists and organized groups.

Chapter 9 once again demonstrates the increasing homogeneity of information and consulting that seems to typify the post–term limits House. We looked at two very different types of issues, school choice bills and bills licensing or regulating health care professionals. We found that sources that legislators relied on most for information about the more politically salient school choice bills changed markedly after term limits. The most frequently mentioned "most important source" of information on school choice bills after term limits was "no one but myself," a phenomenon we dubbed self-referential consulting. Additionally, almost twice as many representatives after term limits said that lobbyists or organized groups were their "most important source" of information on a school choice bill. On the more technical issue of licensing or regulating health care professionals, the most important sources of information were nearly identical before and after term limits. This suggests to us that some of the changes in the House revolve around politicized issues instead of more mundane ones.

In addition, we found that information and consulting networks after term limits had more prominent hubs or choke points. This could make these consulting networks more vulnerable to biased information, but could also make it more efficient to disseminate information throughout the House. The more dispersed, distributed networks of the pre–term limits House would be better able to provide a range of competing views and information, but it would have been more difficult to disseminate a particular idea or viewpoint quickly. Disseminating information efficiently is more consistent with a House that is more hierarchically constructed with more power centered in the leadership.

In chapter 10 we explore relationships between other key players in State Government and the House. This includes relationships between the House and the Governor's office, between the House and the Senate, and between the House and the state agencies. After term limits, we found overwhelmingly that legislators say that the House lost power in its relationship with each of these groups. Now that State Senators and the veteran governor have been expelled by term limits, the House may be able to recoup part of its power with respect to these. But the loss of power to bureaucrats is likely to persist. Some citizens say that if the House lost power to these other branches of government that it would be a "bad thing." We concur with their assessment, and unfortunately the evidence we found overwhelming supports the conclusion that the House is a weakened chamber after term limits. Given the important role that the lower chamber plays as the "people's chamber," we are concerned about the impact this may have on state government. One of the difficulties in governing Michigan effectively is representing divergent interests inherent in Michigan's diverse regions and competing economic bases. This regional and economic diversity has produced a two-party political system that traditionally has balanced these interests by accommodating multiple factions. Increased single-party control or executive branch dominance could undermine this structure.

An Assessment of Term Limits Based on Advocates' Promises

In table 11.1 we summarize claims about term limits from the "Yes on B" campaign available through the Michigan State Archives, claims reported in the Detroit Free Press and claims compiled by Niven (2000) from national newspapers. Given the current penchant for accountability, we have given term limits a "report card." We awarded grades as follows. If term limits achieved its promised outcomes, we gave it an "A." If it did not achieve its promised outcome, but did nothing to make matters worse or to undermine democratic governance in the state, we gave it a "C." If it made matters worse, we gave it an "F." Obviously such grades require us to make judgments. We do not shy from doing so because we have more than five years of research effort standing behind each of these judgments.

Looking at the first section of factors, those affecting who is elected and how they are chosen, we find that term limits have not increased

Table 11.1 The promises of term limits

	Yes on B	Niven	D.F.P.	Achieved in Michigan	Grades
Changes in who's elected and how they're chosen					
Increased electoral competition	✔	✔	✔	No-may decrease	F
Increase number of citizen legislators	✔	✔	✔	No-decreased	F
Increase electoral opportunities for women and minorities	✔	✔	✔	Only in Democratic Party	C
New faces	✔	✔	✔	Yes	A
To whom elected officials respond					
Increase elected officials' sensitivity/ accountability to constituents	✔			Only when it helps them get a future job	C
Increased energy and enthusiasm	✔			Yes	A
Independence from bureaucratic influence	✔			No-gave bureaucrats more power	F
Independence from special interest and lobbyists' influence	✔	✔	✔	No-gave lobbyists' more power	F
How government operates					
Merit-based system for legislative leadership positions	✔			No-money matters more	F
More opportunities for officials to move to higher offices	✔		✔	Yes	A
Less gridlock	✔			Only when legislature was dominated by the Governor	C

Source: Articles on which these data were based on listed within the reference pages and include material available in the State Archives of Michigan.

electoral competition. Indeed, we find that they may have decreased competition. Clearly after term limits overwhelming economic resources were focused on a few highly competitive districts, to the detriment of electoral competition throughout the state as a whole. Most citizens have less choice among viable candidates than they did prior to term limits, and there is less likelihood that an incumbent who deserves to be replaced will confront a viable challenger during the six-year term that he or she can serve. We give term limits a grade of F for its impact on electoral competition.

Term limits proponents promised that they would attract a new breed of citizen legislator. In chapter 5 we demonstrated unequivocally that citizen legislators have become even more rare after term limits. We give term limits another F.

Term limits advocates claimed that by removing the "drag of incumbency" they would provide more opportunities for women and ethnic minority group members to win legislative seats. Term limits seem to help ethnic minority group members and women win elections in California. In Michigan, they had a limited, ephemeral effect on ethnic minority group members' electoral prospects, but they undermined a decade of gains for women, especially in the Republican Party. Term limits appear to increase electoral opportunities for ethnic minority groups members in states where the group was substantially underrepresented. Term limits' effects on women's electoral prospects seem to rest on the fortunes of the Democratic Party. If the Democrats gain seats, more women are elected. If the Republicans gain seats, the representativeness ratio for women declines. These mixed results lead us to give term limits a C for this.

Finally term limits get a clear A for bringing "new faces" to the legislature. As open seats increased, it would have been possible to flood the House with former legislators taken out of mothballs. That has not happened. As opportunities for newcomers to run for office increased, local political actors and others have been recruited for service in the state's capital. This is one promise that term limits clearly achieve, and we award them an A.

The next section on the report card deals with the promised changes in the system of democratic governance. First we assess term limits' ability to increase legislators' accountability to their constituents— another promise made by some term limits advocates. We found that sometimes term limits decoupled legislators from their constituents, especially when they planned to run for another political office in which responding to their current constituents would be a liability. At other times, term limits focused legislators' attention on the district and the local jobs to which they might return. In chapter 6 we found that legislators, especially lame ducks, are differentially responsive to constituents in their district depending on what their future career plans are. Therefore, we give term limits a C to indicate that sometimes electoral accountability is strengthened and sometimes weakened by term limits.

Term limits proponents promised that newcomers would exude energy and enthusiasm. Based on comments made during our interviews, we conclude that they do. We give term limits an A here.

Term limits advocates promised to make legislatures more independent from bureaucratic agencies. Instead they made state agencies more powerful and less accountable to the legislature as the ability of novice legislators proved no match for career bureaucrats. The effect has been the opposite of the one promised by term limits advocates, and the consequences we believe seriously undermine an important set of checks and balances fundamentally important to our political system. We give them an F.

Term limits proponents were especially confident that they would sever the ties between legislators and special interests. Throughout this book we have described the vast increase in the amount of money needed to run for office, the increased importance of money in elections for state legislature, and the increased reliance by legislators on interest groups for information while making them less able to assess the credibility of that information. All these effects of term limits lead us to conclude that term limits seem to have done the opposite of what they promised. Again we give them an F.

We turn now to the section on the internal operations of legislatures. Term limits proponents promised a merit-based system for selecting legislative leaders within the chamber. The system that has developed appears to stress money and help to candidates on the campaign trail. Legislators express frustration with voting for caucus leaders just days after winning election before they were sworn in to office and before they really knew the candidates for whom they were voting. A shot in the dark is a far cry from merit-based selection. Given the number of times we were told by representatives that they would not vote for the same person if they had it to do over again, we give this an F.

Finally, term limits supporters asserted that they would reduce legislative gridlock. With a veteran governor who was described repeatedly as the "most influential member of the House," it would appear that gridlock decreased. It is not clear that this would have been true if the governor had not been a member of the party controlling the legislature, however. It is also unclear whether this would have happened had the governor not been a highly adept career politician. Additionally, it is not clear that having the governor dictate to a theoretically coequal branch of government is what ending gridlock means. If that is what it means, perhaps the goal should be questioned. Further, to some of us who sat in the gallery watching, there appears to have been a lot of times in which the majority party caucused to try to persuade a few members to change their votes. Thus the gridlock that occurred was intraparty "gridlock." Given the difficulty in assessing what does and does not qualify as gridlock, it is difficult to assess term limits ability to promote or inhibit this. Based on these mixed indications, we give term limits a grade of C here. This may be a case of overly generous grade inflation given that empowering the governor to the detriment of the House undermines our system of checks and balances.

Overall, term limits get 3 As, 3 Cs, and 5 Fs. The grade point average is an unimpressive D to D plus. This in and of itself should cause voters and term limits advocates themselves to reconsider whether this is an experiment worth keeping, at least in Michigan in its current form. Yet, this report card is less worrisome to us than what we feel are term limits' overarching effects on democratic governance.

Three Implications

There are three areas in which we are particularly concerned about the implications of term limits for democracy in the State of Michigan and in other term-limited states. These are representation of citizens' interests throughout the state, the state of deliberative policy-making, and the system of checks and balances fundamental to American democracy.

Representing a Diverse Citizenry

We found that term limits increased the advantages of incumbency, raised the cost of elections, especially in competitive districts, and may have reduced competition in elections. Additionally they seem to handicap Republican women and favor candidates with family or personal wealth. These trends suggest to us that various sources of bias in elections may be surfacing or at least become more prominent in the term limits era. As we noted throughout the book, the fundamental responsibility of the legislature is to represent the citizens of the state—all of them. This means not only that voters should have some choice among candidates to represent them, but that elected representatives need to consider and balance the interests of their own constituents with the interests of the state as a whole.

Given the diversity of Michigan and its resulting two-party system of government, representation of the state as a whole implies compromise and negotiation. The shift to one-party control of Michigan's state government that coincided with the implementation of term limits makes it difficult for us to disentangle the effects of these two changes. Therefore, it is plausible that some of the problems that surfaced should not be attributed solely to term limits.

Michigan historically has avoided what Elazar (1984) calls traditionalist political culture in which elites exert control over government institutions and through them preserve their privileged position in society.

Michigan's more populist political traditions have led to strong, but relatively moderate political parties that have successfully balanced various interests. This includes a range of economic groups and regional interests, from the highly industrialized southeastern region to the tourism and agricultural bases of the Lake Michigan shore and the more northern and western regions of the state. As Ballenger (1998) notes, previously, with experience, legislators moderated their ideological positions moving from both ends of the ideological spectrum toward the middle. After term limits, there is a large, 25 percentage point, gap between the ideological positions of legislators from the two political parties (Ballinger, 2003). We are hopeful with the return to divided government (specifically a Democratic governor and Republican-controlled legislative chambers) that partisan politics will resume their more moderate tone in Michigan. We are uncertain whether this will prompt legislators to moderate their political impulses, but it may at least precipitate more bipartisan compromise.

The Demise of Deliberative Policy-Making

Throughout our research we have heard about debate in committees that was limited to an hour on major legislation, an accelerated pace of bill reading and floor deliberations, dissent in committees being suppressed, and dissent during floor debates "fast gaveled" into silence. We have also demonstrated that friendships and coalition building across party lines have decreased and that conflict has sometimes become personalized. We were alarmed by reports from members of both political parties that major pieces of legislation have seen limited debate (sometimes as little as one hour) in committee hearings and been rushed through the chamber. In Michigan, bills receive what is called three readings. Having watched these readings from the gallery, we can attest that having someone stand and read the bill aloud to a virtually empty chamber seems pointless and inefficient. Yet it is precisely this "inefficiency" that provides legislators and their staffs with time to work through sections of a bill and explore its implications. As some people are fond of saying, the devil's in the details. Tales of voting on bills that were still warm from the copy machine suggest to us that deliberative policy-making has suffered and that many devilish details may be intentionally or inadvertently lurking in these laws.

Here again, there are factors other than term limits that at least contribute to this frenetic pace. Legislators were provided with laptop computers at their desks in the chamber in close proximity to the implementation of term limits. The electronic distribution of bill analysis and text has the potential to speed the legislative process. Yet it would still be possible to separate the reading of bills by periods of time that would allow legislators to inform themselves about what they are voting on. This however raises another aspect of deliberative policy-making that we wish to discuss—reliance on the caucus positions. There are many pros and cons of weak and strong parties, and that debate would extend well beyond the scope of our discussion here. Given Michigan's history of moderation within its parties, there has often been nearly the same level of conflict within the caucus as between the two parties. With the advent of highly expensive campaigns, especially for "vulnerable" members (those elected from the handful of truly competitive house districts), the party caucus controls a resource that is the lifeblood of these expensive campaigns—money. As we noted in chapter 2, with the advent of term limits, the role of the chamber's party caucus skyrocketed in distributing money raised by the political parties. This enables the parties' caucuses to enforce party discipline (voting for the caucus position if the vote is needed to pass a bill) even when the representative does not support the bill and his or her constituents would not support it. Yet despite the elevated importance of the caucus leadership, the election of these leaders is often a "shot in the dark" for newly elected representatives who don't know much if anything about their colleagues running for leadership positions. Thus we found that the fundraising ability of a representative was a major factor in his or her selection for a party leadership position within the chamber.

Trust, honesty, and credibility are the coin of the realm of good policymaking. Under term limits, the shortened terms of service with a known endpoint provide incentives for both legislators and other actors in the system to defect from compromises they've agreed to, to break promises, or to misrepresent either through errors of omission or commission the impact of policies. This is another facet of deliberative policy-making that has suffered in the term limits milieu. This undermines the ability of honest brokers to bridge the divide between the various constituencies in the state and address the needs and concerns of all factions.

Uncertainty about the credibility of information in the face of acute needs for information makes legislators vulnerable to biased or at least incomplete information. This empowers the actors with knowledge and information—the state agency officials, the representatives of organized groups or special interests, the staff, the Governor's office and, compared to the House, the Senate. This means that members of the

State House will continue to operate with a serious information disadvantage that is likely to weaken their ability to deliberate and negotiate policy. This relative disadvantage of the House compared to the other parties involved in government leads directly to our next area of concern.

Shortening One Leg of a Three-Legged Stool

Repeatedly throughout our research legislators gave us examples of ways in which the House was losing power to other branches of government and to other political actors, such as lobbyists. We discussed many of these in chapter 10. Although these comments could be seen as a self-serving way for legislators to undermine public perception that term limits should be retained, we are inclined to believe that they also accurately portray a major impact of term limits. One reason we find them credible is that other parties share the perception that the House is less powerful. Often when we go to interviews, the chamber session or a committee meeting has exceeded its scheduled time. So we sit and wait in the legislator's office, often chatting informally with their staff. On several occasions veteran staff confided in us about the latest gaffes of their boss or other representatives. We also interviewed most members of the pre–term limits State Senate to prepare to extend our research to the State Senate. So we heard from veteran Senators about their relationship with the novices in the lower chamber. Finally, as part of our academic teaching responsibilities, we train public administrators (a.k.a. bureaucrats), so we run into people who work in Michigan's state agencies. These people have mentioned situations that confirm information we have heard elsewhere. Therefore, we are inclined to believe representatives' comments about their loss of power, despite the potential for these to be self-serving comments.

Part of this weakening of the House probably results from the staggered implementation of term limits in Michigan. Part of it is systemic, however, given the tendency of the lower legislative chamber to be the entry point into state politics for career politicians, who have become so numerous after term limits.

As small "d" democrats, we are concerned about weakening the "people's chamber," as the lower chamber of a legislature is often called. We are even more concerned when it appears, as it does in our research, that this has strengthened the ability of the executive branch to dictate or at least heavily influence state policy-making. Here again, we acknowledge that the staggered implementation of term limits probably magnified this impact, but we also are concerned that term limits will permanently alter the checks and balances of Michigan's government. Once again, we are worried that a political system in which the "people's chamber" has lost some of its ability to check the excesses of other parts of government will increase unilateral policy-making dominated by one or a few key actors. It is unlikely that such a system would be able to balance Michigan's broad range of interests successfully.

Prospects for the Future

Increase Experience of Legislators, Especially in the House

Voters are likely to be asked to revisit term limits at the ballot box at some point in the future. When they do, we would encourage them to lengthen the limits. The shortness of Michigan's limits enhances the power of incumbency in ways that longer limits would not. Additionally, longer limits would allow caucus leaders to develop a track record on which legislators could make an informed choice. Further, longer limits would allow committee chairs to develop expertise in the areas under the jurisdiction of their committees and would allow them to develop skills in managing legislative debate—a prerequisite of deliberative policy-making. Finally, longer limits would restore some of the power to the House especially, but also to the legislature as a whole. More experience would enable representatives to oversee the work of state agencies, learn who to trust among the lobbyists, and to bargain more effectively with the executive branch. The suggestion of State Representative John Pappageorge, that overall legislative service be limited to 14 years in either chamber,[1] offers one possible way to develop some expertise within the House. Admittedly this would reduce the number of open seat elections as some representatives might continue to run for their seat for seven terms instead of three. Past evidence in Michigan's elections suggests that some of these incumbents would be challenged in primary elections and in the general election and would lose to the challengers. Indeed, we suspect that longer limits would increase the number of challengers that incumbents would face. This would seem to restore some accountability as well as some competition that has been lost with term limits. We would also support other suggestions that lengthen the limits on legislative service, such as increasing the length of service to 12 years in each chamber or simply repealing the limits altogether.

Ways to Increase Legislators' Accountability to Voters and Voters' Participation

Term limits advocates hoped that more open seat elections would reinvigorate the electorate. We applaud this sentiment. An engaged, informed electorate is one way to encourage elected officials to be responsive to voters' needs and concerns. Lack of voter participation is a major concern for us as political scientists committed to a healthy democracy. To our surprise, term limits decreased some forms of electoral competition. Less competitive elections will do little to resolve the problem of low voter turnout.

There are, however, other reforms that could be adopted by those concerned about increasing citizen participation. For example nested districts in which the extent of overlap between House and Senate districts increased would insure greater accountability to voters. In Michigan, with little overlap between State House and State Senate districts, politically ambitious legislators (and after term limits most of them are) have incentives in some districts to ignore the interests of current constituents in favor of their future constituents. In California with General Assembly districts that are an exact multiple of the State Senate districts, current constituents are always future constituents. Michigan's House districts are not multiples of the State Senate districts, so voters cannot adopt that approach without some fairly contentious debates over changing the number of House and Senate districts statewide. However, voters could try to amend the constitution to require that a certain percentage of House districts be included in State Senate districts. This might additionally reduce the ability of either political party to gerrymander voters into districts that concentrate the voting strength of one or the other political party into a few districts. This is facilitated by current computer models that allow district boundaries to be adjusted much more precisely than they were in the past. This practice often leads to underrepresentation of some citizens' views in the state legislature as a whole—a practice that appears to be gaining popularity most notably in Texas and a practice that we find particularly troubling.

Reducing the Power of Money and the Special Interests Who Provide It

The role of money in politics seems to be magnified by term limits. Although there are many campaign disclosure changes that we would advocate, we are not optimistic about the prospects for "true" campaign finance reform. Money like water always seems to find the cracks in any system meant to contain it. We do however think that more campaign contribution disclosure would at least help citizens learn about which interests their elected officials might be listening to.

We would make several specific recommendations. First and foremost it is important for the Secretary of State's office to "key in" candidates' campaign finance reports when they are not available electronically. This was an established practice prior to term limits that has been discontinued. Additionally, with the increased importance of caucus contributions and the increased importance of "leadership PACs" in the intraparty battles for legislative leadership positions, we believe it is important for these leadership PACs to be clearly identified and linked to the candidate involved and that records about these contributions need to be readily available. The prospects for achieving these reforms are low however given the incentives that exist for some elected officials and some interest groups to be discreet about these connections.

We think that the most promising form of campaign finance reform involves citizen participation. Donors don't need to have deep pockets if there are enough of them. As one of the authors tells students in an Introduction to American Government class, if every citizen in the State of Michigan had given the money equivalent to the cost of one six-pack of pop to a State House candidate, we could have outspent all the other donors in the 1998 State House races. We suspect that that might be the most effective form of campaign finance reform, and it requires no additional legislation. Based on the success of Howard Dean's internet fundraising, grassroots campaign finance has potential.

Changes to the Internal Rules of the Chamber

Finally, within the House, legislators complain bitterly about the leadership selection process. Although longer terms clearly would help this selection process, legislators themselves could make one change that would result in a minor improvement. Instead of electing these leaders during the week after the general election, they could wait and campaign for these internal leadership positions for three or four weeks between the general election and the caucus votes. This would provide newcomers with some opportunity to come to Lansing and watch the leadership candidates in action and to learn more about the candidates for these positions. The House has complete control over the rules governing its internal operation, and until voters make other changes in term limits, this would provide some limited help with one of the major problems legislators confront in doing the work of the House—and we would remind them the work of all the citizens of Michigan.

In the three areas of concern we addressed earlier in this chapter, we described a lack of negotiation, compromise, and deliberation over policy in the term-limited House. This problem could be addressed by fairly simple changes in the House rules that would require time for representatives to read and consider legislation. Additionally, if the House were required to consider bills proposed but not supported by a majority of the committee members, it would end the biased representation of Michigan's citizens in which only the citizen's whose representatives control the majority of the seats have their needs and concerns addressed. Although there are generally too many bills introduced in each session to consider them all (although the legislature in Maine does just that), the House could change its rules so that each representative had an opportunity to have at least one of his or her bills considered during each session. This would be likely to increase the number of new ideas considered by the legislature more dramatically than term limits have.

Evaluating Initiatives

Term limits achieved only a few of the goals its advocates hoped it would. Like many social and political experiments that seem simple on the surface, it had many unanticipated as well as unintended consequences—some positive, but unfortunately more negative. Making a change in a social or political system sends ripples through other parts of the system that may magnify instead of ameliorate the problems that motivated the reform effort. Thus, term limits produced results that are in several instances exactly the opposite of the effects voters were promised. This is a common problem with social and political experiments. Consequently many public policy scholars advise that change needs to be made incrementally. That means that small steps are initiated and then expanded gradually if the trajectory of the change seems to be moving in the desired direction.

Further, most public programs or policy innovations include some mechanism to assess their effects or evaluate their impacts. This is true of welfare reform, charter schools, prisoner education programs, and a host of other policy initiatives. Therefore, we believe it is important to study the impacts of social experiments such as term limits and, further, we believe that laws passed by citizen initiative should be subject to monitoring, oversight, and evaluation in the same way that other public programs would be (Barber, 1984). If public programs are found wanting, they often are revised or discontinued—as they should be. Unfortunately, citizen initiatives tend not to include evaluative components. We have advocated elsewhere (Trpovski et al., 2001b) that citizen initiatives should include sunset clauses. We reiterate that advice here, but also encourage voters, absent such clauses, to inform themselves and revisit term limits at the ballot box.

Ideally, Michigan's initial encounter with term limits would have been a modest, incremental program limiting service to a longer number of years. Then, citizens could have decided to shorten the limits if they found that there were mainly positive impacts. Unfortunately, Michigan leapt headlong into term limits and now needs to decide whether to abandon the experiment altogether or whether it might be worth another try, but with longer limits. Some of the unintended, detrimental effects we found result precisely because the service in Michigan is so short (e.g., the increased power of incumbency). Others may persist even with longer limits simply because the limits themselves, by signaling an endpoint in a relationship, tell "rational" actors when they should begin acting in a less than trustworthy manner.

We plan to continue our investigation of term limits effects, and we hope that reformers and other citizens, elected officials and other government actors, and other academics find our ongoing evaluation of term limits helpful and informative. We also hope that these actors will use the evidence we have amassed to "hold term limits accountable" for their impacts on state government.

Appendix

Interview Questions for Members of the Michigan House of Representatives

Form A

Introduction

Thank you for agreeing to talk with us. As you know, we are interviewing members of the House as part of a study to see how term limits may affect the House and the way members go about their work. To do so, we need to know as much as possible about how things are currently done prior to the imposition of term limits. We are asking essentially the same questions of all members of the House. Your participation is voluntary, and if there are any questions you do not wish to respond to, please feel free to say so. I assure you that everything you say will be kept confidential and that you will not be identified in any way in any of our reports on the research. Shall we begin?

1. When you initially ran for the House, what were your reasons for running?
2. Did some person or group ask you to run?
3. What groups do you consider among your strongest supporters?
4. Did any experienced legislator help you learn the job or coach you when you first came to the House?
5. Who do you consider to be the most influential members of the House? Why?
6. Do you have any especially good friends among the members of the House?
6a. Do friendships affect the work of the House? How?
7. I'd like to find out how you make up your mind on a bill that reaches the House floor. Let's take Schools of Choice, for example. Are there any fellow House members whom you would rely on for information and guidance on a bill about Schools of Choice?
8. I'd like to find out about sources other than fellow House members. Are there any sources outside the House membership that you would rely on for information and guidance on a bill about Schools of Choice?
9. In making up your mind on a bill about Schools of Choice, which of the sources of information and guidance that you have mentioned would you rely on most?
10. Let's consider a bill in another area. Let's talk about a bill licensing or regulating heath care professionals. Are there any fellow House members whom

you would rely on for information and guidance about a bill licensing or regulating health care professionals?

11. What about sources other than fellow House members? Are there any sources outside the House membership that you would rely on for information and guidance on a bill licensing or regulating heath care professionals?

12. Which of the sources that you have mentioned would you rely on most in making up your mind about a bill licensing or regulating heath care professionals?

13. I understand that you are a member of the ———— Committee. I would like to find out a number of things about the Committee and your work on it. In several of the questions I am going to ask, I would like you to tell me things about the Committee in terms of this continuum [hand the respondent a card with a scale of categories ranging from an enormous amount to none]. How much control would you say that the Chair of the ———— Committee has over the work of the committee? Why do you say that?

14. How much conflict would you say there is on the ———— Committee?

15. What are the sources of conflict? How is conflict dealt with?

16. What do you think was the most difficult issue that the ———— Committee seriously considered this term? Why was this difficult?

17. Thinking about this issue you just mentioned, I would like to know the extent to which you rely on various possible sources of information and guidance within the House in making up your mind on the issue. We will use the continuum we used before.

17.1 Let's begin with the Speaker. How much would say you relied upon the Speaker for information and guidance in making up your mind about the issue mentioned above?

17.2 What about the Party Caucus?

17.3 The Minority Party Leader?

17.4 The Committee Chair?

17.5 Other House members?

17.6 The Partisan Staff (Caucus or Committee if your party has staff)?

17.7 The Non-Partisan Staff (Legislative Service Bureau)?

17.8 The House Fiscal Agency?

18. Now I would like to know something about outside sources. Still thinking about the same issue you mentioned earlier, to what extent did you rely upon the sources outside of the House listed here for information and guidance in making up your mind on the issue?

18.1 Let's start with the Governor's Office? How much would you say you relied upon the Governor's Office for information and guidance in making up your mind about the issue mentioned above?

18.2 What about State Agency people?

18.3 State Senators?

18.4 Organized groups or Lobbyists?

18.5 Key local officials?

18.6 Advisors in your district?

18.7 Other constituents?

18.8 National Conference of State Legislatures?

18.9 Were there any other external sources that you rely on for information and guidance? Who?

19. How do you decide who to support for party leadership positions?

20. Now I am going to ask you about some things legislators typically spend time doing. Thinking about your work in the House, I'd like you to tell me the amount of time you personally spend on each of these, again using the continuum running from "An enormous amount" to "None".

20.1 What about studying proposed legislation? How much time would you say that you spend studying proposed legislation?

20.2 Developing new legislation?

20.3 Building coalitions in your own Party to pass legislation?

20.4 Building coalitions across party lines to pass legislation?

20.5 Monitoring state agencies?

20.6 Communicating with constituents?

20.7 Attending meetings and functions in your district?

20.8 Helping constituents with problems?

20.9 Making sure your district gets its fair share of government money and projects?

20.10 Fundraising?

20.11 Attending events sponsored by groups in Lansing?

21. Now I'd like you to give the House as a whole a letter grade (A to F) on the following things. You may add pluses or minuses if you like.

Passing good legislation;
Monitoring the implementation of programs;
Responding to constituents needs and concerns.

22. If there were a conflict between what you feel best and what the people in your district want, what would you do? Would you always do what the district wants, always do what you think is best, or would you be somewhere in between? [Provide card with scale running from 1 (always do what people in the district want) to 7 (always do what you think best)].

23. If there were a conflict between what is best for your district and best for the state, as a whole, what would you do? Would you always look after the needs of your district, always look after the needs of the state as whole, or would you be somewhere in between? [Provide card with scale running from 1 (always look after my district) to 7 (always look after the state)].

24. What do you think will be the most important impact of term limits on the House?

25. What do you think will be the most important impact of term limits on state government generally?

26. What do you plan to do when you are termed out of the House? Do you plan to run for another public office?

Notes

Introduction

1. This initiative also limited to eight years the terms of State Senators, the Governor, Lt. Governor, Attorney General, and Secretary of State.
2. Based on a survey of 600 registered voters conducted during the week of March 18–21, 2001. Forty-seven percent of those surveyed would have voted yes or were leaning toward voting yes if a repeal of term limits had been on the ballot at that time. An equal number would have voted no or were leaning toward no. Six percent of those surveyed were undecided. Margin of error 4%. EPIC-MRA Report, March 2001.
3. Based on a survey of 770 adults conducted by Wayne State University's Center for Urban Studies between June 27, 2003 and August 1, 2003. Margin of error of 3.5% with a 95% confidence interval.
4. Based on information from Rep. Pappageorge, which refers to a poll conducted by Mitchell Research and Communications, Inc.
5. California is the other.
6. The other two states that have equally truncated legislative service in the lower chamber are California and Arkansas. In all other states with term limits, it is possible to serve for eight or more years in the lower chamber.
7. We treat our "ordinal" data as interval appearing data, where increments exist between numbers such as 3 and 4. We do this because we actually collected responses falling between these points, permitting legislators to say 3.5 or even 3.75. Often, a legislator would say "Between 3 and 4." We do understand that there are controversies about the reliability of using interval level statistics on these kind of data, but given our face-to-face data collection mode and the encouragements we provided, our procedures seem justified.
8. Because these difference measures produce ratio-level data in which zero denotes the average amount of consulting, positive values denote more than average consulting and negative values denote less than average, we are able to use a broader array of statistically procedures on them with greater confidence in our results. These advantages come at a cost, however. The difference measure is difficult to interpret. Therefore we often report the mean values from the ordinal scale. By combining the two measures, we try to

capitalize on the strength of both. The difference measure, additionally, allows us to rely heavily on analysis of variance, which is a statistical technique that is particularly well suited for investigating interaction effects, which we suspected and found to be the most profound effects of term limits.

9. Herrick et al. (1994) found last-term effects among U.S. Representatives no longer seeking reelection. Carey (1996) in his early comparative work on term limits also found substantial evidence of last-term effects in the Latin American legislatures he studied. It is perhaps not surprising that people's motivations and behavior tend to change in their last term in office. Elsewhere, we have found last-term effects on constituency relations in the Michigan House and noted that such effects become much more pronounced and consequential when institutionalized through term limits (Wilson et al., 2001). Stratmann (2000) has found significant first-term effects in congressional voting behavior. We have also found evidence in the Michigan House of first-term effects with respect to reliance on partisan cues, a pattern that is also accentuated by term limits (Rader, Elder and Elling, 2001). In our conversations with House members, there have also been suggestions of possible second-term effects under Michigan's three-term limitation rule. More specifically, it has been suggested that power and responsibility have tended to gravitate to second-term legislators. If so, this may affect how they relate to organized interests in comparison to their first-term and their last-term peers.

1   Electoral Competition and Incumbency Advantages

1. Authorship of this chapter includes Dr. Jean-Philippe Faletta, University of Saint Thomas, Houston, TX.
2. The vast majority of House seats in Michigan are safe for one party or the other (source: Bill Ballenger's *Inside Michigan Politics*).
3. In previous work, we concentrated on the number of open seat general election races. Here we focus on primary elections, and we adjust for special elections.
4. Based on voting age population.
5. In California the primaries for state offices coincide with the presidential primary. In Michigan, primaries are segregated by party and are held during the first week in August, well after its Republican presidential primary and Democratic presidential caucus. In Michigan, registered independents may vote in either party's primary.
6. For example, Gierzynski and Breaux (1998) find that in the mid-1980s and early 1990s, state party organizations targeted campaign resources at candidates running for open seats and in districts that are highly competitive.

2   Funding Campaigns in a Term-Limited House

1. Authorship of this chapter includes Lisa Marckini, doctoral candidate at Wayne State University.

2. See Eismeier & Pollock (1986), Gordon & Unmack (2003), Thompson & Cassie (1992), Thompson, Cassie, & Jewell (1994).
3. See Dow, Endrsby, & Menifield (1998), Grier & Munger (1986, 1991 and 1993), Gopoian (1984), Endersby & Munger (1992).
4. See Poole, Romer, & Rosenthal (1987), Evans (1996), Poole and Romer (1985), Gopoian (1984).
5. We assume that soft money was about as likely to flow to candidates for either legislative chamber. Although we acknowledge that this assumption could be wrong, we have no evidence to indicate that it is.
6. This "soft money" issue presents a less serious problem for our analysis to the extent that Gierzinski and Breaux (1998) are correct in their judgment that only a relatively small percentage of nonfederal soft money was contributed directly to state and local candidates (p. 204). On the other hand, it appears that a much more substantial amount was contributed to state party committees. These committees most certainly must have used some of these dollars in ways that freed up "hard money" that could then be contributed to various candidates for state office.
7. Beginning in 2000, data for candidates raising more than $50,000 will be kept for fifiteen years.
8. Candidates who raise less than $1,000 per election (primary and general elections are separate elections) do not have to file campaign contribution reports. They do however have to request a filing waiver from the Secretary of State's office.
9. We knew several characteristics of the candidates for whom campaign contribution data were missing. These included their vote totals, their party, whether they were running for an open seat or not, and whether they were running for a competitive seat or not. So, we used these variables to predict the contributions for each of these candidates. This was done four times—for each session and each chamber. Based upon these equations, we also predicted contributions for the candidates for whom we did not have reports. Using these predicted amounts, we estimated total contribution for each chamber. The equations varied by chamber and by election. Given that equations used logs, we had to take the antilogs of the predictions to get our final results.

For the 1990 House the equation was:

$$\text{Logged Total Contributions} = 8.079 + (0.000092 * \text{total vote}) + (0.962 * \text{Democratic Party dummy}).$$

The R^2 was 0.326. All variables in this and the other final equations were significant at least at the 0.05 level.

For the 1990 Senate the equation was:

$$\text{Logged Total Contributions} = 9.591 + (0.00003782 * \text{total vote}) + (-0.615 * \text{Democratic Party dummy}) + (0.706 * \text{competitive race dummy}).$$

The R^2 was 0.459.

For the 1998 House the equation was:

Logged Total Contributions = 8.059 + (0.0001005 * total vote) + (−0.278 * Democratic Party dummy) + (0.249 * competitive race dummy) + (0.469 * open seat dummy).

The R^2 was 0.379.

For the 1998 Senate the equation was:

Logged Total Contributions = 9.493 + (0.00003643 * total vote) + (−1.019 * Democratic Party dummy).

The R^2 was 0.351.

10. This value was 1.23454 to deflate 1998 dollars to 1990 dollars.
11. Time is the quintessential zero–sum commodity. If I spend time at a movie, I have less time to do something else.
12. We rely on a rolling average of base party voting strength provided by Bill Balenger of Inside Michigan Politics to determine which districts are competitive.
13. This is a question we hope to explore in the future.

3   The Interest Group Connection: Money, Access, and Support

1. In order to compare campaign contributions from different years it is necessary to adjust for inflation. We do this using the July Consumer Price Index in each year. Given that we sometimes discuss 1990 contributions, we use this as our baseline year and "deflate" all other dollars to their 1990 value.
2. These reports, called annual reports by the Michigan Secretary of State's Office, are filed in January after the calendar year in which the contributions are given. Therefore, contributions listed on the 1998 annual report were given to the last pre–term limits representatives during the calendar year 1997, not an election year. Similarly, contributions listed on the 2000 annual report were given to the first post–term limits cohort of representatives in 1999, the year after they were elected. The 2002 annual report records contributions given during calendar year 2001.
3. Using a log to the base ten of these contributions minimizes the effect of these few outliers, and produces a very small, but statistically significant difference between the majority and minority parties. Without this adjustment, the average amount given to the two political parties' members does not differ significantly.
4. Using two-way analysis of variance, we found that the interaction effect between term limits and the legislator's terms of experience was statistically significant at $p < 0.04$ using an F-test statistic. Dependent variable: difference between average time and time spent in Lansing attending events sponsored by groups.

Term limits	Length of service	Mean	Std. error	95% confidence interval	
				Lower bound	Upper bound
Pre–term limits	1st term	−0.374	0.156	−0.680	−0.068
	2nd term	−0.099	0.163	−0.420	0.223
	Lame duck	−0.551	0.101	−0.750	−0.352
Post–term limits	1st term	−0.227	0.085	−0.394	−0.060
	2nd term	−0.439	0.085	−0.607	−0.271
	Lame duck	−0.274	0.123	−0.516	−0.031

5. Pearson correlation coefficient was 0.42 before term limits, significant at $p < 0.001$ and 0.24 after term limits, significant at $p < 0.001$.

6. A particularly accessible discussion of this strategy by elected officials is available on the PBS Video called the "Power Game" with Hedrick Smith. The part of the series about the "unelected" discusses the efforts by Tom DeLay to extract large contributions from organized groups and to signal them in meetings with them that he was keeping track of the amount they had given.

7. Using two-way analysis of variance, we found no main effect of term limits and no interaction effect between term limits and the number of terms of service. The main effect of terms of service was only slightly statistically significant at $p < 0.14$ using an F-test statistic. Dependent variable: difference between average time and time spent fundraising

Terms served	Mean	Std. error	95% confidence interval	
			Lower bound	Upper bound
1st term	−0.656	0.103	−0.860	−0.453
2nd term	−0.429	0.107	−0.640	−0.217
Lame duck	−0.696	0.094	−0.881	−0.512

8. Pearson correlation coefficient was .31 before term limits, significant at $p < 0.001$ and .22 after term limits, significant at $p < 0.002$.

9. Using two-way analysis of variance, we found that the interaction effect between term limits and the legislator's terms of experience was statistically significant at $p < 0.07$ using an F-test statistic. Dependent variable: difference between extent of consulting of lobbyists and average consulting

Level of experience	Term limits	Mean	Std. error	95% confidence interval	
				Lower bound	Upper bound
1st term	Pre–term limits	0.540	0.217	0.114	0.967
	Post–term limits	0.702	0.120	0.466	0.938

Continued

2nd term	Pre–term limits	0.401	0.227	−0.046	0.848
	Post–term limits	0.759	0.125	0.513	1.005
Lame duck	Pre–term limits	0.915	0.148	0.624	1.207
	Post–term limits	0.490	0.185	0.125	0.855

4 The New Breed of Term-Limited State Legislators

1. Authorship of this chapter includes Dr. Jean-Philippe Faletta, University of Saint Thomas, Houstan, TX and Eric Rader, doctoral candidate, Wayne State University.

2. Based on information generously provided to the authors by the National Conference of State Legislatures.

3. Prompted by a concern with the diminished attractiveness of seats in the legislature, the state commission responsible for recommending salary adjustments for state officials recommended a substantial salary increase for Michigan legislators. The recommendation was accepted by default under rules that have since been changed via a statewide initiative, and state legislators in Michigan commanded an annual salary in 2001 of $77,400 and $79,650 in 2002.

4. Discussions of the extent to which particular groups are over- or underrepresented typically make use of ratio measures, where the numerator is the percentage of members of a particular group that are present in a particular institutions (a legislative body, an administrative agency, the enrollment of a particular university etc.) and the denominator is the proportion of a larger reference population that consists of members of the focal group. In discussing how term limits have impacted on the composition of state legislatures, we will make use of such a measure. Thus, if African Americans, e.g., constitute 2% of the membership of a given legislative body, but they comprise 12.5% of the population of the state in which this legislative body is located, the index of representation for African Americans would be 2% divided by 12.5%, or 0.16. This measure has a lower bound of 0.00. If the composition of a given legislative body with respect to a particular group exactly matches their presence in a state's population, the index value would be 1.00. If a group is "overrepresented" in a given body, the index for such a group would exceed 1.00 by some amount.

5. Although there is some debate about this among political scientists (e.g., Lublin, 1999 and Cameron et al., 1996), African American candidates do not seem to be dependent upon majority-minority districts to win elections, except in the deep south.

6. Speaker Pro Tempore currently receives an additional salary increment, but this was not true in the early years that we compare. To maintain consistency across the terms we compare, we only examined the top five leadership positions.

5 Career Paths of Term-Limited State Legislators

1. One of the theories behind term limits advocates' preference for citizen legislators was that they would be more responsive to their constituents because
   they would go back to live among them. Alternatively, the prospect of
   running for another political office could be viewed as insurance that lame
   ducks will still respond to the constituents.
2. Some of these offices (e.g., township supervisor or school board member), are
   not full-time positions while others are (e.g., mayor of a large city or service
   on county commissions in large, heavily populated counties).
3. We relied on the Michigan Manual, 1990–2002, and Inside Michigan
   Politics, special issues on House Freshmen, 1998, 2000, and 2002.
4. Given the potentially mixed motives of those elected in 1994 and 1996 and
   the ambiguous status of term limits during this time, they form a unique
   cohort. Thus, we excluded them from some of our comparisons between the
   pre–term limits veterans and the post–term limits cohort.
5. Although several representatives were elected in two or more of these sessions,
   we count their prior experience only once during the year that they were first
   elected. Additionally, although we have not yet interviewed the 2003–2004
   legislators, we have information from their biographies about their prior
   political experience that we include in this section. The increase in prior
   political experience was statistically significant at the $p < 0.001$ level using a
   contingency coefficient.
6. Some respondents has served both in Lansing and at the local level.
7. This difference is statistically significant at the $p < 0.07$ level using
   Chi-squared.
8. Given that we interviewed three cohorts of representatives and that most
   representatives served in two or more of these legislative terms, we interviewed some respondents more than once. For example, in a few cases we
   interviewed a legislator in 1998 as a newcomer to the House, in 2000 as a
   second-term representative, and again in 2002 as a lame duck. In most analyses in this chapter we avoided double counting representatives who were
   interviewed about more than one term of House service because we were
   analyzing things that did not change, such as their prior career or the first
   time they ran for the House. Therefore it was important to count their
   responses only once. In analyzing future career plans, however, we noticed
   changes across time for the same respondents and treated each level of experience in the legislature separately. Thus we will discuss the sort of future
   career plans people have at the end of their first term in the House separately
   from the plans they have at the end of their second term and so on. By doing
   so we compare newcomers, serving their first term in the 1997–1998 session
   to newcomers serving in the 1999–2000 and 2001–2002 sessions. We also
   can trace two cohorts through time, one serving their first term in
   1997–1998 can be traced through three sessions, and another cohort, those
   serving their first session in 1999–2000, can be traced through two sessions,

to see how their plans changed along the way through their brief careers in the State House.

9. Progressive ambition technically refers to moving up the electoral ladder from local, to State, to national, or statewide office. We coined the term "sustained ambition" to denote the patterns of moving from the local to the State level and back to the local level.

10. We checked primary elections for state-level offices, for judges and for county commission races in large counties, and local elections in large cities. We also used personal contacts and connections to trace the career paths of termed-out legislators. We suspect that some local elections and other races may have been missed. We continue to collect additional data about the career paths of termed-out legislators, and we suspect that we may have understated the number who continued in some form of elected public service.

11. The reason this was unique to Democrats was the Republicans controlled the redistricting based on the 2000 census, so Democrats in the House were often pitted against an incumbent Republican in a district drawn to provide the advantage to the Republican—in other words the districts were gerrymandered.

6 Home Style Under Term Limits: Responsiveness to Constituents

1. Members of the Costa Rican national Legislative Assembly are elected to serve four-year terms. Since 1949, they have not been permitted to immediately stand for reelection following the end of their terms. They can, however, seek election to additional terms at some point in the future and there is no limit on the number of nonconsecutive terms that they can serve. Carey finds, however, that the proportion of Costa Rican legislators serving more than a single term is quite small (pp. 77–78).

2. These results are based on a three-way analysis of variance including categories based on pre– and post–term limits expulsions, lame duck status versus more allowable terms in the State House, and whether the respondent said that he or she was considering running for another elected office after he or she could no longer serve in the State House. The main effect of lame duck status was the only statistically significant effect found. It was significant at the $p < 0.05$ level.

3. Again these findings are based on a three-way analysis of variance including status of term limits, lame duck status and plans to run for another elected office. The main effect of lame duck status and the main effect of plans to run for another elected office were both statistically significant at the $p < 0.05$ level.

4. The main effect of lame duck status was statistically significant at $p < 0.1$ and the main effect of plans to run for another office was statistically significant at $p < 0.01$.

5. The main effect for term limits was statistically significant at the $p < 0.13$ level and the interaction effect between term limits and plan to run for another elected office was statistically significant at the $p < 0.08$ level.

6. As noted elsewhere, given that we have interviewed approximately 85% of the population for these three House sessions, we report findings at the $p < 0.15$ level to avoid accepting the null hypothesis when there is indeed an effect. In this instance, the main effect of lame duck status on time spending getting money and projects for the district is significant at the 0.12 level.

7. Before term limits expulsions the mean was 1.07 and afterward it was 1.48, with 1 signifying "a little" and 2 signifying "some." For those able to serve again in the House, the mean was 1.10 and for lame ducks it was 1.45. In both cases these increases were statistically significant at $p < 0.05$.

8. The interaction effect between term limits expulsions and plans to seek another elected office was statistically significant at $p < 0.07$.

9. These effects are statistically significant only at the very relaxed level ($p < 0.15$) we adopted given that we have interviewed more than 85 % of the population.

10. This main effect was statistically significant at $p < 0.05$.

11. This main effect was statistically significant at $p < 0.07$.

12. Based on a two-way analysis of variance using an F test statistic, we found that both main effects and the interaction effect were statistically significant at $p < 0.1$ for the effect of term limits and at $p < 0.001$ for minority or majority party and for the interaction between term limits and majority or minority party.

Dependent variable: 22-grade given to the entire House for responding to the needs and concerns of voters

Term limits	Opposition party	Mean	Std. error	95% confidence interval	
				Lower bound	Upper bound
Pre–term limits	Majority party members	8.375	0.367	7.651	9.099
	Minority party members	7.825	0.403	7.032	8.618
Post–term limits	Majority party members	8.968	0.288	8.400	9.536
	Minority party members	6.043	0.283	5.486	6.600

7 Networking in the House: Winning Friends and Influencing People

1. This term refers to those legislators whose districts are so closely divided between the two major political parties that they are always vulnerable to defeat in the next election.

2. A newly built house office building assigned representatives' offices by district number. Although this was unrelated to term limits, it coincided with their adoption and may have contributed to more regional friendships or at least reinforced those friendships.

3. Given that members of the majority party are much more likely to consult the speaker than are members of the minority party, we limited the following analyses to members of the majority party. Using the difference between consulting the speaker and the average level of consulting as the dependent variable and service on appropriations and the status of term limits as the two categorical variables, we found that the direct effects of both variables were statistically significant at $p < 0.1$ and $p < 0.01$ respectively. Additionally, the interaction between being term-limited and service on appropriations was statistically significant at $p < 0.12$. The means for the four categories were: -0.121 and -0.136 for the pre–term limits cohort for those not on appropriations and those on appropriations and -0.313 and -0.886 for the post–term-limits cohorts for those not on appropriations and those on appropriations. The negative values indicate that the amount of consulting directed toward the speaker is less than the average level of consulting, and it is the lowest for the post–term limits appropriation committee members. The dependent variable ranges from -2.4 to 3.5. We also investigated the effect of these categorical variables on the amount of consulting reported. The interaction effect was statistically significant at $p < 0.05$. Means for those not on the appropriations committee were identical, 0.99, regardless of term limits. This indicates that those not on the appropriations committee consulted the speaker slightly less than a little regardless of whether they served before or after term limits expulsions. Those on the appropriations committee prior to term limits expulsions consulted the speaker at a mean level of 1.5, half way between a little and some. Those on appropriations after term limits consulted the speaker on a difficult issue considered in their committee at a mean level of 0.72, less than "a little."

4. The means for coalition building within the same party were 2.48 before term limits and 2.46 after term limits. The means for building coalitions across party lines were 2.49 before term limits and 2.22 after. As we have done in earlier chapters, we used a difference measure to explore changes in the priority of these activities compared to the average amount of time spent on the entire series of activities. The mean difference for building coalitions within the same party was -0.06 before term limits and -0.09 after term limits, neither substantively nor statistically significantly different. The mean

difference for building coalitions across party lines was −0.06 but dropped to –0.33 after term limits, a statistically significant difference ($t = 2.9$, significant at $p < 0.004$.

8 Conflict, Compromise, and Partisanship: Committees Under Term Limits

1. Authorship of this chapter includes Jovan Trpovski, a doctoral candidate at Wayne State University and Professor of Political Science at Valencia Community College, Orlando, FL 32825.

2. When we asked respondents the questions about committees, we selected a committee on which each representative served and asked several of the committee questions described earlier specifically about that committee. We did this to provide concrete referents for respondents and to avoid having them respond hypothetically. In choosing which committees to ask about, we balanced two competing factors: broad coverage of the full range of different types of committees and enough responses about a committee to feel confident that the perceptions reported were not highly skewed. We chose five committees: appropriations, taxation, transportation, tourism and consumer protection, to ask about when interviewing representatives who served on one of them. These committees were chosen because they included two highly partisan issue areas, consumer protection and taxation, and two that concern issues that cross party lines and tend to form coalitions based on geographic and regional alliances, transportation and tourism. Finally, the crucial role played by the Appropriations Committee convinced us that it was important to cover that committee extensively. If a representative did not serve on any of these five committees, we asked about another committee on which he or she served. We chose these other committees to insure that we covered a broad range of the standing committees in the House. This is particularly important for these analyses to use a measure of relative importance because not only did the committee we asked about differ from respondent to respondent, but the respondent him or herself picked the "difficult issue" that we used to focus the questions. Therefore, some respondents might have picked issues about which they consulted very extensively, so that a response of "some" might be relatively low. Other respondents might have picked issues about which they consulted only to a limited extent. Therefore the same response of "some" might be a relatively high or even the highest level of consulting on that issue. Thus, we analyze the relative prominence of the source in the respondent's overall consulting on the specific issue instead of the absolute value on the scale.

3. In 1999–2000 one Michigan Committee chair had been elected for 3.5 terms in the 1980s prior to being reelected in the 1990s. Those terms of service did not count toward his maximum of 3 House terms because they occurred before the term limits law passed in 1992.

4. This is consistent with levels of pre– and post–term limits chair experience found in California (Clucas, 2000). Moen & Palmer (2000) looking at the part-time Maine legislature finds much lower levels of pre–term limits chair experience and thus a smaller change after term limits.

5. This difference is statistically significant at the $p < 0.01$ level using an F-test statistic.

6. Typically we would follow the same pattern of multivariate analysis that we did in chapter 6 when we explore the combination of term limits and lame duck status on representatives' responsiveness to constituents. But we cannot disentangle these two effects with respect to committees because there are so many veteran chairs and so few first- and second-term chairs before term limits. There were no third-term chairs in the 1997–1998 House and only one freshman chair. Therefore, the two variables we would like to include in the multivariate analyses are too highly correlated for us to disentangle their effects. Therefore, we can compare only the second-term legislators before and after term limits.

7. Even before term limits, Clucas (1998) ranks Michigan's House Speaker as the fourth most powerful in the nation.

8. Using a t-test to compare the two parties after term limits, the difference found was statistically significant at the $p < 0.05$ level.

9. We do not have enough cases to subdivide the Appropriations Committee members into subgroups to perform the comparable analyses on their reliance on subcommittee chairs.

10. These results are based on a two-way analysis of variance. The means reported were for the interaction between the status of term limits and membership in the opposition party. The analysis was limited to members of the policy committees. Using an F-test, the interaction effect was found to be statistically significant at $p < 0.03$.

11.

Session	1991–1992	1993–1994	1995–1996	1997–1998	1999–2000	2001–2002
Maximum sessions of service	3	4	5	6	3	3
Mean of means for sessions of committee service	2.18	2.02	2.19	2.23	1.24	1.51

12. It is worth noting that the means for each committee across all six pre–term limits sessions differ only slightly from a high of 2.14 sessions of prior service on the Appropriations Committee to a low of 1.22 on committees with jurisdiction over senior citizens' issues.

13. We analyzed 17 of these sources of information and guidance here. Other sources of information and guidance are discussed in other chapters.

14. Using an F-test to measure the interaction effect between the status of term limits and opposition party members, the interaction effect is statistically

significant at $p < 0.03$. Using a t-test to compare means the difference between newcomers and more seasoned committee members was statistically significant at $p < 0.15$. There were too few newcomers in the 1997–1998 session to test for an interaction effect with the status of term limits.

15. In 1991 Democrats controlled the House, in 1993 there was split control (the infamous stereo speakers), in 1995 the Republicans controlled the House, in 1997 the Democrats were back in control, and in 1999 and 2001 the Republicans resumed control.

9   How Legislators Decide to Vote

1. The exact wording of these questions follows: "Are there any fellow House members whom you would rely on for information and guidance in making up your mind about a bill about Schools of Choice?" Are there any sources outside the House on which you would rely for information and guidance on a bill about Schools of Choice? Which of all these sources of information that you've mentioned would you rely on most for information and guidance on Schools of Choice? And "Are there any fellow House members whom you would rely on for information and guidance in making up your mind about a bill licensing or regulating health care professionals?" Are there any sources outside the House on which you would rely for information and guidance on a bill about licensing or regulating health care professionals? Which of all these sources of information that you've mentioned would you rely on most for information and guidance on licensing or regulating health care professionals?

2. We treated this response as distinct from those representatives who said that after listening to a wide range of sources they would weigh and balance the information. Those who said they would integrate multiple sources of information decreased from 13.3% before term limits to 9.3% after term limits.

3. Compared to the pre–term limits session, the betweenness of actors increased dramatically in both post–term limits sessions, but especially in the 2001–2002. High betweenness indicates critical links in a consulting network with the potential for restricting or disseminating information throughout the system—in other words gatekeepers. Technically the betweenness of a node in a network is the proportion of the geodesics connecting a pair of points that include the node. This could be visualized by thinking of two sets of triangles. One set is connected by one common vertex. The second is connected by two common vertices. The first has the highest beteweenness because the one common vertex is the only path through which information can flow between the two triangles. The highest betweenness score in the pre–term limits school choice consulting network was 28.5 units. The maximum betweenness for the 1999–2000 and 2001–2002 session was 155.5 units and 406.33 units respectively. This is evidence of choke points or key information disseminators in the post–term limits school choice consulting networks. We confirmed this using another measure of the connectedness of a network, the number of other

representatives (alters) within two links of a focal representative (ego). We found that in the pre–term limits House an average of 23.6 other representatives were within two links of each "ego." In the two post–term limits session, an average of only 18.8 and 18.7 representatives were within two links of each "ego." This suggests post–term limits school choice consulting networks in which information flows less freely than it did prior to term limits. Further, we found a correlation of $r = 0.3$ (statistically significant at $p < 0.01$) between the betweenness of actors in the friendship network and the number of times the actor was named as a source of information and guidance on school choice.

4. This difference was statistically significant at $p < 0.10$ using a contingency coefficient.

5. This difference was statistically significant at $p < 0.11$ using a contingency coefficient.

6. On the other hand, the number of other representatives that can be linked with a given representative (ego) within two connections increased from nearly 11 before term limits to nearly 22 and 27.5 in 1999–2000 and 2001–2002 respectively.

7. To do this we calculated a point connectivity matrix for each matrix for each session. Point connectivity is the number of vertices that would have to be removed from the matrix to isolate the node from all other actors. The number of vertices that would have to be removed enumerates the number of paths in the network that connect the pair of actors. Large sample sizes make it relatively easy to achieve statistical significance for substantively trivial relationships. Given that a 110 by 110 produces 11,990 nodes, an exceedingly large sample size, we are less concerned about the statistical significance of the correlation between these matrices than with the size of the correlation.

10   Checks and Balances: Intragovernmental Relationships and Outside Influences

1. Based on a one-way analysis of variance.

2. Both main effects were statistically significant at $p < 0.01$, but the interaction effect between term limits and service on the appropriations committee was not statistically significant. Dependent variable: difference of average time and time spent monitoring state agencies

Term limits	On appropriations	Mean	Std. error	95% confidence interval	
				Lower bound	Upper bound
Pre–term limits	Not on the approps. committee	−0.740	0.102	−0.940	−0.540
	On appropriations	0.069	0.169	−0.264	0.401
Post–term limits	Not on the approps. committee	−0.960	0.072	−1.102	−0.818
	On appropriations	−0.380	0.126	−0.628	−0.132

3. Both the main effects and the interaction effect of term limits and majority or minority party were statistically significantly different at $p < 0.01$ for the main effects and $p < 0.05$ for the interaction effect, based on an F-test statistic. Dependent variable: grade given to the House for monitoring implementation of programs

Term limits	Opposition party	Mean	Std. error	95% confidence interval	
				Lower bound	Upper bound
Pre–term limits	Majority party members	5.588	0.338	4.922	6.254
	Minority party members	4.425	0.382	3.673	5.177
Post–term limits	Majority party members	5.392	0.265	4.870	5.913
	Minority party members	3.012	.262	2.496	3.528

4. Democrats reported spending nearly "some" time on this (mean of 1.9) compared to Republicans (1.7). This difference was statistically significant using one-way analysis of variance at the $p < 0.7$ level using an F-test statistic.

5. We will continue our investigation of the impact of term limits on bureaucratic oversight during the 2003-2004 legislative term, now that Michigan's chief executive officer is Democratic Governor Jennifer Granholm.

6. When asked about increased power for the governor and decreased power for legislators, 10.9% of the respondents said this would be a good thing, 20.2% said it would be a bad thing and 58.9% said they were uncertain. When asked about increased power going to bureaucrats at the expense of legislators, 7.11% said this would be a good thing, 29.4% said it would be a bad thing, and 56.7% said they were uncertain. Finally, when asked about increased power for the lobbyists and decreased power for legislators, 9.7% said this would be a good thing, 38.9% said it would be a bad thing and 46.1% were uncertain. (Based a Center for Urban Studies Survey conducted in summer of 2003 with 770 Michigan adults. Margin of error 3.5% with a 95% confidence interval.)

11 Conclusions: Term Limits' Report Card

1. Currently legislators can achieve 14 years of service total, but it must be split between the two chambers with six years permitted in the House and eight years permitted in the Senate.

References

Ainsworth, S.H. "The Role of Legislators in the Determination of Interest Group Influence." *Legislative Studies Quarterly* 22, no. 4 (1997): 517–533.

Axelrod, Robert. *The Evolution of Cooperation.* New York: Basic Books, 1984.

Ballenger, William S. "Base Party Strength: How Important Is It?" *Inside Michigan Politics* 6.35 (1998): 1–4. Copyright Inside Michigan Politics, 2029 South Waverly Road, Lansing, MI 48917.

Ballenger, William S. "State Representatives: Hoogendyke 'perfectly conservative,' Cheeks, Clack Most Liberal." *Inside Michigan Politics* 9.20 (2003): 1–4. Copyright Inside Michigan Politics, 2029 South Waverly Road, Lansing, MI 48917.

Barber, Benjamin. *Strong Democracy.* University of California Press, 1984.

Barnard, C.I. *The Function of the Executive.* Cambridge, MA: Harvard University Press, 1938.

Barnhart, Michael. "A Study of Term Limitation and the House." Ph.D. diss., Wayne State University, 1999.

Bearry, B., Julie Harrelson-Stephens, & Lisa Uhlir. "Legislators' Perceptions: Interest Group Reward and Punishment." Paper presented at the annual meeting of the Midwest Political Science Association Annual Meeting, Chicago, April 2001.

Bell, Dawson. "Term Limits, B Yes: Likely Shake-up now Likely in Lansing, Congress." *Detroit Free Press,* November 4, 1992, sec. A.

Benjamin, Gerald & Michael J. Malbin, eds. "California Ballot Pamphlet: Pros and Cons of Proposition 140." In *Limiting Legislative Terms.* Washington, DC: CQ Press, 1992.

Bienenstock, E.J. "New Models for Exchange Networks: A Research Proposal." Paper Presented at the Conference on Social Networks, University of California at Santa Barbara, Social Networks, 2, 1990.

Bienenstock, E.J., P. Bonacich, & M.L. Oliver. "The Effect of Network Density and Homogeneity on Attitude Polarization." *Social Networks* 12 (1990): 153–172.

Bledsoe, Timothy & Mary Herring. "Victims of Circumstances: Women in Pursuit of Political Office." *American Political Science Review* 84, no. 1 (1990): 213–223.

Brace, Paul and Daniel S. Ward. "The Institutionalized Legislature and the Rise of the Antipolitics Era." *In American state and Local Politics.* Chapter 4. New York: Chatham House Publishers, 1999.

Breaux, David & M.E. Jewell. "Winning Big: The Incumbency Advantage in State Legislative Races." In *Changing Patterns in State Legislative Careers.* Edited by G.F. Moncrief and J.A. Thompson. Ann Arbor: University of Michigan Press, 1992.

Brown, Clifford W., Lynda W. Powell, and Clyde Wilcox. *Serious Money: Fundraising and Contributing in Presidential Nomination Campaigns.* New York: Cambridge University Press, 1995.

Burrell, Barbara. "The Political Opportunity of Women Candidates for the U.S. House of Representatives in 1984." *Women and Politics* (1988): 51–68.

Burrell, Barbara. "The Presence of Women Candidates and the Role of Gender in Campaigns for the State Legislature in an Urban Setting: The Case of Massachusetts." *Women and Politics* 19 (1990): 85–102.

Cain, Bruce E., John Ferejohn, and Morris Fiorina. *The Personal Vote: Constituency Service and Electoral Independence.* Cambridge, MA: Harvard University Press, 1987.

California Journal, "Up Front." (November 1991): 490.

Caldeira, G.A., J.A. Clark, & S.C. Patterson. "Political Respect in the Legislature" *Legislative Studies Quarterly* 18, no. 1 (1993): 3–28.

Cameron, Charles, David Epstein, Sharyn O'Halloran. "Do Majority-Minority Districts Maximize Substantive Black Representation in Congress?" *American Political Science Review* 90, no. 4 (1996): 794–812.

Caress, Stanley, Charles Elder, Richard Elling, Jean-Philippe Faletta, Shannon Orr, Eric Rader, Marjorie Sarbaugh-Thompson, John Strate, & Lyke Thompson. "Effect of Term Limits on the Election of Minority State Legislators" *State and Local Government Review,* 2003.

Carey, J.M., R.G. Niemi, & L.W. Powell. "The Effects of Term Limits on State Legislatures." *Legislative Studies Quarterly* 23, no. 2 (1998): 271–300.

Carey, John. *Term Limits and Legislative Representation.* New York: Cambridge University Press, 1996.

Carey, John R.G. Niemi, & Lynda Powell. *Term Limits in State Legislatures.* Ann Arbor: University of Michigan Press, 2000.

Carson, C. "Public Policy Dispute Settlement: A Best Practice Model." Paper presented at the Dispute Resolution Study Circle, Mediating Theory and Democratic Systems, Wayne State University, Detroit, Michigan, February 1998.

Clucas, Richard A. 1998. "Institutional Context and Power of State House Speakers." Paper presented at the Annual Meetings of the American Political Science Association, Boston, MA, September 1998.

Clucas, Richard A. "California: The New Amateur Politics." Paper presented at "Coping with Term Limits: Ohio and the Nation." Sponsored by the Ray C. Bliss Institute of Applied Politics, Columbus, OH, April 2000.

Cobb, Roger W. and Charles D. Elder. *Participation in American Politics: The Dynamics of Agenda Building.* 2nd ed. Baltimore: Johns Hopkins University Press, 1983.

Daniel, Kermit and John R. Lott, Jr. "Term Limits and Electoral Competitiveness: Evidence from California's State Legislative Races." *Public Choice* 90 (1997): 165–184.

DeBow, Kenneth & John C. Syer. *Power and Politics in California.* 6th ed. New York: Longman, 2000.

Detroit Free Press, "Proposal B—Yes Term Limits Will End Gridlock, Sleaze." Richard Headlee, October 12, 1992, p. 7A.

Detriot Free Press, "Term Limits Would Put More Power in Voters' Hands," April 2, 1992, p. 12A.

Dougan, W.R. & M.C. Munger. "The Rationality of Ideology." *Journal of Law and Economics* 32 (1989): 119–142.

Dow, Jay K., James Enderby, & Charles E. Menifield. "The Industrial Structure of the California Assembly: Committee Assignments, Economic Interests, and Campaign Contributions." *Public Choice* 94 (1998): 67–83.

Ehrenhalt, Alan. *The United States of Ambition: Politicians, Power and the Pursuit of Office.* New York: Random House, 1991.

Eismeier, Theodore J. & Philip H. Pollock III. "Strategy and Choice in Congressional Elections: The Role of Political Action Committees." *American Journal of Political Science* 30 (1986): 197–121.

Elazar, Daniel. *American Federalism: A View from the States.* New York: Harper & Row, 1984.

Epic-MRA, The Epic-MRA Report, 9 (3), March 2001, 4710W. Saginaw, Lansing, MI 48917.

Evans, Diana. "Before the Roll Call: Interest Group Lobbying and Public Policy Outcomes in House Committees." *Political Research Quarterly* 49 (1996): 287–304.

Faletta, J.P., Lyke Thompson, John Strate, Marjorie Sarbaugh-Thompson, & Shannon Orr. *Leadership Without Seniority.* Paper delivered at the annual meeting of the American Political Science Association., Washington, DC, August 30–September 3, 2000.

Faletta, J.P., Charles D. Elder, Marjorie Sarbaugh-Thompson, Mary Herring, Eric Rader, & Shannon Orr with Stanley Caress. "Term Limits Effects on the Electoral Environment and Composition of the California State Assemble and Michigan State House of Representatives." *The American Review of Political Science* 22 (2001): 445–469.

Fowler, Linda L. "A Comment on Competition and Careers." In *Limiting Legislative Terms.* Edited by Gerald Benjamin and Michael J. Malgin. Washington, DC: CQ Press, 1992.

Francis, W. "Influence and Interaction in a State Legislative Body." *American Political Science Review* 56 (1962): 953–960.

Francis, W.L. "Leadership, Party Caucuses, and Committees in U.S. State Legislatures." *Legislative Studies Quarterly* 10, no. 2 (1985): 243–257.

Francis, W.L. *The Legislative Committee Game.* Columbus, OH: Ohio State University Press, 1989.

French, J.R.P. & B.H. Raven. *The Bases of Social Power, in Studies of Social Power.* Edited by D. Cartwright. Ann Arbor: University of Michigan Press, 1959.

Gaddie, R.K. & C. Bullock III. *Elections to Open Seats in the U.S. House.* Lanham, MD: Rowman and Littlefield Publishers, Inc., 2000.

Glazer, Amihai & Martin P. Wattenberg. "How Will Term Limits Affect Legislative Work." In *Legislative Term Limits: Public Choice Perspectives.* Edited by Bernard Grofman. Boston: Kluwer, 1996.

Gierzynski, Anthony. "A Framework for the Study of Campaign Finance." In *Campaign Finance in State Legislative Elections.* Chapter 2. Edited by Joel Thompson and Gary Moncrief. Washington, DC: Congressional Quarterly Press, 1998.

Gierzynski, R.K. & David A. Breaux. "The Financing Role of Parties." In *Campaign Finance in State Legislative Elections.* Edited by Joel Thompson and Gary Moncrief. Washington, DC: Congressional Quarterly Press, 1998.

Glazer, Amihai & Martin P. Wattenberg. "Promoting Legislative Work: A Case for Term Limits." Working paper presented at the Conference on Term Limits, University of California, Irvine, June 1991.

Gopoian, J. David. "What Makes PACs Tick? An Analysis of the Allocation Patterns of Economic Interest Groups." *American Journal of Political Science* 30 (1984): 197–213.

Gordon, Stacy B. & Cynthia L. Unmack. "The Effect of Term Limits on PAC Allocation Patterns: The More Things Change..." *State and Local Government Review* 35, no. 1 (2003).

Granovetter, M. "The Strength of Weak Ties." *American Journal of Sociology* 81 (1973): 1360–1380.

Granovetter, M. *Getting a Job.* Cambridge: Harvard University Press, 1974.

Grier, Kevin B. & Michael C. Munger. "The Impact of Legislator Attributes on Interest Group Campaign Contributions." *Journal of Labor Research* 7 (1986): 349–361.

Grier, Kevin B. & Michael C. Munger. "Committee Assignments, Constituent Preferences, and Campaign Contributions." *Economic Inquiry* 29 (1991): 24–43.

Grier, Kevin B. & Michael C. Munger. "Comparing Interest Group PAC Contributions to House and Senate Incumbents, 1980–1986." *Journal of Politics* 55 (1993): 615–643.

Haider-Markel, D.P. "Redistributing values in Congress: Interest Group Influence Under Sub-Optimal Conditions." *Political Research Quarterly* 52, no.1 (1999): 113–144.

Hamm, K.E. "Consistency Between Committee and Floor Voting in U.S. State Legislatures." *Legislative Studies Quarterly* 7 (1982): 473–490.

Hamm, K.E. and R.D. Hedlund. "Accounting for Change in the Number of State Legislative Committee Positions." *Legislative Studies Quarterly* 15, no. 2 (1990): 201–226.

Hamm, K.E., R.D. Hedlund, & N. Martorano. "The Evolution of Committee Structure, Powers and Procedures in Twentieth Century State Legislatures."

Paper presented at the annual meeting of the American Political Science Association, Atlanta, September 1999.

Harrison, Brigid C. *Women in American Politics.* Belmont, CA: Wadsworth, 2003.

Hedlund, R.D. "Organizational Attributes of Legislatures: Structure, Rules, Norms, Resources." *Legislative Studies Quarterly* 9, no.1 (1984): 51–119.

Hero, Rodney E. & Caroline Tolbert. "Latinos and Substantive Representation in the U.S. House of Representatives: Direct, Indirect, or Nonexistent?" *American Journal of Political Science* 39, no. 3 (1995): 640–652.

Herrick, Rebekah & David L. Nixon. "Is There Life After Congress? Patterns and Determinants of Post-Congressional Careers." Paper delivered at the annual meeting of the American Political Science Association. New York City, 1994.

Herrick, Rebekah, Michael K. Moore, & John R. Hibbing. "Unfastening the Electoral Connection: The Behavior of U.S. Representatives When Reelection is No Longer a Factor." *Journal of Politics* 56, no.1 (1994): 214–227.

Herring, Mary & John Forbes. "The Overrepresentation of a White Minority: Detroit's At-Large City Council, 1961–1989." *Social Science Quarterly* 75, no. 2 (1994): 431–445.

Herrnson, Paul S. & Atiya Kai Stokes. "Race Matters: 'Exploring Differences in the Campaigns of Minority and White State Legislative Candidates.'" Paper presented at the Annual Meeting of the American Political Science Association, San Francisco, August 2001.

Hyink, Bernard L. & David H. Provost. *Politics and Government in California.* 15th ed. New York: Longman, 2001.

Jewell, Malcolm E. *Representation in State Legislatures.* Lexington: University Press of Kentucky, 1982.

Jewell, Malcom E. "Political Party Recruiting of State Legislative Candidates." Paper presented at the annual meeting of the American Political Science Association, Boston, September 1998.

Jewell, M.E. & M.L. Whicker. *Legislative Leadership in the American States.* Ann Arbor: University of Michigan Press, 1994.

Johnson, James B. & Philip E. Secret. "Focus and Style Representational Roles of Congressional Black and Hispanic Caucus Members" *Journal of Black Studies* 26, no. 3 (1996): 245–273.

Karnig, Albert & B.O. Walter. "Election of Women to City Councils." *Social Science Quarterly* 56 (1976): 605–613.

Kesler, Charles. "Bad Housekeeping: The Case Against Congressional Term Limitations." *Policy Review* 53 (1990): 20–25.

Kingdon, J.W. *Congressmen's Voting Decisions.* 3rd ed. Ann Arbor, MI: University of Michigan Press, 1989.

Kingdon, J.W. *Agendas, Alternatives, and Public Policies.* 2nd ed. New York: Longman, 1995.

Kobrak, Peter. "Michigan." In *The Political Life of the American States.* Edited by Alan Rosenthal and Maureen Moakley. New York: Praeger, 1984.

Lott, J.R., Jr. & W.R. Reed. "Shirking and Sorting in a Political Market with Finite-Lived Politicians." *Public Choice* 74, no. 4 (1989): 461–484.

Lublin, David. "Racial Redistricting and African-American Representation: A Critique of 'Do Majority–Minority Districts Maximize Substantive Black Representation in Congress?'" *American Political Science Review* 93, no.1 (1999): 183–186.

Malbin, Michael J. & Gerald Benjamin. "Legislatures after Term Limits." In *Limiting Legislative Terms*. Edited by Gerald Benjamin and Michael J. Malbin. Washington, DC: Congressional Quarterly Press, 1992.

Marsden, P.V. & N.E. Friedkin. "Network Studies of Social Influence." *Sociological Methods and Research* 22, no. 1 (1993): 127–151.

Mayhew, David. *Congress: The Electoral Connection*. New Haven, CT: Yale University Press, 1974.

McAnaw, Richard & Noelle Schiffer. "Legislative Quandary Leaders or Followers?" In *Michigan Politics and Government*. Chapter 5. Edited by William P. Browne and Kenneth VerBurg. Lincoln, NE: University of Nebraska Press, 1995.

Milbrath, L.W. "Lobbying as a Communication Process." *Public Opinion Quarterly* 24 (1960): 32–53.

Milliken, William G. "Proposal B No: Democracy's Power Rests with Voters, not Arbitrary Laws." *Detroit Free Press*, October 12, 1992, sec. A.

Mitchell, Cleta Deatherage. 1991. "Term Limits? Yes!" Extensions. Norman, OK: Carl Albert Research Center, Spring, 1991.

Moen, M.C. & K.T. Palmer. "Maine: The Cutting Edge of Term Limits." Paper presented at "Coping with Term Limits: Ohio and the Nation," sponsored by the Ray C. Bliss Institute of Applied Politics, Columbus, April 2000.

Moncrief, G., Peverill Squire, & Malcolm E. Jewell. *Who Runs for the Legislature*. Upper Saddle River, NJ: Prentice Hall, 2001.

Moncrief, G. & J. Thompson. "On the Outside Looking In: Lobbyists Perspectives on the Effects of State Legislative Term Limits." *State Politics and Policy Quarterly* 1, no. 4 (2001): 394–411.

Montgomery, Peter. 1990. "Should Congressional Terms Be Limited?" *Common Cause* (July/August 1990): 31–33.

Nakamura, Robert T. & Frank Smallwood. *The Politics of Policy Implementation*. New York: St. Martin's Press, 1980.

National Conference of State Legislatures (2003) http://www.ncsl.org/programs/legman/about/states.htm.

Niven, David. 2000. "Revolutionary Headlines: Media Coverage of Legislative Term Limits." Paper presented at Coping with Term Limits: Ohio and the Nation, sponsored by the Ray C. Bliss Institute of Applied Politics, Columbus, April 2000.

Pappageorge, John. "Setting a Lifetime Limit of 14 Years in Legislature Gives Lawmakers More Experience to Lead in House." *Detroit News*, December 28, 2003, http://www.detnews.com/2003/editorial/ 0312/29/a19- 19728.htm.

Palm, Albert F. & Gregg W. Smith. "Inescapable Partisanship in a Ticket-splitting State." In *Michigan Politics and Government.* Chapter 8. Edited by William P. Browne and Kenneth VerBurg. Lincoln, NE: University of Nebraska Press, 1995.

Patterson, S.C. "Patterns of Interpersonal Relations in a State Legislative Group: The Wisconsin Assembly." *Public Opinion Quarterly* 23 (1959): 101–109.

Petracca, Mark P. 1991. "The Poison of Professional Politics." *Cato Institute.* On-line posting, May 10, 1991, www.cato.org/pubs/pas/pa-151es.html.

Petracca, Mark P. "A Legislature in Transition: The California Experience with Term Limits." Paper presented at the annual meeting of the American Political Science Association, San Francisco, September 1996.

Polsby, Nelson. "Some Arguments Against Congressional Term Limitations." *Harvard Journal of Law and Public Policy* 16, no. 1 (1993): 1515–1526.

Poole, Keith T. & Thomas Romer. "Patterns of Political Action Committee Contributions to the 1980 Campaigns for the United States House of Representatives." *Public Choice* 47 (1985): 63–111.

Poole, Keith T., Thomas Romer & Howard Rosenthal. "The Revealed Preferences of Political Action Committees." *American Economic Review* 77 (1987): 289–302.

Porter, H.O. & Leuthold, D.A. "Legislative Expertise in Michigan: Formal and Informal Patterns Over Time." *The Michigan Academician* 3, no. 2 (1970): 71–83.

Porter, H.O. "Legislative Experts and Outsiders: The Two-Step Flow of Communication." *Journal of Politics* 36 (1974): 703–730.

Price, D. "Policy Making in Congressional Committees: The Impact of Environmental Factors." *American Political Science Review* 72 (1978): 548–574.

Rader, Eric, Charles D. Elder & Richard C. Elling. "Motivations and Behaviors of the 'New Breed' of Term Limited Legislators." *American Review of Politics* 22 (Winter 2001): 471–490.

Rae, Douglas W. *The Political Consequences of Electoral Laws.* New Haven, CT: Yale University Press, 1971.

Rozell, Mark J. Clyde Wilcox. *Interest Groups in American Campaigns: The New Face of Electioneering.* Washington, DC: CQ Press, 1999.

Sarbaugh-Thompson, Marjorie, Lyke Thompson, Lisa Marckini, John Strate, Richard C. Elling, & Charles D. Elder. "Term Limits and Campaign Finance Reform in Michigan: More Money, More Candidates, More Wealth." In *Money, Politics, and Campaign Finance Reform Law in the States.* Chapter 11. Durham, NC: Carolina Academic Press, 2002.

Schlesinger, Joseph. *Ambition and Politics.* Chicago: Rand McNally, 1966.

Schlozman, Kay Lahman, & John T. Tierney. *Organized Interests and American Democracy.* New York: Harper and Row, 1986.

Squire, Peverill. "Career Opportunities and Membership Stability in Legislatures." *Legislative Studies Quarterly* 13 (1988): 65–82.

Squire, Peverill. "Legislative Professionalism and Membership Diversity in State Legislatures." *Legislative Studies Quarterly* 17 (1992): 69–79.

States Archives of Michigan, Bureau of History, Department of State, Patrick L. Anderson Papers, Box 1, 1992.

Thomas, G. Scott. *The Rating Guide to Life in America's Fifty States.* New York: Prometheus Books, 1994.

Thompson, Joel A. & William E. Cassie. "Party and PAC Contributions to North Carolina State Legislative Candidates." *Legislative Studies Quarterly* 17 (1992): 409–416.

Thompson, Joel A., William E. Cassie, & Malcolm E. Jewell. "A Sacred Cow or Just A Lot of Bull: Party and PAC Money in State Legislative Elections." *Political Research Quarterly* 47, no. 1 (1994): 223–237.

Thurber, J. "Dynamics of Policy Subsystems in American Politics." In *Interest Group Politics.* Edited by A. Cigler and B. Loomis. Washington: CQ Press, 1991.

Trpovski, Jovan, Marjorie Sarbaugh-Thompson, & John Strate. "Conflict and Control on Committee." Paper presented at the annual meeting of the American Political Science Association, San Francisco, August 2001a.

Trpovski, Jovan, Marjorie Sarbaugh-Thompson, & Charles D. Elder "Term Limits in Michigan: Expectations for Citizen Initiatives." Paper presented at the annual meeting of the Midwest Political Science Association, Chicago, April 2001b.

UCINET VI Columbia, SC: Analytic Technologies, 2002.

Wahlke, John C. Heinz Eulau, William Buchanan, & Leroy C. Ferguson. *The Legislative System.* New York: Wiley, 1962.

Welch, S. & D.T. Studlar. "The Opportunity Structure for Women's Candidacies and Electability in Britain and the United States." *Political Science Research Quarterly* 49 (1996): 861–875.

Will, Gary E. *Restoration: Congress, Term Limits and the Recovery of Deliberative Democracy.* New York, NY: The Free Press, 1992.

Williamson, O.E. *Markets and Hierarchies.* New York: Free Press, 1975.

Wilson, Chris D., Charles D. Elder, Lyke Thompson, & Richard C. Elling. "Term-limited Legislators' Responsiveness to Constituents: The Case of the Michigan House of Representatives." Paper presented at the annual meeting of the American Political Science Association, San Francisco, August 2001.

Wright, John. *Interest Groups and Congress: Lobbying, Contributions and Influence.* Boston: Allyn and Bacon, 1996.

Author Index

Subject Index